Birnbaum's 97
Miami &
Ft. Lauderdale

A BIRNBAUM TRAVEL GUIDE

Alexandra Mayes Birnbaum
EDITORIAL CONSULTANT

Lois Spritzer
Editorial Director

Laura L. Brengelman
Managing Editor

Mary Callahan
Beth Schlau
Senior Editors

Patricia Canole
Gene Gold
Susan McClung
Associate Editors

Marcy S. Pritchard
Map Coordinator

Susan Cutter Snyder
Editorial Assistant

HarperPerennial
A *Division* of HarperCollins*Publishers*

For Stephen, who merely made all this possible.

FIRST EDITION

ISSN 0749-2561 (Birnbaum Travel Guides)
ISSN 1056-4454 (Miami)
ISBN 0-06-278256-8 (pbk.)
96 97 98 99 ❖/RRD 5 4 3 2 1

Cover design © Drenttel Doyle Partners
Cover photograph © Paul Chesley

BIRNBAUM TRAVEL GUIDES

Bahamas, and Turks & Caicos
Bermuda
Canada
Cancun, Cozumel & Isla Mujeres
Caribbean
Country Inns and Back Roads
Disneyland
Hawaii
Mexico
Miami & Ft. Lauderdale
United States
Walt Disney World
Walt Disney World for Kids, By Kids
Walt Disney World Without Kids

Contributing Editors

David Klein
Marilyn A. Moore
Molly Arost Staub

Maps

Mark Carlson
Susan Carlson

Contents

Getting Ready to Go

Practical information for planning your trip.

The Cities

*Thorough, qualitative guides to Miami and Ft.
Lauderdale, highlighting both cities' attractions,
services, hotels, and restaurants.*

Miami–Miami Beach

Miami–Miami Beach At-a-Glance

Sources and Resources

Diversions

A selective guide to a variety of unexpected pleasures, pinpointing the best places to pursue them.

Directions

Nine of the best walks and drives through Miami and Ft. Lauderdale, and beyond.

Foreword

It's hard to think of a resort destination that has undergone a greater metamorphosis in recent years than southeastern Florida.

For decades the temperature alone was a powerful lure, and the existence of glitzy hotels, beckoning beach, and other such attractions was just frosting (actually thawing) on the cake. But the vendors of travel services in this area failed to heed the competitive call that was luring longtime Miami visitors to other, equally appealing beaches in the Caribbean, Mexico, and Hawaii. Promotional airfares and discounted package programs made these new destinations delightfully affordable, and it wasn't long before hotel occupancy levels in southeastern Florida began to plummet.

The impetus for the turnaround in Miami's fortunes can be traced directly to the influx of ambitious, energetic Cubans who literally jump-started the city of Miami, long known as a poor relation to the glamour and glitz of Miami Beach. New development followed suit as the city became the natural headquarters for virtually all financial and commercial activities relating to Latin America, and suddenly, Miami was a throbbing force in the expansion of the entire US economy.

Tourism has been a major beneficiary of this growth, and a new, heartfelt sense of civic pride continues to cause the citizenry to re-examine local assets. Blocks of run-down hotels have been rediscovered (and restored) as the nation's most compelling areas of Art Deco architecture. Concurrently, the city has emerged as an important art center; good restaurants abound; and nightclubs pulse. Foreigners are investing in high-priced condos, and celebrities from the worlds of film and fashion now choose Miami as their alternate address—and tourists arrive in record numbers.

We would be foolish to say that crime here (as in other tourist areas) hasn't affected prospective visitors' perceptions. But some of us who once predicted Miami's demise have happily rethought our conclusions.

Toward this end we've tried to create a guide to Miami that's specifically organized, written, and edited for today's demanding traveler, one for whom qualitative information is infinitely more desirable than mere quantities of unappraised data. We realize that it's impossible for any single travel writer to visit hundreds of restaurants (and nearly as many hotels) in any given year and provide accurate appraisals of each. And even if it were physically possible for one human being to survive such an itinerary, it would of necessity have to be done at a dead sprint, and the perceptions derived therefrom would probably be less valid than those of any other intelligent individual visiting the same establishments. It is, therefore, both impractical and undesirable (especially in an annually revised and updated guidebook series such as we offer) to have only one person provide all the data on the entire world. Instead, we have chosen what we like to describe as the "thee and me" approach to restaurant and hotel evaluation and, to a somewhat more limited degree, to the sites and sights we have included in the other sections of our text. What this really reflects is a personal sampling tempered by intelligent counsel from informed local sources.

This guidebook is directed to the "visitor," and such elements as restaurants have been specifically picked to provide the visitor with a representative and, above all, pleasant experience. Since so many extraneous considerations can affect the reception and service accorded a regular restaurant patron, our choices can in no way be construed as an exhaustive guide to resident dining. We think we've listed all the best places, in various price ranges, but they were chosen with a visitor's enjoyment in mind.

Other evidence of how we've tried to tailor our text to reflect modern travel habits is apparent in the section we call DIVERSIONS. Today's traveler is likely to want to pursue a special interest or to venture off the beaten path, and in response to this trend, we have collected a series of special experiences so that it is no longer necessary to wade through a pound or two of superfluous prose just to find exceptional pleasures and treasures.

Finally, I also should point out that every good travel guide is a living enterprise. In our annual revisions, we refine, expand, and further hone all our material to serve your travel needs better. To this end, no contribution is of greater value to us than your personal reaction to what we have written, as well as information reflecting your own experiences while using the book. Please write to us at 10 E. 53rd St., New York, NY 10022.

We sincerely hope to hear from you.

Alexandra Mayes Birnbaum

ALEXANDRA MAYES BIRNBAUM, editorial consultant to the *Birnbaum Travel Guides,* worked with her late husband, Stephen Birnbaum, as co-editor of the series. She has been a world traveler since childhood and is known for her travel reports on radio on what's hot and what's not.

Miami &
Ft. Lauderdale

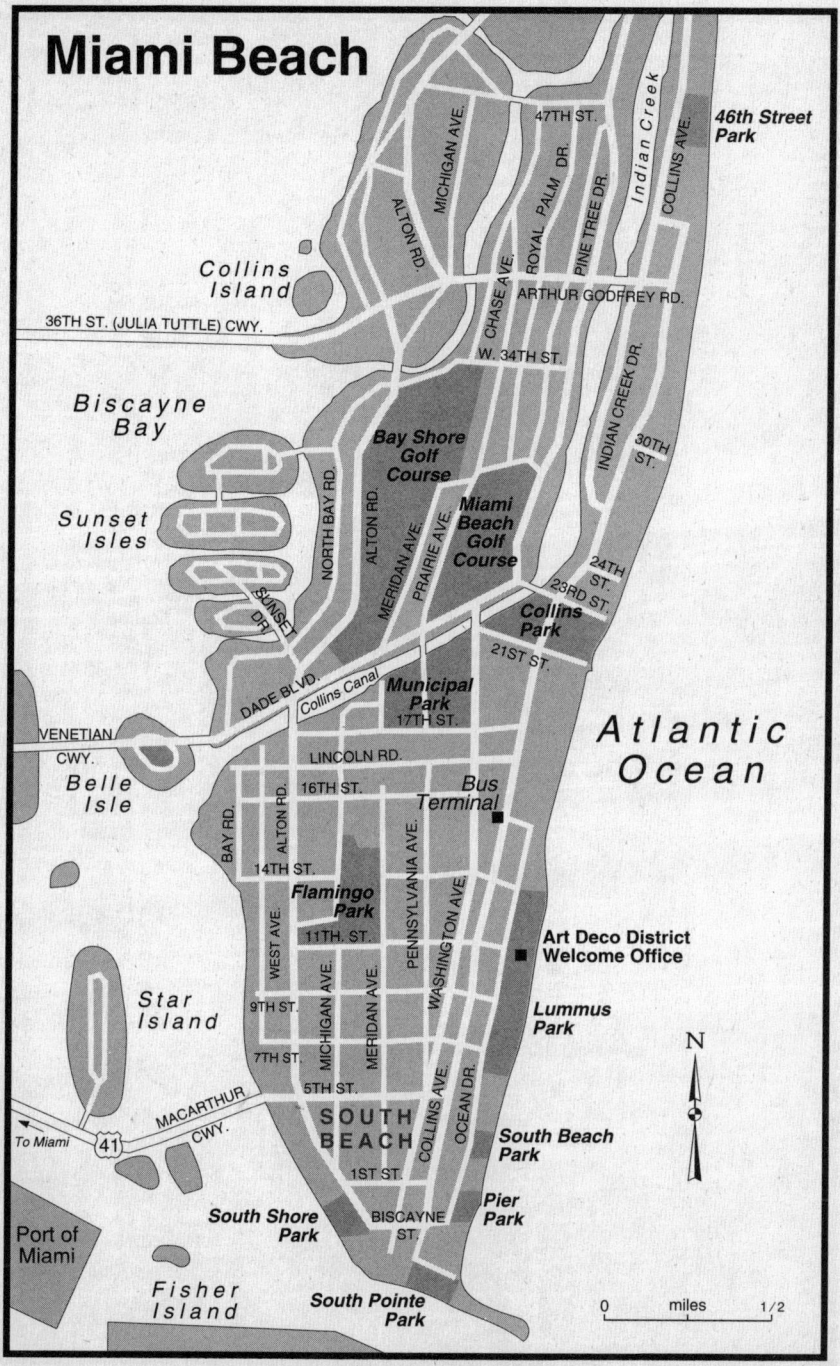

Ft. Lauderdale

NE 17TH CT.
NE 16TH ST.
DIXIE HWY.
NW 14TH CT.
NW 13TH CT.
845
NE 13TH ST.
CHATEAU PARK
NE 11TH ST.
NW 11TH ST.
NW 10TH PL.
Warfield Park
N ANDREWS AVE.
W SUNRISE BLVD.
838
Sunland Park
Holiday Park
FLAGLER DR.
FEDERAL HWY.
NW 8TH ST.
NE 7TH ST.
NW 6TH ST.
NE 6TH ST.
NE 5TH ST.
NW 4TH ST.
NE 4TH ST.
City Hall
NE 3RD ST.
NE 2ND ST.
Bus Station
Bus Station
NW 2ND ST.
Public Golf Course
BROWARD BLVD.
Museum of Discovery and Science
SW 2ND ST.
LAS OLAS BLVD.
Museum of Art
SE 5TH ST.
SE 6TH ST.
SW 5TH PL.
SE 7TH ST.
SE 9TH ST.
SW 9TH ST.
SE 12TH ST.
DAVIE BLVD.
82
SE 14TH ST.
1
SW 14TH ST.
SW 14TH CT.
SW 15TH ST.
SE 17TH ST.
SW 17TH ST.
SE 20TH ST.
SW 20TH ST.
SE 22ND ST.
95
MIAMI RD.
S FEDERAL HWY.
SW 24TH ST.
84

NW 22ND AVE.
95
NW 22ND ST.
NW 19TH AVE.
NW 18TH AVE.
NW 15TH AVE.
NW 12TH AVE.
NW 11TH TERR.
NW 9TH AVE.
NW 7TH AVE.
NW 5TH AVE.
NW 3RD AVE.
SW 20TH AVE.
SW 18TH ST.
NW 1ST AVE.
S ANDREWS AVE.
NE 3RD AVE.
SW 22ND AVE.
SW 15TH AVE.
SW 6TH AVE.
SW 4TH AVE.
SW 9TH AVE.
SW 15TH AVE.
SW 3RD AVE.
S ANDREWS AVE.
S 3RD AVE.
SE 4TH AVE.

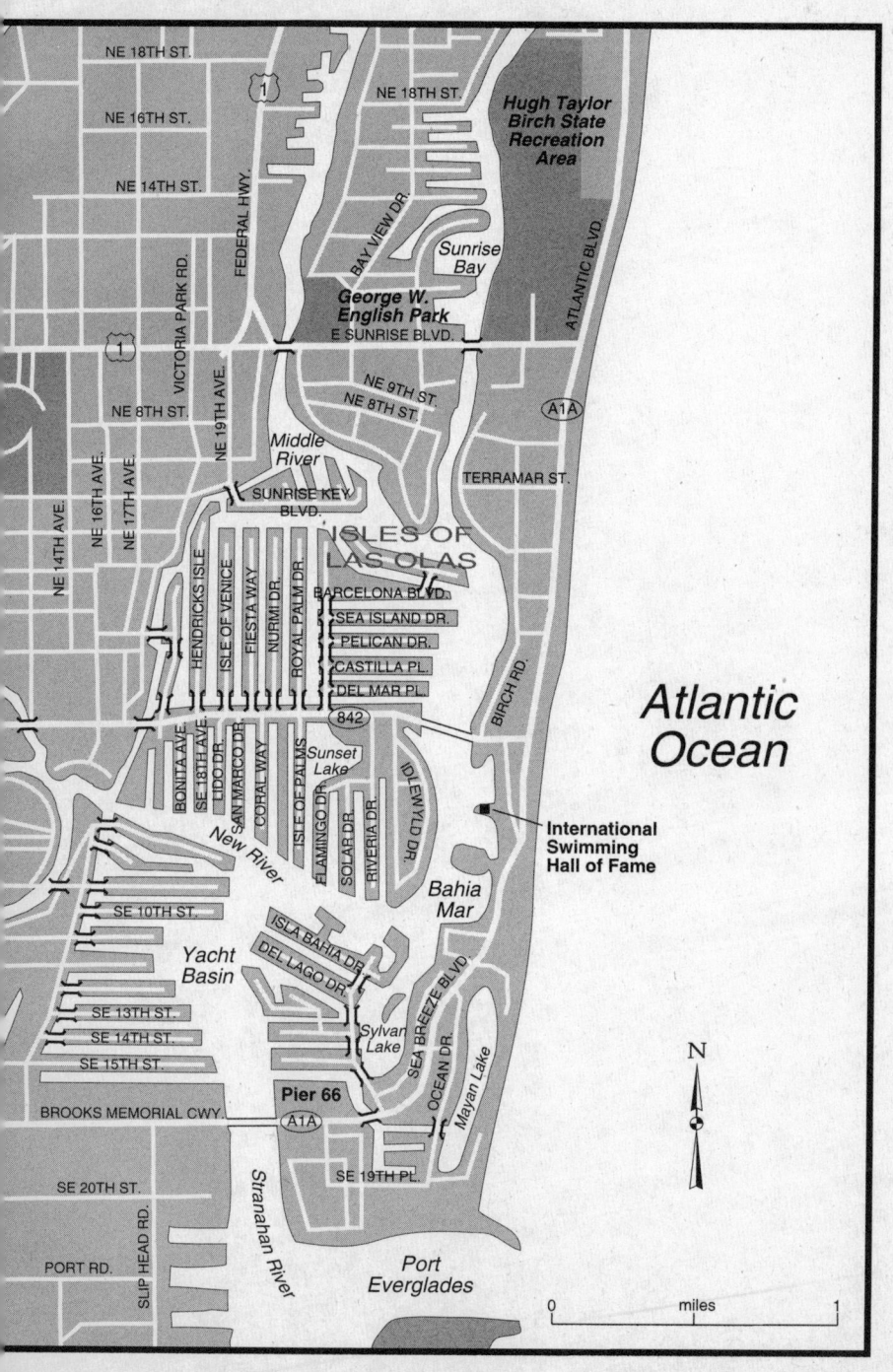

How to Use This Guide

A great deal of care has gone into the special organization of this guide-book, and we believe it represents a real breakthrough in the presentation of travel material.

Our text is divided into four basic sections in order to present information in the best way on every possible aspect of a vacation to Miami and/or Ft. Lauderdale. Our aim is to highlight what's where and to provide basic information—how, when, where, how much, and what's best—to assist you in making the most intelligent choices possible.

Here is a brief summary of what you can expect to find in each section. We believe that you will find both your travel planning and en route enjoyment enhanced by having this book at your side.

GETTING READY TO GO

A mini-encyclopedia of practical travel facts with all the precise data necessary to create a successful trip to Miami and Ft. Lauderdale. Here you will find how to get where you're going, plus selected resources—including useful publications, and companies and organizations specializing in discount and special-interest travel—providing a wealth of information and assistance useful both before and during your trip.

THE CITIES

Our individual reports on Miami and Ft. Lauderdale offer a short-stay guide, including an essay introducing each city as a historic entity and a contemporary place to visit; an *At-a-Glance* section that's a site-by-site survey of the most important, interesting, and unique sights to see and things to do; *Sources and Resources,* a concise listing of pertinent tourism information, such as the address of the local tourist office, which sightseeing tours to take, where to find the best nightspots, which shops have the finest merchandise and/or the most irresistible bargains, and where the best museums and theaters are to be found; and *Best in Town,* which lists our collection of cost-and-quality choices of the best places to eat and sleep on a variety of budgets.

DIVERSIONS

This section is designed to help travelers find the best places in which to engage in a variety of exceptional experiences, without having to wade through endless pages of unrelated text. In every case, our particular suggestions are intended to guide you to that special place where the quality of experience is likely to be highest.

DIRECTIONS

Here are walks that cover Miami and Ft. Lauderdale—their main thoroughfares and side streets, their most spectacular landmarks and lovely parks—and drives through the most interesting communities nearby. We also suggest two one-day or overnight drives: to the Florida Keys and to *Everglades National Park*.

To use this book to full advantage, take a few minutes to read the table of contents and random entries in each section to get a firsthand feel for how it all fits together. You will find that the sections of this book are building blocks designed to help you put together the best possible trip. Use them selectively as a tool, a source of ideas, a reference work for accurate facts, and a guidebook to the best buys, the most exciting sights, the most pleasant accommodations, and the tastiest foods—*the best travel experience* that you can possibly have.

Getting Ready to Go

Getting Ready to Go

When to Go

Miami and Ft. Lauderdale enjoy mild weather all year, although the temperature does occasionally dip into the 50s F or lower in winter, and summers can be uncomfortably hot and humid, with frequent showers. The best weather is during the peak winter travel season; however, travel during the off-season and shoulder seasons (the months immediately before and after the peak months) offers relatively fair weather and smaller crowds, and often is less expensive.

If you have a touch-tone phone, you can call *The Weather Channel Connection* (phone: 900-WEATHER) for current weather forecasts. This service, available from *The Weather Channel* (2600 Cumberland Pkwy., Atlanta, GA 30339), costs 95¢ per minute; the charge will appear on your phone bill.

Traveling by Plane

SCHEDULED FLIGHTS

Unless indicated otherwise, the following airlines offer flights to both *Miami International Airport* and *Ft. Lauderdale/Hollywood International Airport*: *American, American Eagle, American Trans Air (ATA), Carnival Air Lines, Continental, Delta, Delta Connection, Midway* (to Ft. Lauderdale only), *Northwest, Spirit Airlines* (to Ft. Lauderdale only), *Sunjet International* (to Ft. Lauderdale only), *Tower Air* (to Miami only), *TWA, United, USAir, USAir Express,* and *ValuJet.*

FARES The great variety of airfares can be reduced to the following basic categories: first class, business class, coach (also called economy or tourist class), excursion or discount, and standby, as well as various promotional fares. For information on applicable fares and restrictions, contact the airlines listed above or ask your travel agent. Most airfares are offered for a limited time and sell out quickly; once you've found the lowest fare for which you can qualify, purchase your ticket as soon as possible.

RESERVATIONS Reconfirmation is not generally required on domestic flights, although it is wise to call ahead to make sure that the airline has your reservation and any special requests in its computer.

SEATING You usually can reserve a specific seat when purchasing your ticket; otherwise, seats are assigned on a first-come, first-served basis at check-in. Seating charts may be available from airlines and are included in the *Desktop Flight Guide* (Official Airline Guides, PO Box 51703, Boulder, CO 80321;

phone: 800-323-3537 for orders; 708-574-6000 for information; fax: 708-574-6565).

SMOKING US law prohibits smoking on flights scheduled for six hours or less within the US and its territories on both US and foreign carriers. In addition, the major US carriers flying to Miami and Ft. Lauderdale have banned smoking on all their domestic flights—including those of more than six hours in duration. A free wallet-size guide that describes the rights of nonsmokers under current regulations is available from *ASH (Action on Smoking and Health;* DOT Card, 2013 H St. NW, Washington, DC 20006; phone: 202-659-4310).

SPECIAL MEALS When making your reservation, you can request one of the airline's alternate menu choices for no additional charge. Though not always required, it's a good idea to reconfirm your meal request the day before departure.

BAGGAGE On major US carriers, passengers usually are allowed to carry on board one or two bags that will fit under a seat or in an overhead compartment and to check two bags in the cargo hold. Specific regulations regarding dimensions and weight restrictions vary among airlines, but a checked bag usually cannot exceed 62 inches in combined dimensions (length, width, and depth) or weigh more than 70 pounds. There may be charges for additional, oversize, or overweight luggage, and for special equipment or sporting gear. When checking your bags, make sure that the tags the airline attaches are correctly coded for your destination.

CHARTER FLIGHTS

By booking a block of seats on a specially arranged flight, charter operators frequently can offer travelers bargain airfares. If you do fly on a charter, however, read the contract's fine print carefully. Federal regulations permit charter operators to cancel a flight or assess surcharges of as much as 10% of the airfare up to 10 days before departure. You usually must book in advance, and once booked, you may not be able to change your flight—a good reason to buy trip cancellation insurance (see *Insurance,* below). Also, make your check out to the company's escrow account, which provides some protection for your investment in the event that the charter operator fails. Additional information on charter flights is provided in the publication *Jax Fax* (397 Post Rd., Darien, CT 06820; phone: 800-952-9329 for subscriptions; 203-655-8746 for information; fax: 203-655-6257).

DISCOUNTS ON SCHEDULED FLIGHTS

CONSOLIDATORS AND BUCKET SHOPS These companies buy blocks of tickets from airlines and sell them at a discount to travel agents or directly to consumers. Since many bucket shops operate on a thin margin, be sure to check a company's record with the *Better Business Bureau*—before parting with any money.

Cheap Tickets (6151 W. Century Blvd., Los Angeles, CA 90045; phone: 800-377-1000; fax: 800-454-2555).

Fare Deals Travel (9350 E. Arapahoe Rd., Suite 330, Englewood, CO 80112; phone: 800-878-2929 or 303-792-2929; fax: 303-792-2954).

Southwest Travel Systems (1001 N. Central Ave., Suite 575, Phoenix, AZ 85004; phone: 800-STS-TRAVEL or 602-255-0234; fax: 602-255-0220).

STT Worldwide Travel (9880 SW Beaverton Hillsdale Hwy., Beaverton, OR 97005; phone: 800-348-0886 or 503-641-8866; fax: 503-641-2171).

Unitravel (1177 N. Warson Rd., St. Louis, MO 63132; phone: 800-325-2222 or 314-569-0900; fax: 314-569-2503).

LAST-MINUTE TRAVEL SERVICES These are clubs or agencies that provide members or clients with information on imminent trips and other bargain travel opportunities. Some of the clubs charge an annual fee; others offer free membership. Note that despite the names of some of the services listed below, you don't have to wait until literally the last minute to make travel plans.

Discount Travel International (169 W. 81st St., New York, NY 10024; phone: 212-362-3636; fax: 212-362-3236).

FLY ASAP (PO Box 9808, Scottsdale, AZ 85252-3808; phone: 800-FLY-ASAP or 602-224-9504; fax: 602-224-9533).

Last Minute Travel (1249 Boylston St., Boston, MA 02215; phone: 800-LAST-MIN or 617-267-9800; fax: 617-424-1943).

Moment's Notice (7301 New Utrecht Ave., Brooklyn, NY 11204-5137; phone: 718-234-6295; fax: 718-234-6450).

Spur of the Moment Cruises (411 N. Harbor Blvd., Suite 302, San Pedro, CA 90731; phone: 800-4-CRUISE or 310-521-1070 in California; 800-343-1991 elsewhere in the US; 24-hour hotline: 310-521-1060; fax: 310-521-1061).

Traveler's Advantage (3033 S. Parker Rd., Suite 900, Aurora, CO 80014; phone: 800-548-1116 for information; 800-835-8747 for member services; fax: 303-368-3985).

Vacations to Go (1502 Augusta Dr., Suite 415, Houston, TX 77057; phone: 713-974-2121 in Texas; 800-338-4962 elsewhere in the US; fax: 713-974-0445).

Worldwide Discount Travel Club (1674 Meridian Ave., Miami Beach, FL 33139; phone: 305-534-2082).

GENERIC AIR TRAVEL These organizations offer a service similar to airline standby service, except that they sell seats on not one but several scheduled and charter airlines. One pioneer of generic flights is *Airhitch* (2472 Broadway, Suite 200, New York, NY 10025; phone: 212-864-2000 in New York City; 800-326-2009 elsewhere in the US; fax: 212-864-5489).

BARTERED TRAVEL SOURCES Barter—the exchange of commodities or services in lieu of cash payment—is a common practice among travel suppliers. Companies that have obtained travel services through barter may sell these services at substantial discounts to travel clubs, who pass along the savings to members. One organization offering bartered travel opportunities is *Travel World Leisure Club* (225 W. 34th St., Suite 909, New York, NY 10122; phone: 800-444-TWLC or 212-239-4855; fax: 212-564-5158).

CONSUMER PROTECTION

Passengers whose complaints have not been satisfactorily addressed by the airline can contact the *US Department of Transportation* (*DOT;* Consumer Affairs Division, 400 Seventh St. SW, Room 10405, Washington, DC 20590; phone: 202-366-2220). Also see *Fly Rights* (*Consumer Information Center,* Department 133B, Pueblo, CO 81009; phone: 719-948-3334; fax: 719-948-9724). If you have safety-related questions or concerns, write to the *Federal Aviation Administration* (*FAA;* 800 Independence Ave. SW, Washington, DC 20591) or call or fax the *FAA Consumer Hotline* (phone: 800-322-7873; fax: 202-267-5087).

Renting a Car

You can rent a car through a travel agent or national rental firm before leaving home, or from a regional or local company once in Miami or Ft. Lauderdale. Reserve in advance.

Most car rental companies require a credit card, although some will accept a substantial cash deposit. The minimum age to rent a car is set by the company; some also may impose special conditions on drivers above a certain age. Electing to pay for collision or loss damage waiver (CDW or LDW) protection will add to the cost of renting a car, but releases you from financial liability for the vehicle. Additional costs include drop-off charges or one-way service fees.

National Car Rental Companies

Agency Rent-A-Car (phone: 216-349-1000 for main office; 305-238-6617 for Miami office; 954-735-4880 for Ft. Lauderdale office).

Alamo Rent A Car (phone: 800-327-9633).

Avis Rent A Car (phone: 800-331-1212).

Budget Rent A Car (phone: 800-527-0700).

Dollar Rent A Car (phone: 800-800-4000).

Enterprise Rent-A-Car (phone: 800-325-8007).

Hertz Rent A Car (phone: 800-654-3131).

National Car Rental (phone: 800-CAR-RENT).

Payless Car Rental (phone: 800-PAYLESS).

Sears Rent A Car (phone: 800-527-0770).

Value Rent-A-Car (phone: 800-327-2501).

Regional and Local Car Rental Companies

In Miami
A-Jiffy Rent-A-Car (phone: 305-621-5566).
Delta Auto Rental Systems (phone: 800-423-0702 in Florida; 305-871-2500 elsewhere in the US).
Florida Auto Rental (phone: 800-327-3791 or 305-764-1008).
InterAmerican Car Rental (phone: 800-327-1278 or 305-871-3030).
Snappy Car Rental (phone: 800-669-4802)

In Ft. Lauderdale
Florida Auto Rental (phone above).
Lauderdale-by-the-Sea Rent-A-Car (phone: 800-828-3261 or 954-776-4950).
Slaton Rent-A-Car (phone: 954-561-5222).

NOTE

Rent-a-Wreck (phone: 800-421-7253 for locations of franchises nationwide; 954-978-3673 for Ft. Lauderdale area office) rents cars that are well worn but (presumably) mechanically sound. *Prestige Auto Rental and Leasing* (phone: 305-895-0854 for N. Miami office) rents luxury models.

Package Tours

A package tour is a collection of travel services that can be purchased in a single transaction. Its principal advantages are convenience and economy—you don't have to make individual arrangements for each service, and the cost usually is lower than that of the same services purchased separately. Tour programs generally can be divided into two categories: escorted or locally hosted (with a set itinerary) and independent (usually more flexible).

When considering a package tour, read the brochure *carefully* to determine exactly what is included and any conditions that may apply, and check the company's record with the *Better Business Bureau.* The *United States Tour Operators Association* (*USTOA;* 211 E. 51st St., Suite 12B, New York, NY 10022; phone: 212-750-7371; fax: 212-421-1285) also can be helpful in determining a package tour operator's reliability. As with charter flights, to safeguard your funds, always make your check out to the company's escrow account.

Tour operators may offer packages focused on special interests such as the arts, local history, or sports. *All Adventure Vacations* (5589 Arapahoe, Suite 208, Boulder, CO 80303; phone: 800-537-4025 or 303-440-7924; fax: 303-440-4160) represents such specialized packagers. Many also are listed in the *Specialty Travel Index* (305 San Anselmo Ave., Suite 313, San Anselmo, CA 94960; phone: 415-459-4900 in California; 800-442-4922 elsewhere in the US; fax: 415-459-4974).

Below is a list of companies offering package tours to Miami and/or Ft. Lauderdale. Note that companies described as wholesalers accept bookings only through travel agents. For information on local companies offering day tours in Miami and Ft. Lauderdale, see THE CITIES. Information on local tour operators also is available from the *Greater Miami Convention and Visitors Bureau* and the *Greater Ft. Lauderdale Convention and Visitors Bureau* (see *For Further Information* for addresses).

Package Tour Operators

Adventure Vacations (10612 Beaver Dam Rd., Hunt Valley, MD 21030-2205; phone: 410-785-3500 in the Baltimore area; 800-638-9040 elsewhere in the US; fax: 410-584-2771). Wholesaler.

American Airlines FlyAAway Vacations (offices throughout the US; phone: 800-321-2121).

Apple Vacations East (7 Campus Blvd., Newtown Sq., PA 19073; phone: 800-727-3400 or 610-359-6500; fax: 610-359-6524). Wholesaler.

Certified Vacations (110 E. Broward Blvd., Ft. Lauderdale, FL 33301; phone: 800-233-7260 or 954-522-1440; fax: 954-357-4672).

Collette Tours (162 Middle St., Pawtucket, RI 02860; phone: 800-752-2655 in New England; 800-832-4656 elsewhere in the US; fax: 401-727-4745).

Corliss Tours (436 W. Foothill Blvd., Monrovia, CA 91016; phone: 800-456-5717 or 818-359-5358; fax: 818-359-0724).

Dailey-Thorp (330 W. 58th St., New York, NY 10019-1817; phone: 212-307-1555; fax: 212-974-1420).

Delta's Dream Vacations (PO Box 1525, Ft. Lauderdale, FL 33302; phone: 800-872-7786).

Domenico Tours (751 Broadway, Bayonne, NJ 07002; phone: 800-554-8687, 201-823-8687, or 212-757-8687; fax: 201-823-9855).

Globetrotters SuperCities (139 Main St., Cambridge, MA 02142; phone: 800-333-1234 or 617-621-9911; fax: 617-577-8380). Wholesaler.

Le Ob's Tours (4635 Touro St., New Orleans, LA 70122-3933; phone: 800-827-0932 or 504-288-3478; fax: 504-288-8517).

Liberty Travel (for the nearest location, contact the central office: 69 Spring St., Ramsey, NJ 07446; phone: 201-934-3500; fax: 201-934-3888).

Maupintour (PO Box 807, Lawrence, KS 66044; phone: 800-255-4266 or 913-843-1211; fax: 913-843-8351). Wholesaler.

Panorama Tours (600 N. Sprigg St., Cape Girardeau, MO 63701; phone: 800-962-8687 in Missouri and adjacent states; 314-335-9098 elsewhere in the US; fax: 314-335-7824).

Plus Ultra Tours (174 Seventh Ave., New York, NY 10011; phone: 212-242-0393 in New York State; 800-242-0394 elsewhere in the US; fax: 212-633-6652).

Prestige Programs (136 E. 56th St., New York, NY 10022; phone: 212-759-5821; fax: 212-754-5198). Wholesaler.

Travel Impressions (465 Smith St., Farmingdale, NY 11735; phone: 800-284-0044 or 516-845-8000). Wholesaler.

TWA Getaway Vacations (Getaway Vacation Center, 10 E. Stow Rd., Marlton, NJ 08053; phone: 800-GETAWAY; fax: 609-985-4125).

United Vacations (PO Box 24580, Milwaukee, WI 53224-0580; phone: 800-328-6877; fax: 414-351-5256).

Insurance

The first person with whom you should discuss travel insurance is your own insurance broker. You may discover that the insurance you already carry protects you adequately while traveling and that you need little additional coverage. If you charge travel services, the credit card company also may provide some insurance coverage (and other safeguards). Below is a list of the basic types of travel insurance and companies that specialize in such policies.

Types of Insurance

Automobile insurance: Provides collision, theft, property damage, and personal liability protection while driving.

Baggage and personal effects insurance: Protects your bags and their contents in case of damage or theft at any point during your travels.

Default and/or bankruptcy insurance: Provides coverage in the event of default and/or bankruptcy on the part of the tour operator, airline, or other travel supplier.

Flight insurance: Covers accidental injury or death while flying.

Personal accident and sickness insurance: Covers cases of illness, injury, or death in an accident while traveling.

Trip cancellation and interruption insurance: Guarantees a refund if you must cancel a trip; also may reimburse you for additional travel costs incurred in catching up with a tour or traveling home early.

Combination policies: Include any or all of the above.

Travel Insurance Providers

Access America International (PO Box 90315, Richmond, VA 23230; phone: 800-284-8300 or 804-285-3300; fax: 804-673-1491).

Carefree (c/o *Berkely Care,* Arm Coverage, 100 Garden City Plaza, Fifth Floor, PO Box 9366, Garden City, NY 11530; phone: 800-645-2424 or 516-294-0220; fax: 516-294-0268).

NEAR Services (PO Box 1339, Calumet City, IL 60409; phone: 708-868-6700 in the Chicago area; 800-654-6700 elsewhere in the US; fax: 708-868-6706).

Tele-Trip (c/o *Mutual of Omaha,* 3201 Farnam St., Omaha, NE 68131; phone: 800-228-9792 or 402-351-5754; fax: 402-351-2456).

Travel Guard International (1145 Clark St., Stevens Point, WI 54481; phone: 800-826-1300 or 715-345-0505; fax: 800-955-8785).

Travel Insured International (PO Box 280568, E. Hartford, CT 06128-0568; phone: 800-243-3174 or 860-528-7663; fax: 860-528-8005).

Disabled Travelers

Make travel arrangements well in advance. Specify to all services involved the nature of your disability to determine if there are accommodations and facilities that meet your needs. *The Florida Planning Companion for Travelers with Disabilities* provides information on organizations and agencies throughout the state that assist the disabled. Published by the *Florida Division of Tourism,* it also can be obtained from the *Greater Miami Convention and Visitors Bureau* (see *For Further Information* for addresses).

Publications

Access Travel: A Guide to the Accessibility of Airport Terminals (Consumer Information Center, Department 575A, Pueblo, CO 81009; phone: 719-948-3334; fax: 719-948-9724).

Air Transportation of Handicapped Persons (Publication #AC-120-32; *US Department of Transportation,* Distribution Unit, Utilization and Storage Section, M-45.3, 33-410 75th Ave., Landover, MD 20785; phone: 301-322-4961; fax: 301-386-5394).

The Diabetic Traveler (PO Box 8223 RW, Stamford, CT 06905; phone: 203-327-5832; fax: 203-975-1748).

Directory of Travel Agencies for the Disabled and **Travel for the Disabled,** both by Helen Hecker (Twin Peaks Press, PO Box 129, Vancouver, WA 98666; phone: 800-637-2256 for orders; 360-694-2462 for information; fax: 360-696-3210).

The Disabled Driver's Mobility Guide (*American Automobile Association,* Traffic Safety Dept., Department 1000 AAA Dr., Heathrow, FL 32746-5063; phone: 407-444-7961; fax: 407-444-7956).

Handicapped Travel Newsletter (PO Drawer 269, Athens, TX 75751; phone: 941-540-7612; fax: 941-540-7238).

Handi-Travel: A Resource Book for Disabled and Elderly Travellers, by Cinnie Noble (*Easter Seals–March of Dimes National Council,* 45 Sheppard Ave. E., Suite 801, Toronto, Ontario M2N 5W9, Canada; phone/TDD: 416-250-7490; fax: 416-229-1371).

On the Go, Go Safely, Plan Ahead (*American Diabetes Association,* National Service Center, 1660 Duke St., Alexandria, VA 22314; phone: 800-232-3472 or 703-549-1500; fax: 703-549-6995).

Travel for the Patient with Chronic Obstructive Pulmonary Disease (c/o Dr. Harold Silver, 1601 18th St. NW, Washington, DC 20009; phone: 202-667-0134; fax: 202-667-0148).

Travel Tips for Hearing-Impaired People (*American Academy of Otolaryngology,* 1 Prince St., Alexandria, VA 22314; phone: 703-836-4444; fax: 703-683-5100).

Travel Tips for People with Arthritis (*Arthritis Foundation,* 1314 Spring St. NW, Atlanta, GA 30309; phone: 800-283-7800 or 404-872-7100; fax: 404-872-0457).

The Travelin' Talk Newsletter (*Travelin' Talk,* PO Box 3534, Clarksville, TN 37043-3534; phone: 615-552-6670; fax: 615-552-1182).

Traveling Like Everybody Else: A Practical Guide for Disabled Travelers, by Jacqueline Freedman and Susan Gersten (Modan Publishing, PO Box 1202, Bellmore, NY 11710; phone: 516-679-1380; fax: 516-679-1448).

The Wheelchair Traveler, by Douglass R. Annand (123 Ball Hill Rd., Milford, NH 03055; phone: 603-673-4539).

Organizations

ACCENT on Living (PO Box 700, Bloomington, IL 61702; phone: 800-787-8444 or 309-378-2961; fax: 309-378-4420).

Access: The Foundation for Accessibility by the Disabled (1109 Linden St., Valley Stream, NY 11580; phone/fax: 516-568-2715).

American Foundation for the Blind (11 Penn Plaza, Suite 300, New York, NY 10001; phone: 800-232-5463 or 212-502-7600; fax: 212-502-7777).

Mobility International (main office: 25 Rue de Manchester, Brussels B-1070, Belgium; phone: 32-2-410-6297; fax: 32-2-410-6874; US office: *MIUSA,* PO Box 10767, Eugene, OR 97440; phone/TDD: 503-343-1284; fax: 503-343-6812).

MossRehab Hospital Travel Information Service (telephone referrals only; phone: 215-456-9600; TDD: 215-456-9602).

National Rehabilitation Information Center (8455 Colesville Rd., Suite 935, Silver Spring, MD 20910-3319; phone: 301-588-9284; fax: 301-587-1967).

Paralyzed Veterans of America (*PVA;* PVA/Access to the Skies Program, 801 18th St. NW, Washington, DC 20006-3585; phone: 202-872-1300 in Washington, DC; 800-424-8200 elsewhere in the US; fax: 202-785-4452).

Society for the Advancement of Travel for the Handicapped (*SATH;* 347 Fifth Ave., Suite 610, New York, NY 10016; phone: 212-447-7284; fax: 212-725-8253).

Package Tour Operators

Accessible Journeys (35 W. Sellers Ave., Ridley Park, PA 19078; phone: 800-846-4537 or 610-521-0339; fax: 610-521-6959).

Accessible Tours/Directions Unlimited (Attention: Lois Bonanni, 720 N. Bedford Rd., Bedford Hills, NY 10507; phone: 800-533-5343 or 914-241-1700; fax: 914-241-0243).

Beehive Travel (77 W. 200 S., Suite 500, Salt Lake City, UT 84101; phone: 800-777-5727 or 801-578-9000; fax: 801-297-2828).

Classic Travel Service (275 Madison Ave., Suite 2314, New York, NY 10016-1101; phone: 212-843-2900; fax: 212-944-4493).

Dahl's Good Neighbor Travel Service (124 S. Main St., Viroqua, WI 54665; phone: 800-338-3245 or 608-637-2128; fax: 608-637-3030).

Flying Wheels Travel (PO Box 382, Owatonna, MN 55060; phone: 800-535-6790 or 507-451-5005; fax: 507-451-1685).

Hinsdale Travel (201 E. Ogden Ave., Hinsdale, IL 60521; phone: 708-325-1335; fax: 708-325-1342).

MedEscort International (*Lehigh Valley International Airport,* PO Box 8766, Allentown, PA 18105-8766; phone: 800-255-7182 or 610-791-3111; fax: 610-791-9189).

Prestige World Travel (5710-X High Point Rd., Greensboro, NC 27407; phone: 800-476-7737 or 910-292-6690; fax: 910-632-9404).

Sprout (893 Amsterdam Ave., New York, NY 10025; phone: 212-222-9575; fax: 212-222-9768).

Weston Travel Agency (134 N. Cass Ave., PO Box 1050, Westmont, IL 60559; phone: 708-968-2513; fax: 708-968-2539).

NOTE

Wheelchair Getaways (main office: PO Box 605, Versailles, KY 40383; phone: 800-536-5518 or 606-873-4973; fax: 606-873-8039; Florida offices: 12190 SW 46th St., Miami, FL 33175; phone/fax: 305-227-9190; and PO Box 20126, W. Palm Beach, FL 33416; phone: 561-967-9488; fax: 561-641-3658) rents vans designed to accommodate wheelchairs.

Single Travelers

The travel industry is not very fair to people who vacation by themselves—they often end up paying more than those traveling in pairs. There are services catering to single travelers, however, that match travel companions, offer travel arrangements with shared accommodations, and provide information and discounts. Helpful information for those traveling alone also is provided in the newsletter *Going Solo* (Doerfer Communications, PO Box 123, Apalachicola, FL 32329; phone/fax: 904-653-8848).

Organizations and Companies

Contiki Holidays (300 Plaza Alicante, Suite 900, Garden Grove, CA 92640; phone: 800-266-8454 or 714-740-0808; fax: 714-740-0818).

Gallivanting (515 E. 79th St., Suite 20F, New York, NY 10021; phone: 800-933-9699 or 212-988-0617; fax: 212-988-0144).

Globus and Cosmos (5301 S. Federal Circle, Littleton, CO 80123-2980; phone: 800-851-0728 for information; 800-221-0090 for reservations; or 303-797-2800; fax: 303-798-5441).

Jane's International Travel and Sophisticated Women Travelers (2603 Bath Ave., Brooklyn, NY 11214; phone: 800-613-9226 or 718-266-2045; fax: 718-266-4062).

Jens Jurgen's Travel Companion Exchange (PO Box 833, Amityville, NY 11701; phone: 800-392-1256 or 516-454-0880; fax: 516-454-0170).

Marion Smith Professional Singles (611 Prescott Pl., N. Woodmere, NY 11581; phone: 800-698-TRIP, 516-791-4852, 516-791-4865, or 212-944-2112; fax: 516-791-4879).

Partners-in-Travel (11660 Chenault St., Suite 119, Los Angeles, CA 90049; phone: 310-476-4869).

Solo Flights (612 Penfield Rd., Fairfield, CT 06430; phone: 800-266-1566 or 203-256-1235).

Travel Companions (*Atrium Financial Center,* 1515 N. Federal Hwy., Suite 300, Boca Raton, FL 33432; phone: 561-393-6448 in Florida; 800-383-7211 elsewhere in the US; fax: 561-393-6448).

Travel in Two's (239 N. Broadway, Suite 3, N. Tarrytown, NY 10591; phone: 914-631-8301 in New York State; 800-692-5252 elsewhere in the US).

Umbrella Singles (PO Box 157, Woodbourne, NY 12788; phone: 800-537-2797 or 914-434-6871; fax: 914-434-3532).

Older Travelers

Special discounts and more free time are just two factors that have given older travelers a chance to see the world at affordable prices. Many travel suppliers offer senior discounts—sometimes only to members of certain senior citizens organizations (which may offer travel benefits of their own). When considering a particular package, make sure the facilities—and the pace of the tour—match your needs and physical condition.

Publications

The Mature Traveler (GEM Publishing Group, PO Box 50400, Reno, NV 89513-0400; phone: 702-786-7419).

The Senior Citizen's Guide to Budget Travel in the US and Canada, by Paige Palmer (Pilot Books, 103 Cooper St., Babylon, NY 11702; phone: 516-422-2225; fax: 516-422-2227).

Take a Camel to Lunch and Other Adventures for Mature Travelers, by Nancy O'Connell (Bristol Publishing Enterprises, PO Box 1737, San Leandro, CA 94577; phone: 510-895-4461 in California; 800-346-4889 elsewhere in the US; fax: 510-895-4459).

Unbelievably Good Deals & Great Adventures That You Absolutely Can't Get Unless You're Over 50, by Joan Rattner Heilman (Contemporary Books, 180 N. Stetson Ave., Suite 1200, Chicago, IL 60601; phone: 800-621-1918 or 312-540-4500; fax: 800-998-3103 or 312-540-4687).

Organizations

American Association of Retired Persons (*AARP;* 601 E St. NW, Washington, DC 20049; phone: 202-434-2277).

Mature Outlook (Customer Service Center, 6001 N. Clark St., Chicago, IL 60660; phone: 800-336-6330; fax: 312-764-5036).

National Council of Senior Citizens (1331 F St. NW, Washington, DC 20004; phone: 202-347-8800; fax: 202-624-9595).

Package Tour Operators

Elderhostel (75 Federal St., Boston, MA 02110-1941; phone: 617-426-7788).

Gadabout Tours (700 E. Tahquitz Canyon Way, Palm Springs, CA 92262; phone: 800-952-5068 or 619-325-5556; fax: 619-325-5127).

Grand Circle Travel (347 Congress St., Boston, MA 02210; phone: 800-221-2610 or 617-350-7500; fax: 617-346-6700).

Grandtravel (6900 Wisconsin Ave., Suite 706, Chevy Chase, MD 20815; phone: 800-247-7651 or 301-986-0790; fax: 301-913-0166).

Interhostel (*University of New Hampshire,* Division of Continuing Education, 6 Garrison Ave., Durham, NH 03824; phone: 800-733-9753 or 603-862-1147; fax: 603-862-1113).

Mature Tours (10 Greenwood La., Westport, CT 06880; phone: 800-266-1566 or 203-256-1235; fax: 203-259-7113).

OmniTours (104 Wilmot Rd., Deerfield, IL 60015; phone: 800-962-0060 or 708-374-0088; fax: 708-374-9515).

Saga International Holidays (222 Berkeley St., Boston, MA 02116; phone: 800-343-0273 or 617-262-2262; fax: 617-375-5950).

Traveling with Children

Sharing the excitement and discovery of travel with your family can bring special meaning to any trip. Although traveling with your children requires some additional preparation and planning, it does not have to be a burden or an excessive expense. An increasing number of hotels and other travel services cater to families and offer family packages and discounts for children. In addition, numerous publications provide helpful information on family travel.

Publications

Best Places to Go: A Family Destination Guide to the World, by Nan Jeffrey (Menasha Ridge Press, 3169 Cahaba Heights Rd., Birmingham, AL 35243; phone: 800-247-9437 or 205-967-0566; fax: 205-967-0580).

Doing Children's Museums: A Guide to 265 Hands-On Museums, by Joanne Cleaver (Williamson Publishing, PO Box 185, Charlotte, VT 05445; phone: 800-234-8791 or 802-425-2102; fax: 802-425-2199).

The Family Travel Guide: An Inspiring Collection of Family-Friendly Vacations, by Carole T. Meyers (Carousel Press, PO Box 6061, Albany, CA 94706; phone: 800-990-9386 or 510-527-5849; fax: 800-990-9386).

Family Travel Times newsletter (*Travel with Your Children; TWYCH;* 40 Fifth Ave., New York, NY 10011; phone: 212-477-5524; fax: 212-477-5173). Subscription includes copy of the "Airline Guide" issue (also available separately).

50 Great Family Vacations: Eastern North America, by Candyce H. Stapen (Globe Pequot Press, 6 Business Park Rd., PO Box 833, Old Saybrook, CT 06475; phone: 800-243-0495 or 203-395-0440; fax: 203-395-0312).

Flying with Baby: A Parent's Guide to Making Air Travel with an Infant or Toddler Easy, by Scott R. Weinberger (Third Street Press, PO Box 261250, Littleton, CO 80126-1250; phone: 813-360-0795; fax: 414-332-2193).

Fun Family Vacations in the Southeast, by Kent and Sharron Hannon (Peachtree Publishers, Ltd., 494 Armour Circle NE, Atlanta, GA 30324; phone: 800-241-0113 or 404-876-8761; fax: 800-875-8909).

The Penny Whistle Traveling with Kids Book: Whether by Boat, Train, Car or Plane—How to Take the Best Trip Ever with Kids of All Ages, by Meredith Brokaw and Annie Gilbar (Simon & Schuster, 200 Old Tappan Rd., Old Tappan, NJ 07675; phone: 800-223-2348; fax: 800-445-6991).

Places to Go with Children in Miami and South Florida, by Cheryl Lani Juárez and Deborah Ann Johnson (Chronicle Books, 275 Fifth St., San Francisco, CA 94103; phone: 800-722-6657 for orders; 415-777-7240 for information; fax: 800-858-7787).

Travel with Children, by Maureen Wheeler (Lonely Planet Publications, 155 Filbert St., Suite 251, Oakland, CA 94607; phone: 800-275-8555 or 510-893-8555; fax: 510-893-8563).

Trouble-Free Travel with Children: Helpful Hints for Parents on the Go, by Vicki Lansky (The Book Peddlers, 18326 Minnetonka Blvd., Deephaven, MN 55391; phone: 800-255-3379 or 612-475-3527; fax: 612-475-1505).

When Kids Fly (*Massport,* Public Affairs Dept., 10 Park Plaza, Boston, MA 02116-3971; phone: 617-973-5600; fax: 617-973-5611).

Money Matters

CREDIT CARDS AND TRAVELER'S CHECKS

Most major credit cards enjoy wide domestic and international acceptance; however, not every hotel, restaurant, or shop in Miami or Ft. Lauderdale accepts all (or in some cases any) credit cards. It's also wise to carry traveler's checks while on the road, since they are replaceable if stolen or lost and are accepted throughout the US. You can buy traveler's checks at banks and some are available by mail or phone. Keep a separate list of all traveler's checks (noting those that you have cashed) and the names and numbers of your credit cards. Both traveler's check and credit card companies have toll-free numbers to call for information or in the event of loss or theft.

CASH MACHINES

Automated teller machines (ATMs) are increasingly common, and most banks participate in ATM networks such as *MasterCard/Cirrus* (phone: 800-4-CIRRUS) and *Visa/PLUS* (phone: 800-THE-PLUS). Using a card—with an assigned Personal Identification Number (PIN)—from an affiliated bank or credit card company, you can withdraw cash from any machine in the same network. The *MasterCard/Cirrus ATM Location Directory* and the *Visa/PLUS International ATM Directory 1997* provide locations of network ATMs nationwide and are available from banks and other financial institutions.

SENDING MONEY

Should the need arise, you can have money sent to you via the services provided by *American Express MoneyGram* (phone: 800-926-9400 for information; 800-866-8800 for money transfers) or *Western Union Financial Services* (phone: 800-325-6000 or 800-325-4176).

Time Zone

Miami and Ft. Lauderdale are in the eastern standard time zone. Daylight saving time is observed from the first Sunday in April until the last Sunday in October.

Business and Shopping Hours

Miami and Ft. Lauderdale maintain business hours that are fairly standard throughout the US: 9 AM to 5 PM, Mondays through Fridays. Most smaller retail establishments are open weekdays and Saturdays from 9 or 10 AM to 5 or 6 PM. Department stores and malls stay open longer, often until 9 or 9:30 PM, and in some cases as late as 10 or 11 PM; they also may be open on Sundays from noon until around 5 or 6 PM.

Banking hours generally are weekdays from 9 AM to 4 PM, although some banks stay open on Fridays until 6 or 7 PM, and also may offer longer hours on Thursdays. Banks with Saturday hours usually are open from 9 or 10 AM until noon or 1 PM.

Mail

Miami's main post office (2200 NW 72nd Ave., Miami, FL 33152; phone: 305-470-0243; fax: 305-470-0733) is open weekdays from 7 AM to 7 PM, and

Saturdays from 8:30 AM to 1:30 PM. The downtown office (500 NW Second Ave., Miami, FL 33101; phone: 305-371-2911; fax: 305-374-3216) is open weekdays from 8:30 AM to 5 PM, and Saturdays from 9:30 AM to 1:30 PM. Hours for the Miami Beach office (1300 Washington Ave., Miami Beach, FL 33139; phone: 305-531-3763; fax: 305-538-5187) are weekdays from 8:30 AM to 5 PM, and Saturdays from 9:30 AM to 1:30 PM.

In Ft. Lauderdale, the main post office (1900 W. Oakland Park Blvd., Ft. Lauderdale, FL 33310; phone: 954-527-2028 or 954-527-2008; automated information line: 954-735-3596; fax: 954-527-3203) is open weekdays from 7:30 AM to 7 PM, and Saturdays from 8:30 AM to 2 PM. The downtown office (330 SW Second St., Ft. Lauderdale, FL 33302; phone: 954-761-1172; fax: 954-763-9508) is open weekdays from 7:30 AM to 6 PM, and Saturdays from 8:30 AM to 2 PM.

For other post office branches, call the main offices or check the yellow pages. Stamps also can be purchased at most hotel desks and some stores, as well as from public vending machines. For rapid, overnight delivery to other cities, use *Express Mail* (available at post offices) or courier services, such as *DHL Worldwide Express* (phone: 800-225-5345) or *FedEx* (phone: 800-GO-FEDEX).

You can have mail sent to you care of your hotel (marked "Guest Mail, Hold for Arrival") or to *some* post offices—such as the downtown Miami and main Ft. Lauderdale branches (addresses should include "c/o General Delivery"). *American Express* offices also will hold mail for customers ("c/o Client Letter Service"); information is provided in their pamphlet *Worldwide Travelers' Companion.*

Telephone

The area code for Miami is 305. The area code for Ft. Lauderdale recently was changed from 305 to 954.

To make a long-distance call, dial 1 + the area code + the local number. The nationwide number for information is 555-1212; you also can dial 411 for local information. If you need a number in another area code, dial 1 + the area code + 555-1212. (If you don't know an area code, dial 555-1212 or 411 for directory assistance.)

You can use a telephone company calling card number on any phone, and some pay phones take major credit cards (*American Express, MasterCard, Visa,* and so on). Also available are combined telephone calling/bank credit cards, such as the *AT&T Universal Card* (PO Box 44167, Jacksonville, FL 32231-4167; phone: 800-423-4343). Similarly, *Sprint* (8140 Ward Pkwy., Kansas City, MO 64114; phone: 800-226-8472) offers *VisaPhone,* through which you can add phone card privileges to your existing *Visa* card. Companies offering long-distance phone cards without additional credit card privileges include *AT&T* (phone: 800-CALL-ATT), *Executive Telecard International* (4260 E. Evans Ave., Denver, CO 80222; phone: 800-950-

3800), *LDDS/Worldcom* (1 International Center, 100 NE Loop 410, Suite 400, San Antonio, TX 78216; phone: 800-275-0200), *MCI* (323 Third St. SE, Cedar Rapids, IA 52401; phone: 800-444-4444; and 12790 Merit Dr., Dallas, TX 75251; phone: 800-444-3333), and *Sprint* (address above; phone: 800-PIN-DROP).

Some of these companies, such as *AT&T, LDDS/Worldcom,* and *Sprint,* also offer "prepaid" phone cards. These are similar to the long-distance calling cards discussed above, except that the customer purchases a specific dollar amount of credit in advance. Charges for calls made with the card are debited from the credit purchased, and when the credit is used up the card is thrown away. Instructions for using such cards are provided by the issuing companies.

Hotels routinely add surcharges to the cost of phone calls made from their rooms. Long-distance telephone services that may help you avoid this added expense are provided by a number of companies, including *AT&T* (International Information Service, 635 Grant St., Pittsburgh, PA 15219; phone: 800-874-4000), and *LDDS/Worldcom, MCI,* and *Sprint* (addresses above). Note that some of these services can be accessed only with the companies' long-distance calling cards (see above). In addition, even when you use such long-distance services, some hotels still may charge a fee for line usage.

Useful telephone directories for travelers include the *AT&T Toll-Free 800 National Shopper's Guide* and the *AT&T Toll-Free 800 National Business Guide* (phone: 800-426-8686 for orders), the *Toll-Free Travel & Vacation Information Directory* (Pilot Books, 103 Cooper St., Babylon, NY 11702; phone: 516-422-2225; fax: 516-422-2227), and *The Phone Booklet* (Scott American Corporation, PO Box 88, W. Redding, CT 06896; no phone).

Medical Aid

In an emergency: Dial 911 for assistance, 0 for an operator, or go directly to the emergency room of the nearest hospital.

Hospitals

In Miami
Columbia Cedars Medical Center (1400 NW 12th Ave.; phone: 800-327-7386 or 305-325-5511).
Jackson Memorial Hospital (1611 NW 12th Ave.; phone: 305-325-7429).
Mercy Hospital (3663 S. Miami Ave.; phone: 305-854-4400).
Mt. Sinai Medical Center (4300 Alton Rd., Miami Beach; phone: 305-674-2200).

In Ft. Lauderdale
Cleveland Clinic Hospital (2835 N. Ocean Blvd.; phone: 954-568-1000).
Holy Cross Hospital (4725 N. Federal Hwy., phone: 954-771-8000).
Memorial Hospital (3501 Johnson St., Hollywood; phone: 954-987-2000).

24-Hour Pharmacies

Eckerd:

In Miami: 9031 SW 107th Ave. (phone: 305-274-6776); 1825 NE 185th St., N. Miami Beach (phone: 305-932-5740).

In Pembroke Pines (a suburb of Ft. Lauderdale): 154 N. University Dr. (phone: 954-432-5510).

Walgreens:

In Miami: 1845 Alton Rd. (phone: 305-531-8868); 12295 N. Biscayne Blvd., N. Miami (phone: 305-893-6860); 791 NE 167th St., N. Miami Beach (phone: 305-652-7332)

In Hialeah (a suburb of Miami): 500-B W. 49th St. (phone: 305-557-5469).

In Ft. Lauderdale: 3101 N. Ocean Blvd. (phone: 954-563-3800); 2855 Sterling Rd. (phone: 954-981-1104).

Additional Resources

Medic Alert Foundation (2323 Colorado Ave., Turlock, CA 95382; phone: 800-ID-ALERT or 209-668-3333; fax: 209-669-2495).

Travel Care International (PO Box 846, Eagle River, WI 54521; phone: 800-5-AIR-MED or 715-479-8881; fax: 715-479-8178).

Traveler's Emergency Network (*TEN;* PO Box 238, Hyattsville, MD 20797-8108; phone: 800-ASK-4-TEN; fax: 301-559-5167).

Legal Aid

If you don't have, or cannot reach, your own attorney, most cities offer legal referral services maintained by county bar associations. These services ensure that anyone in need of legal representation gets it and can match you with a local attorney. For legal assistance in Miami, contact the *Florida Bar Association* (phone: 800-342-8060 or 305-377-4445); for Ft. Lauderdale, contact the *Broward County Bar Association* (phone: 954-764-8040). If you must appear in court, you are entitled to court-appointed representation if you can't obtain a lawyer or can't afford one.

For Further Information

Tourist information for Miami can be obtained from the *Greater Miami Convention and Visitors Bureau* (701 Brickell Ave., Suite 2700, Miami, FL 33131; phone: 305-539-3000; fax: 305-539-3113). Information for Ft. Lauderdale is available from the *Greater Ft. Lauderdale Convention and Visitors Bureau* (1850 Eller Dr., Suite 303, Ft. Lauderdale, FL 33316; phone: 954-765-4466; fax: 954-765-4467). Tourist information for the state of Florida can be obtained from the *Florida Division of Tourism* (107 W. Gaines St., Suite 501D, Tallahassee, FL 32399-2000; phone: 904-487-1462; fax: 904-921-9158). For local sources of tourist information in Miami and Ft. Lauderdale, see *Sources and Resources* in THE CITIES.

The Cities

Miami–Miami Beach

It's difficult to find adults over 30 who actually were born in Miami. Like California, the city—and all of South Florida—seems to be populated by people who have come from somewhere else, and not just another state. Some two million people live in the greater Miami area year-round, and newcomers escaping economic woes overseas and harsh winters in the northeastern states arrive in droves daily. And few are retirees. The myth that Miami is filled with nothing but senior citizens became outdated long ago—in reality, only 15% of the population of Dade County is over 65.

The area's already large population swells tremendously during the winter months, when millions of "snowbirds" arrive. "Snowbird" is a tricky term that refers primarily to tourists escaping the northeastern freeze, but just as easily could describe South Americans in town for a midsummer shopping spree.

Sprawling across 2,054 square miles of land, Miami is a huge and cosmopolitan city. Despite efforts to market it as the gateway to Latin America or a tropical New York, it still retains a somewhat provincial quality. This is due in part to the way in which the metropolitan area is organized. Greater Miami—actually metropolitan Dade County—comprises 27 municipalities and dozens of neighborhoods in unincorporated areas. As a result, residents have a chauvinistic interest in their own enclaves. While they identify with the whole city, their particular neighborhood is what they care about most—even though many of the residents who have this affinity are recent arrivals or part-time snowbirds.

From an early, small settlement consisting primarily of Native Americans living around the US government's Fort Dallas, Miami grew slowly until one Julia Tuttle tickled the fancy of a railroad tycoon with some orange blossoms. Tuttle was an early settler who was eager to see Miami become part of a railroad hookup with the rest of the state. She petitioned railroad magnate Henry M. Flagler to extend his *Florida East Coast Railroad* south from Palm Beach to Miami. He seemed in no great hurry to do so until the Big Freeze of 1894–95 devastated most—but not all—of Florida's fruit and vegetable crops. When Flagler received a box of frost-free orange blossoms from Tuttle, he suddenly got the message. Soon enough Miami had rail access to the rest of the world.

It wasn't long until the rest of the world was glad of access to South Florida. Attracted by year-round warmth and sunshine, thousands of new residents began pouring into the area, only one step behind hundreds of shrewd entrepreneurs. Once a small village stuck on the side of a swamp, Miami and Miami Beach became glittering wintertime destinations and later began drawing vacationers in the summer as well. While Miami Beach still remains tourist-oriented, the city of Miami has developed into a flourishing international business hub. Together they are an attractive combination that lures a wide variety of visitors.

About 15 years ago, Miami officials—jolted into the realization that their fun-and-sun city had begun to lose its good reputation—launched a series of major programs dedicated to restoration and redevelopment. They began by renewing the beaches, sprucing up oceanfront hotels, dressing up the historic hotel district in Miami Beach, and focusing on clean industry such as international commerce. The Miami River was cleaned up and the parks system was expanded. Ecologists began pushing for strict enforcement of environmental laws to protect the delicate marine ecology, reflecting a determination to keep the good life good in South Florida. Stunning high-rise office towers, bank buildings, and condominiums were built almost overnight to accommodate the Latin Americans and Caribbean islanders who adopted Miami as their capital. The result is truly a new Miami, an exciting place for both residents and visitors—clean, beautiful, and gleaming in the bright Florida sunshine.

That Miami still symbolizes the good life is attested to by the waves of new residents who continue to settle in one or another of Miami's municipalities each year. Many of these new residents are Spanish-speaking, a large number of them refugees from Cuba. Others fled violence in Central America and poverty in the Caribbean; still others are affluent Venezuelans, Brazilians, and Colombians who occupy their Miami homes only part of the year.

This Latin immigration has turned metropolitan Miami into a city where you can buy anything from fried bananas to Chilean wine, and where Spanish is the first language of more than 50% of the year-round residents. More recently, the Latin influence has been felt in Miami's art world. An appreciation of and growing demand for the works of such renowned Latin American artists as Rufino Tamayo, Wilfredo Lam, Roberto Matta, and Armando Morales have made the city the undisputed center of Latin American art in the US. A group of galleries featuring the works of both famous and up-and-coming Latin American artists has had an extraordinary impact on the once-struggling Miami art community.

The only slightly smaller tide of newcomers and regular visitors from the Caribbean, Britain, and Europe gives Miami an even more international aspect, with additions like Jamaican restaurants, Haitian grocery stores, and elegant French dining spots. The city today is a tropical mélange of cultures, offering a rich mix of languages and customs, foods and festivals, attitudes and traditions.

Greater Miami's variety is also a product of its many distinct neighborhoods and municipalities. Coral Gables is one of the metropolitan region's most prestigious planned communities, conceived and built by entrepreneur George Merrick in the 1920s. Elegant gates to the city still stand in various spots around the Gables, relics of Merrick's grand scheme to build "a place where castles in Spain are made real." Strict building codes prevail, and woe to the newcomer who tries to put a flat roof on his home. In a county where almost all the streets are laid out in a simple north-south-east-west numbered grid, Coral Gables sticks to its Spanish and Italian street names and layout; for those unfamiliar with its winding ways, it's easy to get lost here. Just 10 minutes from the airport, Coral Gables also has become a favored locale of more than a hundred multinational corporations doing business in Latin America.

South Miami, adjacent to the Gables, is a crossroads town that might be found in Anywhere, USA. Farther south, in an unincorporated part of Dade County called Kendall, lie expensive estates with pools and tennis courts, where not so long ago there were only vast mango and avocado groves.

Closer to Downtown Miami is Coconut Grove, once a colony of artists and writers, and now a base for wealthy year-round and winter residents. Here a few crafts shops remain next to expensive boutiques and posh restaurants, and a handful of old houses of coral rock nestle close to modern high-rises. Luxurious yachts and sailboats lie in Biscayne Bay, and on weekends Miami's younger generation unwinds at the *CocoWalk* shopping and entertainment complex. The area known as Little Havana is part of the center city, but is really a small world unto itself, with its Latin culture intact. Increasingly, it dominates Miami's political and commercial life.

In a class by themselves are Miami Beach and Key Biscayne. Besides its glittering hotel row, Miami Beach and the small manmade islands between it and the mainland house some of the most luxurious waterfront homes in Greater Miami. The South Beach section has undergone a tremendous renaissance, with the rehabilitation of many Art Deco apartment buildings and hotels, as well as the construction of new high-rise condominiums. Miami's Art Deco District has replaced New York's posh Hampton beach havens as the escape of choice for such luminaries as Sylvester Stallone, Madonna, Gianni Versace, Sophia Loren, Cher, and Whitney Houston. Attracted by the climate and South Beach's churning nightlife scene, models, fashion photographers, movie crews, wannabes, and just plain folks have become the area's newest snowbirds.

Although it was once a coconut plantation, Key Biscayne now has rows of luxury high-rises, enclaves of million-dollar waterfront estates, and wonderful beaches. The island's restaurants and shops bustle with activity.

With a mean annual temperature of 75F, 85,000-plus registered boats, miles of beaches, more than 60 marinas, 11,829 acres of parks, and 354 square miles of water, the Miami area's vital statistics support its reputation as a sunny, water-oriented resort. Yet in the past two decades, the city has become a major urban area, with an economic diversity associated with cities of comparable size. The population has grown by 54% since the early 1970s, and employment has doubled in local business and industry. Indeed, the export trade is expected soon to overtake tourism as the number one local industry.

Nonetheless, Miami remains a major tourist destination. As tourist migration from the Northeast slowed during the 1980s and early 1990s (due in great measure to the growing attractions of the Tampa–*Walt Disney World*–Orlando-Daytona axis), increased numbers of travelers from South America, Europe, and the Orient helped to compensate. Although a number of much-publicized incidents against foreign tourists in the past several years caused a slight drop in the number of visitors from abroad, Miami's steps to make the area safer apparently have been effective in luring them back (see *A Few Words About Crime,* below). The proof: In 1995, tourism to Greater Miami climbed to record levels, up nearly 10% over 1994.

It's probably not true, as an old Florida legend claims, that a race of giants once lived here, but it certainly is true that Miami today possesses a gigantic will that wants more than anything else to grow—and grow and grow and grow. The new, revitalized—and resilient—Miami is sure to have its way.

A FEW WORDS ABOUT CRIME

Like all large cities, Miami has its share of crime. However—despite the recent murders of several tourists in roadway robberies—crimes against both non-residents and residents of Florida actually declined in 1995, according to the *Florida Department of Law Enforcement*.

In the wake of the roadway murders, South Florida has taken several steps to prevent crimes against tourists. Many hotels now offer guests free transportation from the airport and arrange for rental cars to be delivered to hotels. Easier-to-read road signs bearing orange sunbursts direct travelers to the beach and city areas, and special tourist-oriented police units are now stationed at rental car parking lots and around the airport. In addition, rental agencies are prohibited from putting advertising stickers and special license plates on rental cars (to eliminate the obvious signs that a car is being driven by a visitor). Other measures include establishing undercover police patrols and increasing the number of tourist information centers throughout the Miami area.

Nonetheless, travelers should be aware that criminals may deliberately bump a car from behind and then rob the driver when he or she gets out to check for damage. Another common crime is the "smash and grab," where a robber approaches a car at a traffic light, smashes the window, and then grabs for purses or jewelry. To avoid such crimes, drive alertly, make sure you know where you're going, and carry a map. If your car is bumped or you are told you have a flat tire, don't stop until you have reached a safe and well-lit location. If someone suspicious approaches your car at a red light, check for oncoming traffic, and then drive on quickly. Take taxis if you're going out late at night or to an unfamiliar area, and keep valuables in your hotel vault. Remember, it's always wise to err on the side of caution to ensure a safe vacation.

Miami–Miami Beach At-a-Glance

SEEING THE CITY

The *Rusty Pelican* (see *Eating Out*) and *Bayside Seafood* restaurant (3501 Rickenbacker Causeway, Key Biscayne; phone: 361-0808) look across Biscayne Bay at the spectacular Miami skyline and have outdoor seating areas with good views. The *South Pointe Seafood House* (see *Eating Out*), on the southernmost tip of Miami Beach, affords spectacular views of Government Cut, the throughway for the dozens of cruise ships that dock at the Port of Miami.

SPECIAL PLACES

The best way to tour Greater Miami is by car.

MIAMI BEACH

MIAMI BEACH From the late 1920s until the 1960s, this 8-mile-long island east of the mainland was renowned for its glittering seaside resorts. But in the mid-1960s, the wide beaches and the distinctive hotels fell into decline. These days, however, Miami Beach's glitzy reputation, along with its unique architecture, has been restored. Several efforts at renewal and redevelopment over the past few years have brought tourists to the flashy *Fontainebleau Hilton* and the other big hotels that line Collins Avenue, the main drag; a $64-million beach renourishment program has created a 300-foot strand extending from Government Cut to Haulover Inlet; and a boardwalk runs 1.8 miles along the beach from 21st to 46th Streets. South Beach, the southern end of the island between Fifth and 20th Streets, has been designated a National Historic District because of its many Art Deco buildings (see below). Ocean Drive, South Beach's main drag, has been widened and spruced up and is now lined with chic outdoor cafés, shops, galleries—and plenty of tanned, attractive, and trendy pedestrians. For more on Miami Beach, see *Quintessential Miami* in DIVERSIONS.

ART DECO DISTRICT A drive or stroll through this Miami hot spot will forever banish images of the city as a geriatric center. New and restored buildings, hotels, and cafés with façades of bright pink, turquoise, and peach gleam in the sun. The area's name is actually a bit of a misnomer—the fanciful structures here are a mixture of traditional Art Deco, Art Moderne (a French-influenced hybrid), and Spanish-Mediterranean Revival styles. During the mid-1980s, local preservationists fought to upgrade the South Beach area from Ocean Drive to Lenox Court, which was in a state of decay. More than 800 buildings were rehabilitated and redecorated. Española Way, stretching from Drexel to Washington Avenues between 14th and

15th Streets, also has undergone large-scale renovation. Its Spanish-Mediterranean Revival–style buildings, many containing eclectic boutiques and art galleries, have been painted in warm coral tones and adorned with gaily striped awnings; gaslight lamps lend a romantic glow. For more on this area, see *Quintessential Miami* in DIVERSIONS and *Tour 1: South Beach–The Art Deco District* in DIRECTIONS.

BASS MUSEUM OF ART The museum building is listed on the National Register of Historic Places for its classic Art Deco design. Constructed of Key stone (oolitic limestone), the exterior of the building is adorned with carved nautical figures and features whimsical touches inspired by traditional Maya architecture. Inside, the small museum has several gems in its permanent collection, among them works by Botticelli, Ghirlandaio, and Rubens. Changing exhibitions, lectures, concerts, readings, and a film series complete the picture. Closed Sunday mornings and Mondays. No admission charge for children under six. 2121 Park Ave., off Collins Ave. (phone: 673-7533).

HOLOCAUST MEMORIAL This $3-million memorial park is dedicated to the survivors of the Holocaust in Europe during World War II. At the center of the park is the sculpture *Love and Anguish,* a 43-foot bronze outstretched hand that seems to grow from the ground, symbolic of the concentration camp victims' struggle for survival. A walk surrounding the reflecting pool features touching photographs etched into a granite wall by a special chemical process. Open daily. No admission charge. Meridian Ave. and Dade Blvd. (phone: 538-1663).

DOWNTOWN AREA

PORT OF MIAMI Every week thousands of people depart from here on Caribbean cruises, making Miami the world's busiest cruise port. About three million passengers embark annually; more than 16 cruise ships make this their home port, primarily offering three- to seven-day Bahamas-bound trips, three-day to one-week excursions to the eastern and western Caribbean, and day and evening gambling cruises to the Bahamas.

With the rise of terrorism a few years back, increased security measures were taken that now prevent non-cruising visitors from boarding ships. However, you can park your car on the MacArthur Causeway between Downtown Miami and Miami Beach and watch the ships maneuver. Or have a cool drink at an outdoor café in the Art Deco District and watch the behemoths glide out to sea. Ships generally leave port on Fridays, Saturdays, Sundays, or Mondays between 4 and 7 PM; you'll spot the largest outbound fleets on Saturdays and Sundays around 4 or 5 PM.

Among the cruise lines serving the port are *Carnival Cruise Lines* (phone: 800-327-9501); *Dolphin Cruise Line* (phone: 800-222-1003); *Majesty Cruise Line* (phone: 536-0000; 800-532-7788); *Norwegian Cruise Line* (phone: 800-327-7030); and *Royal Caribbean Cruises* (phone: 800-327-6700). For port information, call 371-7678.

BAYSIDE MARKETPLACE On 16 acres of Biscayne Bay shoreline, this shopping and entertainment complex features 150 stores, restaurants, and outdoor cafés, plus great views of the boats docking at the adjacent *Miamarina*. Charter boats may be hired (see *Boating*), and several sightseeing cruises leave from here (see *Sightseeing Tours*). Stroll past two-story, peach-tinted buildings housing merchandise-filled boutiques, or the adjacent open-air *Pier 5 Market,* which offers crafts displayed on pushcarts, stalls filled with artwork, and vendors selling goods from South and Central America and the Caribbean. Open plazas serve as stages for strolling jugglers, street musicians, and cartoon-costumed characters. Among the hot spots here is the *Hard Rock Café* (phone: 377-3110), where burgers and such are served amid rock 'n' roll memorabilia. It's impossible to miss: A huge neon guitar sits atop its roof. The *Warner Brothers* and *Disney* stores do a vigorous business in movie and television paraphernalia. The marketplace is open daily. Visitors may arrive by *Metrorail*'s "Peoplemover," public bus, hotel shuttlebus, car (parking is available), *Water Taxi,* or boat. 401 Biscayne Blvd., entrance at NE Fourth St. and Biscayne Blvd. (phone: 577-3344).

LITTLE HAVANA, CALLE OCHO (EIGHTH STREET) A real Latin flame burns in this Miami community, founded by Cubans who left their native island after Castro's takeover. A few shops feature handmade jewelry, dolls, and works of art, and fruit stands, bakeries, restaurants, and coffee stalls offer authentic Latin food. Many of the eateries are on Southwest Eighth Street, called Calle Ocho in this part of town. Try *Versailles* (3555 Calle Ocho; phone: 445-7614), *Centro Vasco,* or *Málaga* (see *Eating Out* for the latter two) for a typically Cuban or Spanish lunch or dinner—black bean soup, *tapas* or paella, and flan for dessert—then top off your meal with a quick cup of *café cubano* at a sidewalk stall. Watch cigars being hand-rolled by Cuban experts in exile at *La Gloria Cigar Factory* (1872 W. Flagler St.; phone: 642-1653), but never on Sunday. For additional details, see *Quintessential Miami* in DIVERSIONS and *Tour 5: Little Havana* in DIRECTIONS.

METRO-DADE CULTURAL CENTER This huge, $25-million downtown complex, designed by architect Philip Johnson, provides a tranquil Spanish-style oasis in the midst of commercial buildings. It houses the *Center for the Fine Arts,* the *Historical Museum of South Florida,* and the *Miami-Dade Public Library.* 101 W. Flagler St., at NW First Ave.

Center for the Fine Arts Art since World War II and art of the Americas are the focus of this museum, whose name was scheduled at press time to be changed to *The Miami Art Museum of Dade County.* The center hosts major traveling exhibitions of works by artists such as Jasper Johns, but has launched a drive to establish a permanent collection over the next few years. Signs are in English and Spanish. There is a small gift shop. Open extended hours on Thursdays; closed Mondays. Admission charge; voluntary contributions on Tuesdays (phone: 375-1700).

Historical Museum of South Florida The excellent exhibits here chronicle the histories of the various groups that have settled in the region. Numerous displays, including a *chickee* hut, depict Native American life, while the Spanish exploration period comes alive through 17th-century maps and a mock-up of a fort that kids can climb. Maritime history displays include artifacts from treasure fleets. There's also a full-size trolley car that was used in Miami in the 1920s. Exhibitions on the ongoing contributions made by Cubans, blacks, and Jews bring the museum's coverage of the area's history up to date; a sign points out that only "30 years ago, Jews and blacks were barred from part of Dade County." Signs and recorded messages are in both English and Spanish. There's a fine gift shop. Open extended hours on Thursdays; closed Sunday mornings. Admission charge (phone: 375-1492).

Miami-Dade Public Library The main branch of the city's library boasts over one million volumes. In addition, scheduled art exhibitions take place in the first floor auditorium. Open extended hours on Thursdays; closed Sunday mornings October through May; closed all day Sunday June through September (phone: 375-BOOK).

CORAL GABLES

For additional details on this community, see *Tour 4: Cruising through Coral Gables* in DIRECTIONS.

FAIRCHILD TROPICAL GARDEN Founded by a tax attorney with a touch of the poet in him, this just might be one of the most lyrical tax shelters imaginable—83 acres of paradise dotted with lakes and lush with tropical and subtropical plants and trees. Something's always blooming here—it's said to be the largest tropical botanical garden in the continental US. In the wake of Hurricane Andrew, a one-acre plot has been left in its storm-tossed natural state so that students and scientists can observe the natural patterns of regrowth after the fury of the 1992 storm. Other exhibits include the world's largest collection of palms, a rain forest, and a rare-plant house. Complimentary tram rides and walking tours are available, complete with commentary. Visitors also may take a leisurely stroll around the 11 lakes; benches for contemplation are thoughtfully provided. Other features include a snack bar open on weekends from November through April, a gift shop, and a bookstore focusing on horticulture. Closed *Christmas Day*. No admission charge for children under 13. 10901 Old Cutler Rd. (phone: 667-1651).

VENETIAN POOL Once a rock quarry that provided material for many of the stately stone homes in Coral Gables, the *Venetian Pool* is a rare treat. The only swimming pool listed in the National Register of Historic Places, the 822,000-gallon free-form lagoon is fed by underground artesian wells. With its varying levels and waterfalls, coral caves, a palm-fringed island, bridges, and painted gaslight poles, it's a place for Esther Williams fantasies. In fact, movie stars such as Williams, the queen of water ballet, and Johnny "Tarzan" Weismuller once backstroked here, and Paul Whiteman's orchestra performed here. A photo exhibit chronicles beauty pageants and celebrities' visits. Visitors may swim here (amenities include lockers and a café, and swimming and scuba lessons are available), but the pool is extremely crowded during the summer, when kids from local camps come here to splash around. Closed Mondays between *Labor Day* and June 1. Admission charge. 2701 DeSoto Blvd. (phone: 460-5356).

SOUTH MIAMI

For more information on this area, see *Tour 2: South Miami by Car* in DIRECTIONS.

VIZCAYA MUSEUM AND GARDENS This palatial estate is where James Deering, the International Harvester magnate, reaped his personal rewards. Built in 1916, the 70-room Venetian palazzo, with 34 rooms open to the public, is furnished with European antiques, precious china, and artwork from the 15th to the 19th centuries. The Roman sculpture, 17th-century Italian marble tables, and a Chinese snuff-bottle collection are particularly noteworthy. The 10 acres of formal gardens, with fountains, grottoes, statuary, and wonderful plant life, exude an ambience of Italian grandeur and are popular wedding sites. Not surprisingly, this is the site of Miami's annual *Italian Renaissance Festival.* Visitors may explore the house on one of the several guided tours given daily and stroll through the grounds at their leisure. Closed *Christmas Day.* No admission charge for children under five. 3251 S. Miami Ave., just off US 1 (phone: 250-9133).

MIAMI MUSEUM OF SCIENCE AND SPACE TRANSIT PLANETARIUM The exhibitions on coral reefs and the Everglades here are especially enlightening; there's also a participatory science arcade, a wildlife center housing more than 150 live animals, and natural history collections with cases of fossils and butterflies. Kids love the hands-on exhibits and mini-shows on Florida natural life, and visitors inspired by the planetarium show may search for the stars themselves with the *Weintraub Observatory's* telescope. Observatory director Jack Horkheimer is somewhat of a "star" himself; he hosts "Star Hustler," a local PBS TV program that explains what's new in the heavens. The planetarium has several shows daily (laser shows with rock music are scheduled on weekends). The observatory is open Friday and Saturday evenings only, weather permitting. The museum is closed *Thanksgiving* and *Christmas Day.* Separate admission charges to the museum and planetarium; no admission charge to the observatory. 3280 S. Miami Ave. (phone: 854-4247, general information; 854-2222, planetarium).

KEY BISCAYNE

For more information on the island, see *Tour 2: South Miami by Car* in DIRECTIONS.

BILL BAGGS CAPE FLORIDA STATE RECREATION AREA This 400-acre state park was hit hard by Hurricane Andrew in 1992, but it is on the comeback trail. The coconut plantation is gone, and the fallen Australian pines and other trees non-native to Florida have been turned into mulch to support the native cabbage palms, strangler figs, palmetto stands, and sea grape trees planted here as part of a $4-million revegetation project. There's great fishing all along the seawall, and the park is building several fishing platforms on the ocean (due to be completed at press time); bring your own gear and bait. In addition, the beaches, which stretch for $1\frac{1}{4}$ miles, are now wider; a man-made coastal wetlands and mangrove area is being constructed (scheduled to open at press time); there are open-air pavilions for picnickers; and the *El Farito* concession sells sandwiches and rents four-wheel surrey bicycles. Snorkelers will enjoy the underwater scenery just off the beach (bring your own gear). This is also the site of Florida's first lighthouse, a 95-foot-tall structure built in 1825 that has just received a complete renovation. Park facilities include the *Lighthouse Café* (phone: 361-8487), a casual eatery next to the historic lighthouse that features good seafood and stunning ocean views; restrooms; changing areas; and four short boardwalks. Open daily. Admission charge. 1200 Crandon Blvd. (phone: 361-5811).

MIAMI SEAQUARIUM Among the 10,000 sea creatures swimming around the tide pools, jungle islands, and huge reef tank (under a geodesic dome) at South Florida's largest tropical marine aquarium are killer whales, sharks, sea lions, and performing seals and dolphins. The biggest stars of the bunch are Lolita, a killer whale, and Flipper, named after the famous TV dolphin (many episodes of the TV series were filmed here). Four different shows are repeated 15 times throughout the day, including one with Salty, star of the TV film *Salty the Sea Lion.* In addition, a "halfway house" for injured manatees is scheduled to open by the end of this year. Snack stands and a café are on the premises. Open daily. Admission charge. 4400 Rickenbacker Causeway (phone: 361-5705).

SOUTH DADE COUNTY

METROZOO Miami's cageless zoo boasts over 250 different species of rare and exotic animals. Pathways lead through re-creations of Asia, the Eurasian steppes, the European forest, the African jungle, and the African plains—each filled with the area's indigenous animals including elephants, chimpanzees, silverback gorillas, and Bengal tigers (some include the rare white kind). Visitors can enjoy a full day's entertainment by roving through the 290-acre site and attending the daily shows, petting zoo, and feedings. Those who prefer riding to walking can hop aboard the elevated, air conditioned, complimentary monorail that runs every 45 minutes. Several stands offer quick snacks and beverages. Open daily. Admission charge. 12400 SW 152nd St. (phone: 251-0401).

PARROT JUNGLE More of the tropics, but this time, screaming, colorful, and talented. Not only do these parrots, macaws, and cockatoos fly, but they also ride bicycles, roller-skate, and solve math problems—all amid a jungle of huge cypress and live oaks. Don't miss the opportunity to pose for photos with brilliantly plumaged red, turquoise, and yellow parrots poised on your arms and head. Other daily wildlife shows feature snakes, bald eagles, and scorpions. There's also a monkey exhibit and a petting zoo with pigs, goats, and miniature deer. The coffee shop here is a great breakfast stop. Open daily. Admission charge. Two miles south of US 1 at 11000 SW 57th Ave. (Red Rd.) and Killian Dr. (phone: 666-7834). The attraction will move 20 miles away to a new location on Watson Island toward the end of the decade.

MONKEY JUNGLE Four hundred monkeys run free, go swimming, swing from trees, and wander about while visitors watch from encaged walkways. Other attractions include orangutans and gibbons, as well as lush gardens. Naturally, some chimp stars perform (four daily shows rotate continuously). In 1994, an archaeological team uncovered the richest fossil deposit in South Florida here, including more than 5,000 specimens dating back 10,000 years. Open daily. Admission charge. 14805 SW 216th St. (phone: 235-1611).

ELSEWHERE

FRUIT AND SPICE PARK Some 30 tropical acres feature over 500 species of fruit, nut, and spice trees and plants. Guided tours by *Dade County Parks Department* naturalists include samplings of seasonal fruits, and you're free to eat anything that's fallen to the ground. This also is the site of the *Redland Natural Arts Festival* each January and the *Tropical Agricultural Fiesta* each July. Tours are conducted Saturday and Sunday afternoons for a nominal charge. A gift shop sells horticulture-related books, canned and dried tropical fruits, and exotic spices. Closed *Thanksgiving, Christmas Day,* and *New Year's Day.* Admission charge. Thirty-five miles southwest of Miami, at 24801 SW 187th Ave., Homestead (phone: 247-5727).

CORAL CASTLE Hand-built in 1923 by a man who was jilted the day before his wedding, this unusual home is testimony to lost love. More than 1,000 tons of coral rock were dug by hand and fashioned into a two-room tower and a walled-in, roofless courtyard divided into several sections containing outdoor furniture and solar-heated bathtubs. Open daily. No admission charge for children under seven. 28655 US 1, Florida City (phone: 248-6344).

MICCOSUKEE INDIAN VILLAGE Just 25 miles west of Miami, descendants of Florida's original settlers are maintaining the lifestyle of their forebears. Among the attractions are alligator wrestling, crafts demonstrations, a small museum featuring the history of the tribe, and airboat rides that will take you deep into the Everglades. Fresh frogs' legs and catfish dinners are served at the restaurant nearby. Music and arts and crafts festivals are held in July and December. Open daily. Admission charge. US 41 (Tamiami Trail) West (phone: 223-8380, weekdays; 223-8388, weekends).

Sources and Resources

TOURIST INFORMATION

The *Greater Miami Convention and Visitors Bureau* (701 Brickell Ave., Suite 2700, Miami, FL 33131; phone: 539-3000; 800-283-2707; fax: 539-3113) is best for brochures, maps, and general tourist information. It's closed weekends. For information on fairs, art shows, and events in the area's parks, call the *Dade County Parks and Recreation Department*'s information line (phone: 857-6868). Call the *Florida State Parks and Recreation Department* (phone: 904-488-9872) for maps, calendars of events, health updates, and travel advisories. *Activity Line* (phone: 557-5600), a visitor information phone guide in six languages, offers updated schedules of events, plus dining, sports, and shopping tips.

LOCAL COVERAGE The *Miami Herald,* a morning daily, publishes its "Weekend" section, with a full schedule of upcoming events, on Fridays. Also of interest are *New Times,* an alternative weekly; *South Florida* and *Ocean Drive* magazines, both monthly; and the *South Florida Business Journal* and *Miami Today,* both weekly newspapers. Spanish publications include the dailies *El Nuevo Herald* and *Diario de las Américas,* and monthly magazines *Miami Mensual* and *Selecta.*

TELEVISION STATIONS WPBT Channel 2–PBS; WFOR Channel 4–CBS; WTVJ Channel 6–NBC; WSVN Channel 7–Fox; and WPLG Channel 10–ABC.

RADIO STATIONS AM: WIOD 610 (news); and WINZ 940 (news/talk). FM: WLRN 91.3 (public radio); WTMI 93.1 (classical); WLVE 93.9 (mellow jazz); WZTA 94.9 (rock); WKIS 99.9 (country); WMXJ 102.7 (oldies); WSHE 103.5 (alternative); WBGG 106 ('70s); WJQY 106.7 (easy listening); and WQBA 107.5 (Spanish).

TELEPHONE The area code for Miami is 305.

SALES TAX The sales tax is 6.5% in Dade County, 6% in most other counties. There's also a 12.5% Dade County hotel tax, although three municipalities have different rates: the hotel tax is 11.5% in Miami Beach, 9.5% in Bal Harbour, and 10.5% in Surfside. Local meal taxes are generally from 6.5% to 8.5%; in Bal Harbour, the rate is 9.5%, and in Surfside, 8.5%.

GETTING AROUND

AIRPORT *Miami International Airport* is a 15- to 20-minute drive from Downtown Miami and 20 to 30 minutes from Miami Beach—longer during rush hours. Van service between the airport and the city is provided by *Supershuttle* (phone: 800-8-SHUTTL or 871-2000); fares start at $6. *Tri-Rail* (phone: 800-TRI-RAIL in Florida; 305-728-8445 elsewhere in the US) offers free shuttle bus service between *Miami International Airport* and the commuter rail station in Hialeah, a suburb of Miami (also see "Tri-Rail," below).

BUS *Metrobus* serves Downtown Miami, Collins Avenue in Miami Beach, Coral Gables, and Coconut Grove fairly well, but service to other areas tends to be slow and complicated. The fare is $1.25 plus 25¢ for a transfer. For information on routes and schedules, call 638-6700.

CAR RENTAL Miami is served by all the large national firms. Intensive competition makes rates here among the least expensive in the country, but if you want to drive a convertible or minivan during peak season, be sure to reserve one well in advance. For more information, see GETTING READY TO GO.

METRORAIL/METROMOVER *Metrorail,* an elevated rail system, operates from the *Dadeland* shopping mall in the Kendall area to Downtown Miami, and beyond to the *Civic Center* and Hialeah; fare, $1.25. Offering the best views of Miami, the *Metromover* rail system is a 4.3-mile downtown loop; the fare is 25¢, free for those transferring from the *Metrorail.* For information, call 638-6700.

TAXI You sometimes can hail a cab in the street, but it's better to order one on the phone or pick one up in front of any of the big hotels. Major cab companies are *Central Cab* (phone: 532-5555); *Metro Taxi* (phone: 888-8888); *Super Yellow Cab* (phone: 888-7777); and *Yellow Cab* (phone: 444-4444).

TRI-RAIL The 67-mile commuter railroad system began operating in 1989, connecting Dade, Broward, and Palm Beach Counties with increasingly frequent daily routes. The fare ranges from $2 to $5.50 one way and $3.50 to $9.25 round trip, depending on the distance traveled. Passengers board the double-decker trains at any of 15 stops, with connecting passes to *Metrorail/Metromover* and shuttle buses. Transfers to county buses cost 25¢ or less. The train provides access to major sights and, via connecting buses, to the *Miami International, Ft. Lauderdale/Hollywood,* and *Palm Beach International* airports. Extra trains are scheduled for games at the *Joe Robbie* and *Orange Bowl Stadiums* and for special events. There are also guided tours to *Bayside Marketplace* and other attractions. The *Tri-Rail* system is accessible to disabled passengers (phone: 800-TRI-RAIL in Florida; 305-728-8445 elsewhere in the US).

WATER TAXI The *Water Taxi* (phone: 467-6677) runs daily, stopping at major restaurants and other popular landings. The taxis operate on demand as late as 1 AM and must be summoned by phone. Fare is $7 one way; $14 for an all-day pass.

SIGHTSEEING TOURS

Knowledgeable and folksy narrated walking, boat, and *Metromover* rail tours, sponsored by the *Historical Museum of Southern Florida,* are led by Dr. Paul S. George, a local history professor. Itineraries include Little Havana, the Art Deco District, Coconut Grove, Coral Gables, a Miami River boat tour, and a Key Biscayne boat tour (phone: 375-1625).

BOAT Miami is largely a waterfront city, and one good way to get to know it is by boat—excursions range from narrated tours of Millionaires' Row to romantic sunset cruises. Departing from the marina at *Bayside Marketplace* (see *Special Places,* above) are three popular cruises: The *Island Queen* (phone: 379-5119) offers daily hour-and-a-half tours; *Bayside Cruises* (phone: 822-2428) offers six cruises on Fridays, Saturdays, and Sundays on the 49-passenger *Pauhana,* docked next to the *Hard Rock Café;* and the *Heritage of Miami* (phone: 442-9697), a dramatic tall ship, offers daily two-hour tours of Biscayne Bay and also is available for charters. The *Lady Lucille* (phone: 534-7000) docks in front of the *Fontainebleau Hilton Resort & Towers* (see *Checking In*) and offers three 90-minute sightseeing cruises daily.

HELICOPTER/PLANE *Chalk's International Airlines* (phone: 371-8628; 800-4-CHALKS) offers half-hour scenic air tours of Miami on Saturday afternoons, as well as scheduled flights every day to Bimini and Paradise Island in the Bahamas.

WALKING The *Miami Design Preservation League* (phone: 672-1836) sponsors walking tours of Miami Beach's Art Deco District.

SPECIAL EVENTS

On *New Year's Eve,* Miami's annual *Orange Bowl Parade,* which starts from Biscayne Boulevard, serves as a prelude to the *FedEx Orange Bowl,* held on the evening of January 1. This year, the location of the game is scheduled to move from *Orange Bowl Stadium* to *Joe Robbie Stadium* (phone: 371-4600 for information). The *King Mango Strut Parade,* held a few days earlier, pokes fun at the lavish *Orange Bowl* festivities (phone: 444-7270). *Umoja Night—The Lighting of the Community Kinara* is a celebration of *Kwanzaa,* an African-American holiday that falls just before *New Year's;* it features music, dancing, and food (phone: 836-7344). The annual *Art Miami Fair,* which showcases contemporary art, a good percentage of it Latin American, is held at the *Miami Beach Convention Center* in early January (phone: 673-7311). Also in January, an *Art Deco Weekend* takes place on Ocean Drive, in the heart of South Beach's historic Art Deco District (phone: 672-2014). Miami Beach also hosts the *Festival of the Arts* each February (phone: 673-7733). The *Coconut Grove Art Festival* also is held in February (phone: 447-0401), as is the *Miami Film Festival,* 10 days of national and international film premieres with visiting directors, producers, and stars (phone: 377-3456), and the *International Boat Show,* the largest boat show in the world, which is held at the *Miami Beach Convention Center* (phone: 531-8410).

In March, natives and visitors alike head for Calle Ocho (Eighth St.) in Little Havana for *Carnaval Miami,* a nine-day festival featuring a 23-block street party, Latin foods, conga lines, salsa bands, and lots of people (phone: 644-8888). In April, the *Yamaha Miami Billfish Tournament* attracts more than 300 anglers in pursuit of sailfish, vying for South Florida's richest fishing purse (phone: 365-0497 or 561-2868). May ushers in the *Miami Home Show* at the *Miami Beach Convention Center* (phone: 666-5944). Coconut Grove is the site of the *Miami/Bahamas Goombay Festival* in June, celebrating the area's Bahamian heritage. It's considered the country's largest black heritage festival, with *junkanoo* groups (local citizens who form bands and play calypso and reggae music continuously on homemade instruments) and lots of conch chowder and fritters (phone: 372-9966).

July brings the *Tropical Agricultural Fiesta* at the *Fruit and Spice Park* and the *Annual Everglades Music and Crafts Festival* at the *Miccosukee Indian Village* (see *Special Places* for information on both sites). For sailboat enthusiasts, the two-day *Columbus Day Regatta* in October attracts more than 300 entrants (phone: 876-0818). In November, the *Miami Book Fair International,* held at *Miami Dade Community College,* welcomes authors, publishers, booksellers, and street vendors to one of the world's largest week-long celebrations of the printed word, considered the country's premier literary event by *The New York Times* and *Publisher's Weekly* (phone: 237-3258). In November, race cars fire up their engines for the *Nascar Busch Series* at the new *Homestead* race track (phone: 379-RACE). The Miccosukee tribe's annual *Arts Festival* in late December draws members from 20 tribes who perform songs and dances, and demonstrate other skills at the *Miccosukee Indian Village* (phone: 223-8380). Also in late December is the *Carquest Auto Parts Bowl*, a top-ranked collegiate football classic (phone: 564-5000) that only adds to Miami's city-wide football mania leading up to the *Orange Bowl* game on *New Year's Day.*

MUSEUMS

In addition to those described in *Special Places,* other museums to see include the following.

AMERICAN POLICE HALL OF FAME AND MUSEUM A marble monument commemorates more than 7,000 slain officers. Exhibits in the three-story building include law enforcement vehicles and equipment, including a guillotine and an electric chair. At a mock crime scene, visitors are encouraged to solve a murder. Closed *Christmas Day.* Admission charge. 3801 Biscayne Blvd., Miami (phone: 573-0070).

ART MUSEUM AT FLORIDA INTERNATIONAL UNIVERSITY The varied exhibits here include painting retrospectives, photography shows, and displays of university graduates' work. Open extended hours on Mondays; closed Saturday mornings and Sundays. No admission charge. University Park, SW 107th Ave. and Eighth St., Miami (phone: 348-2890).

LOWE ART MUSEUM The highlight here is the *Kress Collection of Italian Renaissance and Baroque Art,* a permanent collection of European and American art from antiquity to the present, and Native American, African, Asian, and pre-Columbian art. There also are visiting exhibits. Closed Sunday mornings and Mondays. Admission charge. 1301 Stanford Dr., on the *University of Miami* campus in Coral Gables (phone: 284-3535).

MIAMI YOUTH MUSEUM Hands-on exhibits, including *Kidscape,* a miniature neighborhood with Dr. Smile's dental office, a fire station, and a supermarket, are fun for kids of all ages. There's also a "Metro-Dade Safe Neighborhood" exhibit and a newspaper exhibit called "Hot off the Press." Guided tours are in both English and Spanish. Closed Mondays and holidays. Admission charge. *Miracle Center,* 3301 Coral Way, Level U, Coral Gables (phone: 661-3046).

WOLFSONIAN MUSEUM For decades, multimillionaire Mitchell Wolfson Jr. collected objets d'art, rare books, and everyday items. When the collection grew too large—it now incorporates 60,000 examples of propaganda and the decorative arts—he bought an Art Deco–style warehouse and opened a museum and study center. The result is a rare documentary of American and European cultural history from 1885 to 1945. Closed Mondays. Admission charge. 1001 Washington Ave., Miami Beach (phone: 531-6287).

MAJOR COLLEGES AND UNIVERSITIES

The *University of Miami* in Coral Gables (1200 San Amaro Dr.; phone: 284-2211), with an enrollment of 13,500, has a four-year college and highly regarded graduate schools (medical campus, 1600 NW 10th Ave.; marine science campus, Rickenbacker Causeway, Key Biscayne). *Florida International University* is a four-year college with two separate campuses (SW Eighth St. and 107th Ave., Miami, and NE 151st St. and Biscayne Blvd., North Miami; phone: 348-2000). *Miami Dade Community College* (main campus: 11380 NW 27th Ave.; phone: 237-1093), is the largest junior college in the country.

SHOPPING

In addition to sparkling blue waters and broad wind-swept beaches, Miami offers some sand-free sports—and the best of them is shopping. The places listed below carry a wide variety of items, and many have interesting restaurants and scenic views as well. For general shopping hours, see GETTING READY TO GO.

Aventura Mall One of South Florida's largest malls, with 200 shops and stores on two levels. Anchors are *Lord & Taylor, Macy's, JC Penney,* and *Sears.* A large food court offers a pause that refreshes. 19501 Biscayne Blvd., North Miami Beach (phone: 935-1110).

Bal Harbour Shops Lovely open-air shopping amid gardens and fountains attracts the international jet set and wannabes. The 100 upscale stores include *Saks Fifth Avenue, Neiman Marcus, Cartier, Gucci, Brooks Brothers, Chanel, Cartier, Bally, Louis Vuitton, Mark Cross, A/X Armani Exchange,* and *Tiffany & Co.* Cutting-edge fashion is available at *Gianni Versace, Romanoff Couture, Caron Cherry,* and *Fendi.* Good snack stops include *Bal Harbour Bistro,*

Coco's Sidewalk Cafe, and *Carpaccio.* 9700 Collins Ave., Bal Harbour (phone: 866-0311).

Bayside Marketplace From the designers of Boston's *Faneuil Hall,* this shopping and entertainment complex overlooking the water has 150 shops and restaurants. There are also pushcarts where you can buy arts and crafts items from South America, Central America, and the Caribbean. Also see *Special Places.* 401 Biscayne Blvd., Miami (phone: 577-3344).

Books & Books Both locations, one in Coral Gables and the other in Miami Beach, offer frequent readings by authors such as Carlos Fuentes and Susan Sontag. The Coral Gables store also features a sizable selection of used and out of print books. 296 Aragon Ave., Coral Gables (phone: 442-4408), and 933 Lincoln Rd., Miami Beach (phone: 532-3222).

CocoWalk An exciting open-air, Mediterranean-style shopping complex in the heart of Coconut Grove, it boasts three dozen shops, several eateries (including *Café Tu-Tu Tango;* see *Eating Out*), and entertainment for the young and young-at-heart. Stores are closed holidays. 3015 Grand Ave., Coconut Grove (phone: 444-0777).

Dadeland Mall This large mall in the Kendall section of southwest Miami claims Florida's largest *Burdines,* along with *Saks Fifth Avenue, Lord & Taylor,* and 165 other shops. 7535 N. Kendall Dr., Kendall (phone: 665-6226).

Elite Fine Art Latin American art by masters and emerging artists. Closed weekends. 3140 Ponce de León Blvd., Coral Gables (phone: 448-3800).

Epicure Market *The* place on the Beach for unusual grocery items and take-out goodies for sand or sea, including three types of smoked salmon, imported caviar, fresh-ground coffee, large cooked shrimp, and prepared meals. 1656 Alton Rd., Miami Beach (phone: 672-1861).

Falls Shopping Center More than 60 upscale stores and restaurants set among splashing waterfalls in the Kendall section of Miami. 8888 SW 136th St., Miami (phone: 255-4570).

Florida Keys Factory Shops Excellent bargains amid a Mediterranean setting complete with fountains. More than 50 shops for browsing in addition to an open-air food court. About 30 miles south of Miami, 250 E. Palm Dr., Florida City (phone: 248-4727).

A Likely Story Children's books and educational toys, including easels, games, and specialty items. 5740 Sunset Dr., South Miami (phone: 667-3730).

Mayfair Shops in the Grove High-fashion shops such as *Polo/Ralph Lauren* and *Ann Taylor* are still found here, but now the mix is more mainstream. Newly renovated, the mall has a 10-screen movie theater, new boutiques and shops, and the trendy *Planet Hollywood* restaurant (see *Eating Out*). This mall is worth a visit if only to bask in the fabulous Alhambresque atmosphere. 2911 Grand Ave., Coconut Grove (phone: 448-1700).

Miami Duty-Free Travelers planning to leave the country, even for a short cruise, may buy items at duty-free prices right in Miami, in this clean, uncluttered shop. Drive into the highly secure parking lot and present either your cruise or flight ticket and passport to the security guard. Select and pay for your goods. *MDF* will deliver your purchases to your plane at *Miami International Airport* or your ship at the Port of Miami on the day of departure. Items include Calvin Klein scents, Cartier watches, Wedgwood china, jewelry, and leather goods. Salespeople speak many languages. Prices are 20% to 40% below retail, and no Florida tax is levied. 125 NE Eighth St., Miami (phone: 358-9774).

Unicorn Village Market This large, trendy shop associated with the *Unicorn Village* restaurant (see *Eating Out*) features enormous displays of organically grown produce, prepared Pritikin Diet items, and wines produced without pesticides or added sulfites. There's also prepared food to go. At *The Shops at the Waterways,* 3595 NE 207th St., North Miami Beach (phone: 933-8829).

Virginia Miller Galleries Features major works by 19th- and 20th-century artists. There's contemporary artwork by Cuban Americans, Latin Americans such as Tamayo and Matta, and European artists such as Karel Appel. Closed Sundays. 169 Madeira Ave., Coral Gables (phone: 444-4493).

SPORTS AND FITNESS

BASEBALL The *National League's* Florida *Marlins* play at *Joe Robbie Stadium* near the north county line (2269 NW 199th St.; phone: 620-2578 or 623-6100). The *University of Miami Hurricanes* play at *Mark Light Stadium* (on campus at 1 Hurricane Dr., corner of Ponce de León and San Amaro, Coral Gables; phone: 284-2655; 800-GO-CANES).

BASKETBALL The *Heat,* Miami's *NBA* entry, burns up the court at the *Miami Arena* (701 Arena Way, Miami; phone: 577-HEAT, tickets; 530-4400, information).

BICYCLING Cyclists have more than 100 miles of bicycle paths at their disposal in the Miami area. A 3½-mile bicycle path on Key Biscayne originates in *Crandon Park* and goes through the beach area, woods, and hammocks of trees and cane grass before ending at *Sundays on the Bay* restaurant. The *Dade County Parks and Recreation Department* has more information (phone: 375-4507). Another favorite spot for cyclists and runners is *Tropical Park.* The 2-mile path winds through a wooded area, along two lakes, and past sports facilities. Pick up a map at the park office (7900 40th Rd., Miami; phone: 226-8315; open weekdays) or the tennis center (same address and phone as the park office; open daily).

Bicycle rentals are available throughout the Greater Miami area. A few places to try: *Dade Cycle Shop* (3216 Grand Ave., Coconut Grove; phone: 443-6075); *Mangrove Cycles* (260 Crandon Blvd., Key Biscayne; phone: 361-5555); and *Miami Beach Bicycle Center* (601 Fifth St., Miami Beach; phone: 673-2055).

BOATING Greater Miami is laced with navigable waters and has many private and public marinas with all kinds of boats for rent. Sailboats and powerboats, along with windsurfers and day sailers, are available from *Easy Sailing* (3400 Pan American Dr., Coconut Grove; phone: 858-4001). Sailboat rentals are available through *Sailboats Miami* (Rickenbacker Causeway, Miami; phone: 361-SAIL) and *Sailboats of Key Biscayne* (*Crandon Marina,* 4000 Crandon Blvd., Miami; phone: 361-0328). The *Pauhana,* a 49-passenger catamaran, is available for charter or sunset tours (401 NE Fourth St. at *Bayside Marketplace,* Miami; phone: 888-3002 or 822-2428). *Club Nautico,* a good choice for powerboat rentals, has docks in Miami (phone: 673-2502) and Coconut Grove (phone: 858-6258). Boat rentals also are available through *Haulover Marine Center* (15000 Collins Ave., Miami Beach; phone: 945-3934). For information on sport fishing charters, see *Fishing,* below.

DOG RACING Greyhound racing is held at the *Flagler Greyhound Track* (401 NW 38th Ct., Miami; phone: 649-3000). Check the racing dates before heading to the track.

FISHING Anglers of every ilk will find their special brand of fishing within reach here. Surf and offshore saltwater fishing is available year-round, and there's also plenty of freshwater action in canals and backwaters, including the Everglades and Florida Bay.

Charter boats offer a choice of half-day or full-day deep-sea fishing. There are dozens of boats listed under "Fishing" in the Miami yellow pages, but the following are among our favorites. *Blue Waters* (16375 Collins Ave., North Miami Beach; phone: 944-4531) rents 50-foot and larger fishing boats with captain, mate, bait, and tackle. Other favorites include the *Kelley Fleet at Haulover* (10800 Collins Ave. Miami Beach; phone: 945-3801 or 949-1173). *Crandon Marina* (4000 Crandon Blvd., Key Biscayne; phone: 361-1281) offers fishing boats; powerboats, speedboats, and overnight cruises are also available. Charter boats for sport fishing are available at *Miami Beach Marina* (300 Alton Rd., phone: 673-6000), where you'll also find the party boat *The Reward. Haulover Marine Center* (15000 Collins Ave., Miami Beach; phone: 945-3934) offers rack storage facilities for boats.

The boardwalks on the Rickenbacker and MacArthur Causeways also are popular fishing spots. The *Holiday Inn Newport Pier* (16701 Collins Ave., Miami Beach; phone: 949-1300) is open 24 hours daily and provides equipment rental; there's an admission charge.

Fishing seasons offshore vary by location, as do regulations on kinds and sizes of fish you're allowed to catch. The *Florida Fishing Handbook* is available at no charge by writing to the *Florida Game and Fresh Water Fish Commission* (620 S. Meridian St., Tallahassee, FL 32399-1600; phone: 904-488-1960). Licenses are required for both freshwater and saltwater fishing, and can be obtained from bait and tackle shops as well as some *Kmart* stores. Long-term licenses may be obtained by contacting the state commission.

Competitive fisherfolk may want to enter the *Yamaha Miami Billfish Tournament,* held in April (see *Special Events*).

FITNESS CENTERS Staying in shape is no problem in Dade County. Try the *YMCA* in the *World Trade Center Building* (90 SW Eighth St.; phone: 577-3091); visitors who are members of a *Y Away Plan* back home (more than 50 miles away) are welcome without charge. The *Cross Training Fitness Centers* (2901 Florida Ave., Coconut Grove; phone: 442-2400); *Downtown Athletic Club* (200 S. Biscayne Blvd., Miami; phone: 358-9988); *Gold's Gym Miami* (1617 SW 107th Ave., Miami; phone: 553-8878); *Washington's Gym* (95 Hook Sq., Miami Springs; phone: 885-8130); and *World Gym* (3737 SW Eighth St., Coral Gables; phone: 445-5161) are also open to visitors for a fee.

FOOTBALL The *NFL Dolphins* are the team, and *Dolphin*-mania sweeps through the entire city during the pro football season, so for good seats call the *Joe Robbie Stadium* in North Miami in advance (2269 NW 199th St.; phone: 620-2578; fax: 620-6596). The *University of Miami Hurricanes* play at *Orange Bowl Stadium* (1501 NW Third St.; phone: 358-5885 for tickets, 643-7100 for other *Orange Bowl* information; fax: 643-7115). Or contact the *University of Miami* ticket office (5821 San Amaro Dr., Coral Gables; phone: 284-2655 or 1-800-GO-CANES).

GOLF Its almost constant sunshine, balmy breezes, and picturesque fairways make Greater Miami a golfer's dream—witness the preponderance of golf tournaments held here. Resorts and hotels without their own courses usually can provide access to other clubs.

TOP TEE-OFF SPOT

Doral Golf Resort & Spa At the moment, this 667-room resort is the grande golfing dame of the Miami–Miami Beach tourist axis. *The Doral*'s superb golf facilities (four 18-hole layouts plus a par 3 executive course) thus far remain unsurpassed. The fabled championship *Blue Monster* course is still one of the most formidable challenges in the state, and the *Gold* course offers little diminution in challenge. The pro is Don Pesant; the *Jim McLean Learning Center* is the pro workshop. 4400 NW 87th Ave., Miami (phone: 592-2000 or 800-71-DORAL; fax: 594-4682).

In addition, Miami has more first-rate courses open to the public than most places you can name. Among the better ones are *Bayshore* (2301 Alton

Rd., Miami Beach; phone: 532-3350); *Kendale Lakes* (6401 Kendale Lakes Dr., Miami; phone: 382-3930); *Keys Gate Golf and Tennis Club* (2300 Palm Dr., Homestead; phone: 230-0362); *The Links at Key Biscayne* (6700 Crandon Blvd., Key Biscayne; phone: 361-9129); *Miami Springs* (650 Curtiss Pkwy., Miami Springs; phone: 888-2377); and *Palmetto* (9300 SW 152nd St., Miami; phone: 238-2922). For more information about golfing in Miami, call *Tee Times,* a 24-hour reservation line (phone: 669-9500), or the parks and recreation departments of Dade County (phone: 857-6868), Miami Beach (phone: 673-7730), or Miami (phone: 575-5240).

The *Honda Golf Classic,* played in March at the *Tournament Players Club at Eagle Trace* in Coral Springs (phone: 954-346-4000), is one of the major US events on the *PGA* circuit. You might spot such pros as Nick Price, Nick Faldo, or Fred Couples attempting a birdie here. The $1.4-million *Doral-Ryder Open* is held annually in late February or early March on the championship *Blue Monster* course at the *Doral Golf Resort & Spa* (see above).

HOCKEY The Florida *Panthers* hockey team is the newest addition to Florida's professional sports teams, and one of the newest expansion teams competing in the *National Hockey League.* Until a permanent stadium is built for them, home games are played at the *Miami Arena* (701 Arena Blvd., Miami; phone: 530-4444).

HORSE RACING The *Hialeah Race Track* (2200 E. Fourth Ave., Hialeah; phone: 885-8000; 800-442-5324), listed on the National Register of Historic Places, is worth a visit just to see the beautiful grounds and clubhouse and the famous flock of pink flamingos. Call for racing times. There also is thoroughbred racing at *Calder Race Course* in North Dade County, next to *Joe Robbie Stadium* (21001 NW 27th Ave.; phone: 625-1311 in Dade County; 523-4324 in Broward County). The country's only all-weather racetrack, it's open from May through January. The track's "Family Sundays" feature clowns, games, face painting, and a petting zoo. Dining is available in the *Clubhouse Dining Room, Blinker's Cafe,* and *Turf Club.*

ICE SKATING If it's too hot outside, consider ice skating. *The Miami Ice Arena* (14770 Biscayne Blvd., North Miami Beach; phone: 940-8222) has skate rentals.

JAI ALAI Almost year-round, there's betting nightly on jai alai (a Basque game resembling a combination of lacrosse, handball, and tennis) at the *Miami Jai-Alai Fronton,* the country's largest (3500 NW 37th Ave., Miami; phone: 633-6400). You can buy tickets at the gate or reserve them in advance.

JET SKIING For action-packed water fun, jet skis are available at *Tony's Jet Ski Rentals* (3501 Rickenbacker Causeway, Key Biscayne; phone: 361-8280) and *Fun Watersports* (*Miami Airport Hilton and Marina,* 5101 Blue Lagoon Dr., Miami; phone: 261-7687).

JOGGING In Miami, run along South Bayshore Drive to *David Kennedy Park,* at 22nd Avenue, and jog the Vita Path. In Miami Beach, run on a wooden boardwalk that extends along the ocean from 21st to 46th Street, or run toward the parcourse track on the southern tip of South Beach. The *Miami Mile,* a world class event fashioned after New York's *Fifth Avenue Mile* and San Francisco's *California Mile,* is off and running the third week of January. For more information, call 759-5990.

MOTORCYCLING Harley-Davidson motorcycles are all the rage with the South Beach crowd, so why not cruise Miami on your own "chrome pony"? Harleys are for rent at *The Biker's Place* (12864 Biscayne Blvd., North Miami; phone: 673-2932); delivery to hotels in South Beach is complimentary.

NATURE WALKS There are nature walks at *Fairchild Tropical Garden* and the *Fruit and Spice Park* (see *Special Places*). In addition, the *Dade County Parks and Recreation Department* (phone: 857-6868) sponsors frequent guided tours through natural hammocks, tree forests, and bird rookeries. For canoe trips and van tours of the Everglades call *The Naturalist Services* (phone: 662-4124).

ROLLER BLADING You'll see in-line skaters all over South Florida, particularly on South Beach and in Coconut Grove. Join them by buying or renting skates at *Skate 2000* (1200 Ocean Dr., Miami Beach; phone: 538-8282). You can skate indoors to a computerized light show—two million lights synchronized to music—at *Hot Wheels Roller Skating Center* (12265 SW 112th St., Kendall; phone: 595-2958).

SCUBA DIVING Diving opportunities abound along the coast, where a three-banded basic reef system extends upward from the Florida Keys, past Miami and Ft. Lauderdale. Although it's broken up in spots, and some areas are polluted, plenty of opportunities exist for spotting elkhorn and brain coral—even bright red soft corals at deeper levels—and colorful tropical fish. The first reef is about 15 feet deep, the second about 40 feet deep, and the third is 60 to 100 feet deep. The practice of sinking freighters and other large objects in the sea to create artificial reefs lures oceans of finny friends at 100- and 200-foot depths. Miami boasts about 150 wrecks, and numerous dive shops operate in this area. Among them are *Diver's Paradise* (*Crandon Marina,* Key Biscayne; phone: 361-DIVE); *The Diving Locker* (223 Sunny Isles Blvd., Miami; phone: 947-6025); and *Team Divers* (300 Alton Rd., Miami Beach; phone: 673-0101; 800-543-7887). Also look in the yellow pages.

SKY DIVING *Skydive Miami* (*Homestead General Airport;* phone: SKYDIVE; 800-759-3483) will fly you up and let you sail down. The company also will provide—for a fee—video or still shots of your dive.

SWIMMING With an average daily temperature of 75F, and miles of ocean beach on the Atlantic, Miami Beach and Key Biscayne offer some great places for swimming, all water sports, and another prime activity: sedentary sun worshiping. A 2-mile stretch of beach is open at *Crandon Park* (Rickenbacker Causeway to Key Biscayne; phone: 361-5421). The southern end of Haulover Beach (A1A north of Bal Harbour; phone: 947-3525) is popular with families, while the northern end is Miami's unofficial clothing-optional beach. There are also a marina, sightseeing boats, charter fishing fleets, kite-flying concessions, and restaurants. Miami Beach has several long stretches of public beach at various places, including South Beach (Fifth St. and Collins Ave.), a favorite of surfers; *Lummus Park* (South Beach on Ocean Ave.), with lots of shade; and North Shore Beach (71st St. and Collins Ave.), with landscaped dunes and an oceanfront walkway. There are also small public beaches at the east ends of streets near major hotels.

TENNIS Mild and sunny weather make South Florida ideal for year-round tennis, as attested to by illustrious part-time residents Gabriela Sabatini and Steffi Graf.

CHOICE COURTS

Doral Golf Resort & Spa A veritable metropolis of a resort, this 2,400-acre establishment offers 15 well-kept clay and hard-surface tennis courts, backboards, ball machines, private lessons, and group clinics. The late Arthur Ashe was director of tennis; the program is currently managed by *Peter Burwash International Clinics.* 4400 NW 87th Ave., Miami (phone: 592-2000; 800-327-6334 or 800-71-DORAL; fax: 594-4682).

Fisher Island Club This exclusive resort's tennis program has two grass, two hard, and 14 clay courts, all lighted. You might bump into a movie star or millionaire working on his or her serve. Private lessons, weekly clinics, and round-robins help tune up your game. There's also a pro shop. 1 Fisher Island Dr., Fisher Island (phone: 535-6021; 800-624-3251 outside Florida; fax: 535-6003).

International Tennis Center The site of the annual *Lipton Championships,* the center is available for play year-round, offering two grass courts, 16 hard and eight clay courts, a pro shop, and lessons. 7300 Crandon Blvd., Key Biscayne (phone: 365-2300).

Turnberry Isle Major Pro-Am tournaments, such as the *Fred Stolle Invitational,* are held here There are 26 tennis courts (16 lighted), including 12 clay, 12 hard, and two grass courts. The teaching staff is under the guidance of Fred Stolle, a winner of *Wimbledon* and the *French, US,* and *Australian Opens.* 19999 W. Country Club Dr., Aventura, Turnberry Isle (phone: 932-6200; 800-327-7028; fax: 931-9256).

Most of Miami's major resort hotels have tennis courts for the use of their guests, and there are also public facilities throughout the county, including those at the *Flamingo Stadium* in Miami Beach's *Flamingo Park Tennis Center* (1200 12th St.; phone: 673-7761), with 19 clay courts; *Tamiami* (11201 SW 24th St., Miami; phone: 223-7076); *North Shore Center* (350 73rd St., Miami Beach; phone: 993-2022); *Miami Springs Tennis Courts* (401 Westward Dr., Miami Springs; phone: 885-3654) and *Tropical Park* (7900 SW 40th St., Miami; phone: 553-3161). In addition, there are over 200 public courts in metropolitan Dade County (phone: 857-6868).

The 11-day *Lipton Championships* tournament is one of the world's largest tennis happenings, with such top players as Boris Becker and Ivan Lendl on hand in March. For information and tickets, contact the *International Tennis Center* (see above) or the tournament office (2 Alhambra Plaza, Coral Gables; phone: 446-2200 or 442-3367).

WATER SKIING Those not staying at a beachfront resort can try the sport at *Fun Watersports* (*Miami Airport Hilton and Marina,* 5101 Blue Lagoon Dr., Miami; phone: 261-7687).

WINDSURFING Major beachfront hotels rent equipment, but Windsurfer Beach at Key Biscayne is considered by many to be the prime spot. Bring your own board or rent from *Sailboards Miami* (Rickenbacker Causeway; phone: 361-SAIL), which offers two-hour lessons guaranteed to teach any novice.

THEATER

For current offerings, check the publications listed in *Tourist Information* in this chapter. The *Coconut Grove Playhouse* (3500 Main Hwy.; phone: 442-4000) imports New York stars for its season of classics that runs from November through May. The *Jackie Gleason Theater of the Performing Arts,* referred to locally as *TOPA* (1700 Washington Ave., Miami Beach; phone: 673-7300), offers touring plays and musicals, including some pre- and post-Broadway shows. The *Gusman Center for the Performing Arts* (174 E. Flagler St., Miami; phone: 372-0925) and the *Dade County Auditorium* (2901 W. Flagler St., Miami; phone: 545-3395) book theatrical and cultural events year-round.

MUSIC

Visiting orchestras and artists perform in Miami at the *Gusman Center for the Performing Arts* and the *Dade County Auditorium,* and in Miami Beach at the *Jackie Gleason Theater of the Performing Arts* (see *Theater,* above, for details on all three). The *Florida Grand Opera* (1200 Coral Way, Miami; phone: 854-7890; 800-741-1010) stages a full complement of major productions during the winter season, as does the *New World Symphony* (541 Lincoln Rd., Miami Beach; phone: 673-3331). The *Cameo Theater*, a nightclub and concert venue (1445 Washington Ave., Miami Beach; phone: 532-0922) hosts all manner of performers year-round. Luminaries such as Gloria Estefan, Madonna, and Billy Joel often perform at the *Miami Arena* (701

Arena Way, Miami; phone: 530-4444) and the *Orange Bowl Stadium* (1501 NW Third St., Miami; phone: 643-7100).

DANCE

The *Miami City Ballet* (905 Lincoln Rd., Miami Beach; phone: 532-7713), headed by Edward Villella, is one of the country's best young companies, and performs a full season beginning each fall at four South Florida venues: the *Jackie Gleason Theater* (1700 Washington Ave., Miami Beach), the *Bailey Concert Hall* (3501 SW Bailey Rd., Ft. Lauderdale), the *Broward Center* (201 SW Fifth Ave., Ft. Lauderdale), and the *Kravits Center* (701 Okeechobee Blvd., West Palm Beach). There are numerous performances of *The Nutcracker* throughout the region around *Christmastime*.

NIGHTCLUBS AND NIGHTLIFE

For night owls interested in Miami's myriad after-dark destinations, there are several 24-hour recorded information lines, among them the *Jazz Hotline* (phone: 382-3938); *Blues Hotline* (phone: 666-MOJO); the *PACE Free Concert Line* (phone: 895-5488); and the *Swing Dance Hotline* (phone: 944-9917).

The *Club Tropigala* show at the *Fontainebleau Hilton Resort & Towers* (phone: 672-7469; see *Checking In*) may make customers think they're watching a lavish "flesh and feathers" production in pre-Castro Havana; *Les Violins* (1751 Biscayne Blvd., Miami; phone: 371-8668) also presents a flashy show with a Cuban twist. Latin jazz and salsa bands enliven *Centro Vasco* (see *Eating Out*) late Friday nights, while Las Vegas–style revues fill two stages at the *Holiday Inn Newport Pier* (16701 Collins Ave., Miami Beach; phone: 949-1300) Wednesdays through Sundays. In Little Havana, shout *olé* to flamenco shows at *Málaga* (see *Eating Out*).

For live blues and a bit of history, stop in at *Tobacco Road* (626 S. Miami Ave., Miami; phone: 374-1198), Miami's oldest bar. If jazz is your bag, try *Greenstreet's* (2051 Le Jeune Rd., Coral Gables; phone: 443-2301) or *MoJazz* (928 71st St., Miami Beach; phone: 865-2636). The *Alcazaba* in the *Hyatt Regency Coral Gables* (50 Alhambra Plaza, Coral Gables; phone: 441-1234) features dancing to Top 40, salsa, and merengue music on Wednesdays, Fridays, and Saturdays. The *Baja Beach Club* (3015 Grand Ave., Coconut Grove; phone: 445-5499) and *Hungry Sailor* (3064 Grand Ave., Coconut Grove; phone: 444-9359) offer live reggae or rock 'n' roll nightly.

But the nightlife scene you're most likely familiar with is on the south end of Miami Beach, known as South Beach or SoBe. World-famous for its cutting-edge impresarios who host themed parties, South Beach draws the party crowd from as far north as New York and as far east as London and the Continent, not to mention points south, like São Paulo and Buenos Aires. The only problem: Nightclubs in this hipper-than-thou milieu have an average lifetime of about one year, so be sure to call ahead.

At this writing, supper clubs to see and be seen in (after 10 PM or even later) include *Mezzanotte* (1200 Washington Ave., Miami Beach; phone:

673-4343) on Saturday nights; *Bang* (1516 Washington Ave., Miami Beach; phone: 531-2361) on Sunday nights; *Amnesia* (136 Collins Ave., Miami Beach; phone: 531-5535); *Cheetah Club* (220 21st St., Miami Beach; phone: 532-0042); *Temptations* (1532 Washington Ave., Miami Beach; phone: 534-4288); and *Penrod's Beach Club* (1 Ocean Dr., Miami Beach; phone: 538-1111). A popular dance spot is *Bash* (655 Washington Ave., Miami Beach; phone: 538-2274), which is owned by Mick Hucknall, the lead singer of the pop group *Simply Red,* and actor Sean Penn. South Beach clubs favored by gays include the *Paragon* (245 22nd St., Miami Beach; phone: 534-1235) and the *Warsaw Ballroom* (1450 Collins Ave., Miami Beach; phone: 531-4555).

Best in Town

CHECKING IN

Winter is the busy season in Miami, and reservations should be made well in advance. In winter, a double room at hotels in the very expensive category will run $230 or more per night; in the expensive category, $160 to $210; in the moderate category, $110 to $160; and in the inexpensive category, $55 to $110. Besides those listed below, there are hundreds of other hotels in the Greater Miami area, including those run by such chains as Howard Johnson and Holiday Inn. Check the yellow pages, call the hotel chains' toll-free 800 numbers, or contact the *Central Reservation Service for Greater Miami* (phone: 800-950-0232). In summer, most hotels cut their rates, some quite substantially, so shop around. For information about bed and breakfast accommodations, contact the *Greater Miami Convention and Visitors Bureau* (see *Tourist Information,* above).

Most of Miami's major hotels have complete facilities for the business traveler. Those hotels listed below as having "business services" usually offer such conveniences as meeting rooms, photocopiers, computers, translation services, and express checkout, among others. Call the hotel for additional information. Unless we note otherwise, rooms in the hotels listed below have air conditioning, private baths, TV sets, and telephones. All telephone and fax numbers are in the 305 area code unless otherwise indicated.

We begin with our favorite places, followed by recommended hotels, listed by price category.

GRAND HOTELS

Grand Bay Everything about this consistent winner of Florida and US hotel awards is done in high style. Strains of Mozart and Mendelssohn fill the elegantly appointed, European-style lobby each afternoon and early evening; lavish fresh flower arrangements and stunning crystal chandeliers are everywhere. Rooms and suites boast bleached oak furnishings and elegant appointments. All of its 180 spacious rooms have private balconies (some overlooking Biscayne Bay), stocked bars and mini-fridges, two-poster beds, fax machines, and stereo entertainment centers with VCRs. Eight suites feature in-room Jacuzzis and baby grand pianos. Attention to individual needs is paramount, which makes this a favorite with celebrities from George Michael to Luciano Pavarotti. There are two restaurants, including the famed *Grand Café* (see *Eating Out*), and two lounges; high tea is served in the lobby. Business services are available. 2669 S. Bayshore Dr., Coconut Grove (phone: 858-9600; 800-327-2788; 800-341-0809 in Florida; fax: 859-2026).

Omni Colonnade Built in the 1920s, this Coral Gables hostelry melds its original Spanish Renaissance façade and a two-story, marble-floored rotunda with a late-19th-century decor and European elegance. Luxurious details in its 157 rooms and suites include carved mahogany furniture, king-size beds, stocked mini-bars, marble vanities, and gold bathroom fixtures. No-smoking rooms are available. Upon arrival, guests are greeted with champagne and orange juice in the dark-paneled, intimate lobby with its overstuffed sofas and Oriental rugs. A room-service breakfast can be delivered to outdoor tables set among lovely gardens at the rooftop pool and Jacuzzi that overlook Coral Gables. *Doc Dammers Bar & Grill* is an informal eatery, with interesting early photos of the area and live music most nights. A small health club, a concierge, 24-hour room service, and business services complete the picture. 180 Aragon Ave., Coral Gables (phone: 441-2600; 800-843-6664; fax: 445-3929).

Turnberry Isle Set on 300 verdant acres on the Intracoastal Waterway in North Miami Beach, this complex of two hotels—each with its own distinct personality—offers a total of 340 rooms and suites, all with spacious marble or tile baths complete with sunken whirlpool tubs and separate shower stalls. The *Country Club* hotel is a stunner. The exterior is Mediterranean, with fountains and barrel-tile roofs, and the lobby/lounge is palatial. The guestrooms are oversized and beautifully decorated, and even the meeting rooms are brighter and airier than most, with French doors opening onto the golf course. The *Veranda* restaurant, open only to hotel guests and members of the country club and the yacht club, serves such innovative dishes as rum-glazed shrimp with passion-fruit sauce, plantain-crusted salmon filet, and fire-roasted ranch veal chops. The *Marina* hotel is favored by such notables as Bill Cosby and Elton John for its no-lobby privacy. The design is Mediterranean and all 70 rooms were recently upgraded as part of a $2-million renovation project. Located on the marina, the yacht club attracts those who revel in things nautical—museum-quality ship models enhance the decor. Among the yachts available for charter is the 140-foot *Miss Turnberry* ($10,000 per day). The marina facilities are superb; as many as 117 150-foot boats can moor here. The roster of sports facilities includes five pools, a beach reachable by free shuttle, two Robert Trent Jones Sr. championship golf courses, and 24 tennis courts. The adjacent spa features beauty and stress-management programs, plus the usual compliment of training machines (for additional details see *Sybaritic Spas* in DIVERSIONS). The complex, linked by a complimentary shuttle, offers a total of 11 restaurants and lounges, a private beach club, 24-hour room service, a concierge, and business services. 19999 W. Country Club Dr., Aventura, Turnberry Isle (phone: 932-6200; 800-327-7028; fax: 937-5736).

VERY EXPENSIVE

Alexander An elegant, yet surprisingly homey place metamorphosed from former luxury apartments into an all-suite condominium hotel. A chandeliered portico, a grand lobby with a curving stairway and antiques from the Cornelius Vanderbilt mansion in New York, and 158 spacious, antiques-filled suites are all impressive; each suite boasts a fully equipped kitchen, a king-size bed, and a sleep sofa in the living room. *Dominique's* restaurant, with a main dining room overlooking the ocean, specializes in rack of lamb and *tarte tatin*. There's also a poolside grill and snack bar and a ballroom. The grounds include an acre of tropical gardens, two lagoon swimming pools—one with its own waterfall—and four soothing whirlpools. A private marina and golf and tennis facilities are nearby. It's actually less expensive for a family to stay in a suite here than to take several rooms in other expensive hotels. Business services are available. 5225 Collins Ave., Miami Beach (phone: 865-6500; 800-327-6121; fax: 864-8525).

Crowne Plaza Miami This recently renovated ($9 million) former *Omni* hotel is located near the bay in Downtown Miami. The lobby's casual, tropical-style elegance is heightened by comfortable public seating areas amid lush greenery, flowers, and floor-to-ceiling windows that offer a view of the almost perpetually bright blue sky. All 528 rooms are furnished in Art Deco style. Guests enjoy a health club, a pool, and sauna facilities. The *Fish Market* (see *Eating Out*) is one of its two restaurants; there's also a sports bar. The hotel sits atop *Omni International Mall*, with 125 stores, and is also convenient to Miami Beach, *Bayside Marketplace*, and the airport. The *Metromover*, with connections to *Metrorail*, stops within walking distance, as does the *Water Taxi* (see *Getting Around*). Business services are available. 1601 Biscayne Blvd., Miami (phone: 374-0000; 800-465-4320; fax: 374-0020).

Delano Famous even before it opened in mid-1995, this refurbished property caters to a sophisticated, glamorous crowd—often celebrities who like to be near other celebrities. And speaking of celebrities, Madonna is a co-owner of the hotel's restaurant, *The Blue Door;* Kelly Klein, wife of Calvin, helped design the spa; and David Barton (the owner of a chain of health clubs based in Manhattan) has opened a branch on the premises, so guests can work out (for an additional fee) next to stars like k.d. lang, Kate Moss, Jack Nicholson, and others. The hotel is owned by Ian Schrager, the New York trendsetter who originated Studio 54 in the 1970s and who brought in French designer Philippe Starck to reinvent this slim, streamlined tower built in 1947. Most striking is a 150-foot-long swimming pool that is one inch deep at one end and five feet at the other; Starck calls it a *salon d'eau.* Rooms are decorated in minimalist style and all are white, from the linens on the beds to the furniture. Besides the 208 more reasonably priced rooms, eight bungalows are available at $450 a night. The hotel has an eat-in "kitchen" for breakfast and lunch; a terrace for lunch; a lounge, the *Rose Bar;* a concierge desk; room service; and business services. 1685 Collins Ave., Miami Beach (phone: 672-2000; 800-555-5001; fax: 532-0099).

Doral Golf Resort & Spa A luxurious $48-million facility modeled after the Terme di Saturnia in Tuscany, this resort's Spa at Doral evokes the feeling of its ancient predecessor, with its clay-tile roofs and Roman arches, yet the equipment is thoroughly 20th-century. There's everything needed by those in search of enhanced fitness, health, and stress management. The Tuscan menu, based on the spa's "Fat Point System of Nutrition," is served in the informal *Ristorante di Saturnia* or the luxurious *Villa Montepaldi.* (For additional details see *Sybaritic Spas* in DIVERSIONS.) But that's only the beginning: There's also world class golf (four championship courses and a par 3 practice course); 15 tennis courts; and essentially unlimited access (and free transportation) to its sister property, the *Doral Ocean Beach*. The resort itself offers 619 rooms and 48 suites, an Olympic-size pool (heated in winter), six restaurants, three lounges, two Jacuzzis, and a fitness center. Virtually no physical or spiritual need is left unattended. Business services are available. 4400 NW 87th Ave., Miami (phone: 592-2000; 800-71-DORAL; fax: 594-4682).

Doral Ocean Beach Relaxed elegance and a friendly staff are the hallmarks of this 420-room high-rise. The lobby sets the stage, with its European-style gold mosaics, marble, and crystal chandelier. Other highlights include exclusive shops, an Olympic-size pool, water sports, two outdoor Jacuzzis, a disco, a lounge with live piano music, a fitness center, a video gameroom, two lighted tennis courts, and an FAA-licensed helipad. On the 18th floor is *Alfredo the Original of Rome,* a restaurant known for its pasta dishes but also heralded for such entrées as veal stuffed with mushrooms. Not to be overlooked is the stunning view of the ocean, the Intracoastal Waterway, Downtown Miami, and the cruise ships at the Port of Miami. All meals are served indoors and out daily at the *Doral Café* in the hotel and the *Sandbar* at the ocean—more than just another beach bar. Business services are available. 4833 Collins Ave., Miami Beach (phone: 532-3600; 800-22-DORAL; fax: 532-2334).

Inn at Fisher Island Just off the southern tip of Miami Beach, this exclusive 216-acre island was once the Spanish-style private winter playground of William Vanderbilt. It's now a private club and elite residential resort refuge with 55 villas and suites, a nine-hole golf course designed by P. B. Dye, 18 superb tennis courts (see *Tennis* in this chapter), croquet, basketball, a beach, two marinas harboring enormous yachts, seven restaurants (one housed in the original Vanderbilt mansion, with marble floors and mahogany paneling), and several shops. The European-style *Spa Internazionale* (see *Sybaritic Spas* in DIVERSIONS) is a good place to unwind. Though the cost for a vacation rental is significant, it's worth it to many for the privacy and distance from "the outside world." Business services are available. Accessible only by helicopter, seaplane, private yacht, or private ferry. 1 Fisher Island Dr., Fisher Island (phone: 535-6021; 800-537-3708 outside Florida; fax: 535-6003).

Mayfair House Located in the heart of Coconut Grove, this five-story, all-suite hotel is built around an open-air atrium with lush foliage, mosaic tile staircases, multiple flowing fountains, and reflecting pools. The first level houses the revitalized *Mayfair Shops in the Grove* complex. Each of the 182 oversized suites is beautifully decorated with hand-carved mahogany wood, Viennese Art Nouveau furnishings, French doors, and calming tones that accentuate the eye-appealing angles of the architectural design. Designed for the ultimate in comfort, each suite features a terrace Jacuzzi; kimonos; a fully stocked mini-bar and mini-fridge; a state-of-the-art marble bathroom with a second telephone, TV set, radio, and hair dryer; a central stereo system; and a VCR. There are antique pianos in 52 of the suites. The lobby boasts two original Tiffany windows. Dining and/or drinking options include the highly regarded *Mayfair Grille* (see *Eating Out*); the private (hotel guests and members only) *Ensign Bitters* lounge; the elegant lobby lounge; the bar at the intimate rooftop pool with view of the bay; and more than 70 restaurants in the mall, just steps away. Guests have privileges at the exclusive *Cross Training* gym across the street. Business services are available. Popular among savvy locals seeking weekend getaways, this hotel offers value packages year-round. 3000 Florida Ave., Coconut Grove (phone: 441-0000; 800-433-4555; 800-341-0809 in Florida; fax: 447-9173).

Sheraton Bal Harbour In 1995, this 668-room property located in the exclusive Bal Harbour area completed a $52-million renovation that added a spectacular 17-foot waterfall and a meandering river-like swimming pool with multiple lagoons. The property sits within a lushly landscaped 10-acre garden leading directly to the five-acre beachfront where enticements include a new spa, two tennis courts, a jogging path along the beach, a *Body By Jake* fitness center, volleyball, water sports, beachside cabañas, and a gameroom. For sipping and supping, there are the acclaimed *al Carbón,* a restaurant with an open-hearth kitchen that combines contemporary South American and Mediterranean fare; an oceanside snack and drink bar; three lounges; and a 24-hour deli. Directly across the street are the elegant *Bal Harbour Shops.* Business services are available. 9701 Collins Ave., Bal Harbour (phone: 865-7511; 800-325-3535; fax: 864-2601).

Sonesta Beach Key Biscayne Just minutes away from Miami's action lies this beach-side eight-story hotel. The sea-at-sunset color scheme (sea green, lavender, turquoise, and pink) extends from the fashionable lobby to the 300 deluxe rooms, which feature private balconies and stocked mini-fridges and bars. Parents rejoice in the complimentary "Just Us Kids" program of daily super-vised activities for children ages five to 13. Adults keep busy by exercising at the fitness center, playing tennis (there are nine courts), or relaxing on the beach or around the Olympic-size pool. Water sports include snorkel-ing, windsurfing, kayaking, and sailing. Bicycle rentals are available; there's complimentary shuttle service to four popular shopping complexes during the day and an evening shuttle to *Bayside Marketplace,* South Beach, and Coconut Grove. Dining options abound: the innovative *Purple Dolphin* (see *Eating Out*); *Two Dragons*, a Chinese restaurant; a café-deli; and a beach-side grill. After dinner, head to *Desire's* disco and lounge, or retire to your room where you can choose from a selection of more than 100 movies. 350 Ocean Dr., Key Biscayne (phone: 361-2021; 800-SONESTA; fax: 361-3096).

EXPENSIVE

Biltmore Originally opened in 1926, this gracious edifice was the creation of George Merrick, who built Coral Gables. Influenced by Seville's Giralda Tower, the 275-room structure is in the ornate, whimsical Mediterranean–Moorish Revival style, which was popular at that time. Now affiliated with Westin hotels, the completely refurbished establishment is listed on the National Register of Historic Places. It boasts gold, green, and blue coffered and vaulted ceilings, French doors, gargoyles, hand-carved mahogany eleva-tors, miles of travertine marble floors and columns, original 1920s chan-deliers, and poolside statues of Roman gods and goddesses. High-living types may choose the bi-level, two-bedroom *Everglades Suite,* also known as the *Al Capone Suite,* after the mobster who lived here for eight years. At the *Cellar Club* level, guests enjoy complimentary hors d'oeuvres and a 20% discount on dining at the hotel's restaurants (but not for room service); in addition, they may purchase a large selection of wines through the *Cellar Club* at reduced prices. While the rooms feature slightly different layouts, color schemes, and furnishings, all are spacious and boast sitting areas and 10-foot-high ceilings. Deluxe rooms offer balconies, complimentary daily newspapers, and the usual special amenities. There's a 22,000-square-foot J-shaped pool (arguably the country's largest hotel pool), an 18-hole Donald

Ross–designed championship golf course, tennis on 10 lighted courts, and the extensive *Biltmore Spa and Fitness Center* (see *Sybaritic Spas* in DIVERSIONS). The hotel also has two restaurants, two lounges, a spectacular Sunday brunch (see *Eating Out*), 24-hour room service, business services, conference facilities, historical tours, free airport transportation, and a car rental desk. 1200 Anastasia Ave., Coral Gables (phone: 445-1926; 800-727-1926 or 800-228-3000; fax: 448-9976).

Eden Roc With the addition of a world class spa, conference center, and complete renovation of its 350 rooms, this property has been restored to its former dominance on Miami Beach's hotel scene. The facility has two restaurants, five bars, and two swimming pools. The state-of-the-art spa is also the site of an indoor sports club equipped with squash, basketball, and racquetball courts, as well as the only rock climbing wall in South Florida. Scenes from Sean Connery's 1995 film *Just Cause* were filmed in the lobby area and penthouse suite, and Madonna is shown enveloped in the hotel's aqua bed linens on the cover of her 1995 album "Bedtime Stories." (See *Sybaritic Spas* in DIVERSIONS.) 4525 Collins Ave., Miami Beach (phone: 531-0000; 800-327-8337; fax: 531-6955).

Fontainebleau Hilton Resort & Towers This Miami Beach grande dame, with 1,206 guestrooms on 20 acres of beachfront real estate, is still glamorous. The lagoon-like pool has a grotto bar inside a cave; there are also three whirlpool baths. The 12 restaurants and lounges include *Kamon,* a Japanese steakhouse and sushi bar, and a kosher kitchen. There's also a fully equipped *Spa Pavilion* (see *Sybaritic Spas* in DIVERSIONS) and seven night-lit tennis courts with pro shop. Business services are available. 4441 Collins Ave., Miami Beach (phone: 538-2000; 800-548-8886 in Florida; 800-HILTONS elsewhere in the US; fax: 532-8145).

Impala One of the best historic renovations on Miami Beach, this 60-year-old Spanish-Mediterranean–style boutique hotel set back one block from the beach boasts fine European service. The 17 rooms and three suites have eclectic furnishings and original artworks; amenities include imported cotton linens, oversized baths, stereos with CD players, speaker phones with voice mail, and computer data ports. *Cafe Impala,* an Italian eatery under separate management, recently opened here. 1228 Collins Ave., Miami Beach (phone: 673-2021; 800-646-7252; fax: 673-5984).

Inter-Continental Miami Built in the grand old hotel tradition, this property is in the city center, near the Brickell Avenue financial district and *Bayside Marketplace.* The 644 rooms in the soaring 34-floor travertine triangle have marble baths and modern furnishings with Oriental accents. Former President George Bush and actor Eddie Murphy are among those who have stayed in the two-story Royal Suite. The lobby, with its 18-foot Henry Moore sculpture, is all beige and bone travertine marble, accented with green rattan furniture and area rugs. There are three restaurants, including the highly regarded *Le Pavillon* and the *Royal Palm Court*. For the fitness-minded there's a swimming pool plus an outdoor jogging trail that takes advantage of the stunning views of Biscayne Bay; three floors are reserved for non-smokers. Business services are available. 100 Chopin Plaza, Miami (phone: 577-1000; 800-327-0200; fax: 577-0384 or 377-3002).

Marlin This Art Deco District hostelry combines 1930s architecture with 1990s amenities in 12 suites complete with kitchens and VCRs. The decor in the public rooms is "Jam-Deco"—classic Art Deco design with hot Jamaican colors. The hotel was developed by Chris Blackwell, founder of Island Records, who included a recording studio on the premises, attracting lots of show-biz types. The *Shabeen* restaurant serves Jamaican food, the bar specializes in exotic drinks, and the beach is just a block away. 1200 Collins Ave., Miami Beach (phone: 673-8770; 800-688-7678; fax: 673-9609).

Pelican In an area where visual excitement is coin of the realm for hoteliers, this place is true to its fashion roots. Owned by Diesel Jeans International, each of the hotel's 25 rooms has a unique decor, from 1950s subthemes to Hollywood plush; the rooms also have oak floors, ceiling fans, CD players, refrigerators, and safes. The penthouse suite ($2,000 a night) occupies the top floor. Public areas include a bar (with TV sets in the men's room) and the *Pelican Cafe,* serving Mediterranean specialties. 826 Ocean Dr., Miami Beach (phone: 673-3373; 800-7-PELICAN; fax: 673-3255).

MODERATE

Beekman Located in Surfside, a cozy oceanside village north of Miami Beach, this 12-story, all-suite hotel offers lodging options that are ideal for families. Studios and one- and two-bedroom apartments are available, all with balconies and fully equipped kitchens. A 150-foot beach is at your doorstep; shopping, tennis, theaters, and restaurants are within walking distance. Complimentary breakfast is served daily in the *Beekman Cafe.* 9499 Collins Ave., Surfside (phone: 861-4801; 800-237-9367; fax: 865-5971).

Cavalier Built in 1936, this 41-room property has a Jamaican-inspired decor done in tangerine, turquoise, and pink. Many rooms have canopy beds; all feature cable TV, VCRs, CD players, and in-closet safes. There's no restaurant on the premises, but there are plenty of eateries nearby. The beach is just across the street. 1320 Ocean Dr., Miami Beach (phone: 534-2135; 800-338-9076; fax: 531-5543).

Miami Airport Hilton Located on a lagoon, the 500-room hostelry offers a pool, a Jacuzzi, a sauna, jet and water skiing (for a fee), and free use of three lighted tennis courts and a lighted basketball court. There's also a concierge floor, restaurant, café/pool grill, nightclub, and bar. Ten floors are reserved for nonsmokers. Free parking and free transportation to the airport are available. 5101 Blue Lagoon Dr., Miami (phone: 262-1000; 800-HILTONS; fax: 267-0038).

Place St. Michel Charming, cozy, and elegant describe this 27-room European-style bed and breakfast establishment built in 1926. In the heart of Coral Gables, it's favored by international architects who appreciate its Art Deco details and antique furnishings. On the premises is *Stuart's,* a jazz bar; *St. Michel,* an excellent dining spot; and a deli that's popular with the local lunch crowd. Continental breakfast is included, room service is available until 11 PM, and there's an obliging concierge desk. 162 Alcazar Ave., Coral Gables (phone: 444-1666; 800-848-HOTEL; fax: 529-0074).

Sol Miami Beach Originally the *Cadillac* hotel, this 271-room, ocean-front property (ca. 1938) is owned by the Spain-based Grupo Sol. The cool turquoise and blue Deco exterior belies its glitzy interior, which features plum and yellow, with lots of neon. There are two restaurants and two lounges. Some units have kitchenettes; all have cable TV. For action, there's a pool, a fitness center, shuffleboard courts, and water sports. Business services are available. 3925 Collins Ave., Miami Beach (phone: 531-3534; 800-336-3542 or 800-531-3534; fax: 531-1765).

INEXPENSIVE

Leslie Another vintage 1930s hotel in South Beach, this one offers 43 rooms decorated in vivid Art Deco prints and equipped with cable TV, VCRs, and CD players. The *Leslie Cafe* has an eclectic menu. Located across the street from the beach. 1244 Ocean Dr., Miami Beach (phone: 534-2135; 800-338-9076; fax: 531-5543).

Miami River Inn Claiming to be the oldest continuously operating inn south of St. Augustine, this charming bed and breakfast establishment on the Miami River was built in 1906. The 40 antiques-furnished rooms in four wooden buildings and the lushly planted pool and whirlpool area make guests feel like they're in another place and time. Close to the *Center for the Fine Arts, Historical Museum,* and *Bayside Marketplace,* the inn is protected by security gates at night. Complimentary continental breakfast is served. Off-street parking is available. 118 SW South River Dr., entrance on SW Second St., Miami (phone: 325-0045; 800-468-3589; fax: 325-9227).

Paradise Inn Located one block from the beach, this two-story motel with a Key lime façade trimmed in orange is a budgeter's delight, with 45 basic and clean rooms and another 45 efficiency units with kitchenettes. All feature remote-control satellite TV and in-room safes. The quietest rooms face the inner courtyards. There's a pool, free parking, complimentary continental breakfast, and laundry facilities, but no restaurant. 8520 Harding Ave., Miami Beach (phone: 865-6216; fax: 865-9028).

Ritz Plaza This 1940s-style hostelry, with its much-photographed Art Deco squared finial, has been restored to its early splendor, with a soaring lobby featuring the original four-color terrazzo floor and a front desk made of coral—one of the few such pieces extant. The 132 rooms and suites retain a 1940s look and feel, with such period details as the original cast-iron tubs (now modernized). Though a bit small and without any views, the standard rooms are great values. An Olympic-size pool overlooks the ocean, and water sports are also available. Meals are served on the terrace and in the *Ritz Café,* a high-ceilinged dining room with a huge crystal chandelier and a window wall facing the ocean. *Harry's Bar* has a vintage look—with lots of chrome and a jukebox playing 1950s music—and offers a light menu. Guests often include photography crews shooting fashion assignments nearby. Near the *Miami Beach Convention Center,* 1701 Collins Ave., Miami Beach (phone: 534-3500; 800-522-6400; fax: 531-6928).

EATING OUT

Much of Miami's socializing centers on eating out, so be prepared for long lines from December through April, when visitors swell the ranks of restaurant diners. Expect to pay $85 or more for a dinner for two at places in the very expensive category; $65 to $85 at places in the expensive category; $40 to $65 at restaurants in the moderate range; and less than $40 at eateries in the inexpensive range. Prices do not include drinks, wine, taxes, or tips. Unless otherwise noted, all restaurants serve lunch and dinner, and all telephone numbers are in the 305 area code.

In a town where destination dining is a major league sport, separating the good from the great, the merely delicious from the unforgettable is part of the game. The range is broad—from sumptuous and sophisticated to homegrown and ethnic; don't be timid about trying it all. We begin with our culinary favorites, followed by our recommendations of cost and quality choices, listed by price category.

INCREDIBLE EDIBLES

Biltmore Café The gastronomic choices are legend at this restaurant's Sunday all-you-can-eat-for-$39.95-a-person brunch ($45 on holidays). To begin with, there are raw oysters, jumbo shrimp, smoked fish, belly lox, three different types of caviar, four types of pâté, raspberry blintzes, eggs Benedict, all types of salads, fresh baked breads and pastries, and pasta. What makes this brunch unique are some unusual extras—grilled Maine lobsters, a sushi and sashimi bar, rack of lamb, a Häagen-Dazs ice-cream sundae station, and a lavishly hedonistic pastry table. Everything is perfect, from the champagne and freshly squeezed orange juice mimosas to the courtyard setting, complete with ice sculptures, a gurgling fountain, and a jazz-playing trio. Bring your appetite. Open Sundays from 11 AM to 4 PM. Reservations necessary. Major credit cards accepted. At the *Biltmore Hotel,* 1200 Anastasia Ave., Coral Gables (phone: 445-1926; 800-727-1926).

Chef Allen's Chef/owner Allen Susser has won deserved national acclaim for his culinary achievements. Featured here is regional South Florida cooking, using local produce and fresh-caught yellowtail, tuna, and snapper. The menu changes daily and may include whole-wheat linguine with lobster or Florida bay scallop ceviche with cilantro. Even the salad of field greens is beautifully presented, with confetti-like squares of colorful peppers. Among the specialties are roasted veal chops enhanced by ginger-baked calabaza (a pumpkin-like vegetable). The white-chocolate–macadamia-nut mousse is as rewarding to the eyes as it is to the taste buds. The decor—handmade Italian furniture and pink neon lights—is as upbeat, fresh, and sophisticated as the food. Open daily for dinner. Reservations advised. Major credit cards accepted. 19088 NE 29th Ave., North Miami Beach (phone: 935-2900).

Fish Market Far more elegant than its name implies, this is possibly South Florida's best seafood restaurant. In the *Crowne Plaza Miami* hotel, the two-room dining area gleams with marble and mirrors. You can order just about any kind of fish grilled, with a broad choice of sauces, but the kitchen also performs magic with such specialties as colossal shrimp (Central American crustaceans as large as baby lobster tails, yet succulent and tender) and grilled snapper with buckwheat pasta. The superb sole filets stuffed with Florida lobster, mussels, and wild mushrooms, and the sumptuous scallops and medaillons of lobster served with *risotto Milanese* (Italian short-grain rice with saffron). For a special treat, try the pâté of tropical fruits and berries with passion-fruit sauce for dessert. Businesspeople love the "executive service" lunch, when a two-course meal is served in less than 30 minutes or there's no charge. Closed Saturday lunch and Sundays. Reservations advised. Major credit cards accepted. In the *Crown Plaza Miami Hotel,* 1601 Biscayne Blvd., Miami (phone: 374-0000).

Grand Café This elegantly European bi-level dining room celebrates both romance and business with style, attentive service, and wonderful culinary creations. Recommended appetizers include the renowned fresh spinach risotto with porcini mushrooms and mascarpone cheese. Incredible entrées range from black bean–encrusted rare tuna with lemongrass sauce to grilled Maine lobster with cilantro zinfandel sauce. Leave room for the dark chocolate and praline *crousillant* (a small round confection consisting of layered hazelnut cake, crisp caramel, dark chocolate mousse, and chocolate ganache). Open daily for breakfast, lunch, and dinner; brunch served Sundays. Reservations necessary for dinner, advised for other meals. Major credit cards accepted. In the *Grand Bay Hotel,* 2669 S. Bayshore Dr., Coconut Grove (phone: 858-9600).

Mark's Place The modern interior—dramatized by vibrant contemporary glass sculptures—serves as an exciting backdrop for this Miami "in" spot. Mark Militello, acclaimed as one of the best chefs in the nation, is on the cutting edge of the movement to merge Caribbean and tropical ingredients with classic European techniques. He whips up such imaginative dishes as grilled yellowtail snapper with Mediterranean salsa; West Indian pumpkin and hearts of palm; and salmon with couscous and crispy leeks. The rich desserts include a terrific apple tart. Closed for lunch weekends. Reservations necessary. Major credit cards accepted. 2286 NE 123rd St., North Miami Beach (phone: 893-6888).

Osteria del Teatro This trendy, crowded spot consistently serves exquisite Italian food with French overtones, attracting movie stars, models, and locals who consider it one of the best restaurants (if not *the* best) on South Beach. Anything on the menu is sure to be excellent, especially the mixed seafood grill. While the early crowd tends to be older and more conservative, the late crowd is the hippest in town. Open for dinner; closed Tuesdays. Reservations necessary. Major credit cards accepted. 1443 Washington Ave., Miami Beach (phone: 538-7850).

Yuca The name derives from both a Miami acronym for Young Upscale Cuban-Americans and a starchy vegetable ("yucca" in English) that is a staple of Cuban cooking. The award-winning restaurant is decorated in gradations of white to beige, providing a subtle backdrop for the chef's visually spectacular creations. The innovative bilingual menu features nouvelle twists on Cuban standards—sweet plantains stuffed with dried cured beef and *salsa verde* (forget what it sounds like; your mouth will thank you), excellent pan-seared yellowtail filet dusted with cumin and pumpkin seeds and served with *poblano* mashed potatoes, and filet of salmon with pistachio-encrusted coconut rice, sweet corn *arepa,* and avocado vinaigrette. Chocoholics will adore the *tres leches de chocolate,* a milk-soaked cake layered with mousse and covered with chocolate meringue. You can diet tomorrow. Open daily. Reservations advised. Major credit cards accepted. 177 Giralda Ave., Coral Gables (phone: 444-4448). Also at 501 Lincoln Rd., Miami Beach (phone: 532-YUCA).

VERY EXPENSIVE

Forge Once more famous for its 300,000-bottle wine collection and its elegance than for its complex dishes, this ornately decorated restaurant—adorned with antique furniture, stained glass, carved ceilings, and crystal chandeliers—has ditched its stodgy steaks and chops for more imaginative, continental fare, including roast duck with black currant sauce. For dessert, regulars love the famed blacksmith pie—alternating layers of chocolate cake, French vanilla custard, and whipped cream—but don't bypass the chocolate cheesecake. Open daily for dinner. Reservations necessary. Major credit cards accepted. 432 Arthur Godfrey Rd., Miami Beach (phone: 538-8533).

Joe's Stone Crab Don't miss this, the ultimate Miami dining experience. Since 1913 the place has been selling tons of the best stone crabs around, along with scrumptious home fries, delectable creamed spinach, and to-die-for Key lime pie. Diners who don't arrive early often have to wait hours to be seated, and service can be rushed and sporadic, but devoted fans say it's well worth the wait—though even that has improved since the completion in 1995 of a multimillion-dollar expansion that includes a parking garage. Besides the crabs, lobster and fresh fish are served. Picnickers can buy lunch from the restaurant's expanded take-out section (with separate entrance) and avoid the lunacy of the dining room. Closed Sunday lunch and from mid-May through mid-October. No reservations. Major credit cards accepted. 227 Biscayne St., Miami Beach (phone: 673-0365; 800-780-CRAB)

EXPENSIVE

Max's South Beach When Miami Beach became too fashionable to be ignored, famed Boca Raton restaurateur Dennis Max looked south. Enlisting chef Kerry Simon, Max soon had another hit on his hands by combining America's popular healthy foods with exotic flavorings from the Far East and Latin America. The restaurant exemplifies the local postmodern style with its dim lighting, mahogany bar, sleek banquettes, high ceilings, and a wait staff of model types. Like most South Beach restaurants, this one is almost painfully noisy, but the food and the experience are worth it. Open daily for dinner. Reservations necessary. Major credit cards accepted. 764 Washington Ave., Miami Beach (phone: 532-0070).

Mayfair Grille Allen Susser of *Chef Allen* fame had a hand in the revamping of this favorite Miami dining spot, and his touch is most evident in the menu. New World fare is served in an elegant atmosphere; specialties are Nantucket bay scallops with lobster polenta and scallion cream, stone crab cassoulet with conch, and rock shrimp with seafood sausage. Open daily for breakfast, lunch, and dinner. Reservations advised for lunch and dinner. Major credit cards accepted. In the *Mayfair House Hotel,* 3000 Florida Ave., Coconut Grove (phone: 441-0000).

Pacific Time Housed in an Art Deco building on Lincoln Road's pedestrian mall, this tall-ceilinged space is a terrific spot for people watching, whether you're inside or out at one of the white-linen covered tables set up on the sidewalk (where it's quieter). But the real attraction here is the food: Chefs Jonathan Eismann and Yves Picot prepare nouvelle American fare with

Asian influences. Among the best entrées are Szechuan grilled black grouper, sweet sake–roasted sea bass, and yellowfin tuna with sushi bar flavors. Open daily for dinner. Reservations necessary. Major credit cards accepted. 915 Lincoln Rd., Miami Beach (phone: 534-5979).

Rusty Pelican For a dynamite view of Downtown Miami across the bay, visit this nautically decorated spot. Meals range from burgers and prime ribs of beef to seafood and tropical fruits. Open daily; brunch served on Sundays. Reservations advised. Major credit cards accepted. 3201 Rickenbacker Causeway, Key Biscayne (phone: 361-3818).

Victor's Café Even in its heyday, Havana didn't offer a restaurant as spectacular as this New Cuban eatery, where Key stone columns, terra cotta tiles, light woods, and a gurgling fountain re-create a Cuban plantation house court-yard—only it's indoors, beneath a three-story-high glass dome. The fare is a blending of the flavors, spices, and dishes of the several cultures that set-tled in Cuba—traditional Spanish, with Chinese, French creole, African, and Taino Indian influences. Begin with a *mojíto* (a delightful house rum drink with crushed mint) or the white sangria. In season, choose the fresh jumbo stone crabs. Year-round specialties include *maravilla de catibia* que-sadillas (yucca flour quesadillas filled with creole spiced shrimp), cassava turnovers filled with Florida lobster fricassee, and yucca French fries served with an out-of-this-world cilantro sauce. Beef dishes include sirloin pre-pared with adobo (a flavorful herb sauce) and served with creamy polenta, and oak-grilled *churrasco* (skirt steak). Seafood lovers can feast on fresh mahimahi filets marinated in *mojo* (a dark, spicy sauce), shellfish casseroles, and shrimp quenelles. The ambience is both romantic and exotic, with strolling guitarists serenading the guests. A Latin band entertains nightly in the *Rumba* lounge, with its popular happy hour and late night *tapas* bar. The same people own New York City's *Victor's Café*. Open daily. Reservations necessary. Major credit cards accepted. 2340 SW 32nd Ave., Coral Gables (phone: 445-1313).

MODERATE

Brasserie L'Entrecôte You'll feel like you're in Paris at this traditional French bistro, which is decorated with hand-painted country tiles and brass and mahogany appointments, and has a terrace that overlooks the *Mayfair Shops in the Grove.* The restaurant, which received a "best French restaurant award" from *South Florida* magazine in 1995, offers an exquisite menu. Favorites are the *L'Entrecôte* steak with mushrooms and *pommes frites,* and blackened swordfish. Leave room for the *crème brûlée.* Open daily. Reservations advised for dinner on Fridays and Saturdays. Major credit cards accepted. 2901 Florida Ave., Coconut Grove (phone: 444-9697).

Centro Vasco Next to jai alai, this is Miami's favorite Basque import. The present owner's father started this restaurant in Havana, then moved it to Miami when Castro came into power. He replicated the traditional Spanish decor, huge portions, and authentic menu, attracting such notable diners as Ronald Reagan, Jimmy Carter, and John Glenn. Specialties are a classic black bean soup that's arguably the best this side of Cuba, seafood paella (clams, lobster, shrimp, and sea bass in a succulent sauce, served over seasoned yellow rice), *rabo encendido* (braised oxtail simmered in a rich red wine sauce), and sea bass served broiled, grilled, baked, or fried. A great sangria is made right at your table. Save room for the *leche frita* (a flan-like fried milk dessert). On weekends there's entertainment in three different rooms, ranging from Latin-jazz bands to flamenco shows to comedians. Open daily for lunch, dinner, and late night *tapas*. Reservations advised for dinner. Major credit cards accepted. 2235 Calle Ocho (Eighth St.), Miami (phone: 643-9606).

Le Festival Dinner at this French restaurant is to be savored. From the plush decor to the outstanding fare, it's one of Miami's finest. Rack of lamb, veal scaloppine in brandy cream sauce, Dover sole, and chateaubriand are favorites. On Thursdays, wild game such as venison is available. The extensive wine list includes Chilean and Spanish selections. Closed Saturday lunch and Sundays. Reservations advised. Major credit cards accepted. 2120 Salzedo St., Coral Gables (phone: 442-8545).

Kaleidoscope Here fine dining is in a romantic enclosed atrium, on a balcony, or in an air conditioned dining room. Menu high points include Bahamian seafood griddle cakes, grilled grouper, bouillabaisse, and fresh fruit tarts with almond pastry made on the premises. Open daily. Reservations advised. Major credit cards accepted. 3112 Commodore Plaza, Second Floor, Coconut Grove (phone: 446-5010).

Monty's Stone Crab Casual and known for serving stone crabs year-round (they're brought in from Virginia during the local off-season), this place also offers a wide array of fresh seafood, steaks, and pasta. Guests can eat dockside at picnic tables, or indoors in a setting with lots of glass windows and a view of the bay. Open daily. Reservations advised. Major credit cards accepted. 2550 S. Bayshore Dr., Coconut Grove (phone: 858-1431).

Las Puertas Here's the place to sample imaginative cuisine in a cozy atmosphere. Dishes have Mexican and Aztec accents: Favorites are lean duck breast *fajitas;* tortilla soup flavored with onion, tomato, carrots, and cilantro and served with *ancho* chili and avocado; and *cochinita pibil,* tender pork stewed in banana leaves with achiote seasoning and sour oranges and topped with chorizo. Open daily for dinner; closed Saturdays and Sundays for lunch. Reservations advised. Major credit cards accepted. 148 Giralda Ave., Coral Gables (phone: 442-0708).

Purple Dolphin Dine either in front of a large mural of frolicking dolphins or on the atrium terrace, which is decked out with potted palms and other tropical greenery. There's live music in the evenings. Hummus and *tapenade* (an addictive black olive, garlic, and anchovy dip) are placed on every table along with freshly baked rolls. Try the seared salmon with black bean salsa and crispy green plantains; meat lovers can choose from rack of lamb with a spinach and goat cheese tart and rosemary sauce or beef tenderloin medaillons with wild mushroom ragout and potato-leek sauce. Reserve early for Friday's fabulous, reasonably priced, all-you-can-eat seafood buffet. And last but not least, the desserts are to die for. Open daily for breakfast, lunch, and dinner. Reservations advised for weekend dinners. Major credit cards accepted. In the *Sonesta Beach Key Biscayne Hotel,* 350 Ocean Dr., Key Biscayne (phone: 361-2021).

South Pointe Seafood House Seafood lovers will find no disappointments at this casual wood-beamed, wharf-styled, Old Florida eatery with 10 dining rooms, each decked out with Tiffany lamps, Victorian curtains, and rustic appointments. There's jumbo shrimp wrapped in bacon; whitewater clams steamed with garlic, corn relish and *ancho* chili butter; fresh stone crab claws; and champagne-poached salmon. For those who want to try it all, there are four different seafood combination platters. Sweets include homemade Key lime pie and apple-walnut upside-down pie with cinnamon ice cream. A microbrewery is on the premises. Open daily; brunch served on Sundays. Reservations advised. Major credit cards accepted. 1 Washington Ave., Miami Beach (phone: 673-1708).

Toni's Sushi Bar Japanese interpretations of grilled salmon, chicken, and steaks, along with shrimp teriyaki, are among the highlights here. The sushi is the best on South Beach. Open daily for dinner. Reservations necessary on weekends. Major credit cards accepted. 1208 Washington Ave., Miami Beach (phone: 673-9368).

INEXPENSIVE

Café Tu-Tu Tango In the *CocoWalk* complex, this jumping eatery decked out as an artist's loft touts its eclectic *tapas*-style specialties as "food for the starving artist." It offers light, multiethnic dishes such as frittatas (Italian omelettes), pizza, smoked-chicken quesadillas, and kebabs. Entrées are appetizer-sized, so most people order three or more to share. Open daily for lunch, dinner, and late snacks. No reservations. Major credit cards accepted. 3015 Grand Ave., Coconut Grove (phone: 529-2222).

Dan Marino's American Sports Bar & Grill This is a sports fan's heaven, with 41 television screens, football paraphernalia lining the walls, and pool tables, dart boards, and video games. The bill of fare includes steaks, seafood, pasta, burgers, and salads. Occasionally you'll spot the famous *Miami Dolphins* quarterback himself. Open daily. Reservations unnecessary. Major credit cards accepted. In *CocoWalk,* 3015 Grand Ave., Coconut Grove (phone: 567-0013).

11th Street Diner This 1948 diner traveled from its home in Wilkes-Barre, Pennsylvania, to trendy South Beach. Old-fashioned favorites such as black cows (root beer floats) and meat loaf and gravy are served, as are such modern dishes as Cobb salad and grilled dolphin (the fish, not the mammal). Open daily 24 hours. No reservations. Major credit cards accepted. 1065 Washington Ave., Miami (phone: 534-6373).

Málaga Located in Little Havana, this traditional Cuban eatery, a favorite gathering spot for Miami's politicians and business executives, is a good place to get acquainted with the island basics. Best are standards like fried whole red snapper, spiced pork, or *arroz con pollo* (rice with chicken). The fried plantains are a must-try. There's live musical entertainment Fridays and Saturdays. Open daily. Reservations advised. Major credit cards accepted. 740 Calle Ocho (SW Eighth St.), Miami (phone: 854-9101 or 858-4224).

News Café An international newsstand-cum–sidewalk café that's an ideal spot for people watching or a pre-beach breakfast. The menu is light, with sandwiches, salads, cheeses, and Middle Eastern fare. Open daily 24 hours. Reservations unnecessary. Major credit cards accepted. Located across from the ocean in the heart of South Beach. 800 Ocean Dr., Miami Beach (phone: 538-6397).

Planet Hollywood Hollywood memorabilia, some of it huge (such as Arnold Schwarzenegger's *Terminator II* motorcycle), is suspended from the ceilings, the walls, and the columns, while four giant TV screens show film clips. The food—primarily pizza, sandwiches, and salads—is better than you'd expect and there's often a line on Fridays and Saturdays. Perhaps you'll catch a glimpse of one of the famous owners such as Schwarzenegger, Bruce Willis, or Sylvester Stallone. Open daily. Reservations necessary for large parties. Major credit cards accepted. In the *Mayfair Shops in the Grove* complex, 3390 Mary St., Coconut Grove (phone: 445-7277).

Rascal House This is one of only two Florida restaurants to make food guru Mimi Sheraton's list of the 50 best US restaurants (the other is *Mark's Place,* above). Lines snaking into the parking lot attest to the delicatessen's popularity for almost 41 years. Try the pastrami on rye or the *rugelach.* Open daily for breakfast, lunch, dinner, and late snacks. No reservations. Major credit cards accepted. 17190 Collins Ave., Miami Beach. (phone: 947-4581).

Tap Tap For years, Miami's thriving Haitian community has been overlooked on the culinary scene, but this place may change all that. This small eatery (named for the elaborately decorated buses that ply the countryside of Haiti) is painted with brightly colored Caribbean murals that just plain make you happy. Favorite dishes include grilled fish marinated in chili, blue crab and vegetable soup (in season), and the traditional goat grilled over *boukannen,* the hardwood and charcoal fire that dates from precolonial days. Open daily. Reservations unnecessary. Major credit cards accepted. 819 Fifth St., Miami Beach (phone: 672-2898).

Tropical Chinese Despite its inauspicious location in a suburban shopping center near an expressway, this place serves the best dim sum in town. Chinese families from all over Miami flock here on weekends to sample these delicate appetizer-size dumplings, which are served one after another as they emerge from the kitchen. Save room for entrées if you can; the baby clams in fresh basil sauce and noodle dishes are first-rate. Open daily. Reservations advised. Major credit cards accepted. 7991 SW 40th St., west of Palmetto Expressway (phone: 262-7576).

Unicorn Village An outstanding natural-food restaurant and marketplace, it's on a marina with dockage for diners arriving by boat. Dining is either inside or out. Creative salads, low-fat and low-sodium dishes, vegetarian lasagna and other pasta, plus fish and stir-fry dishes are featured. A large selection of by-the-glass wines includes seven organically produced choices (with no added sulfites). Note: This is a totally nonsmoking place. Open daily; brunch is served Sundays. No reservations. Major credit cards accepted. At *The Shops at the Waterways,* 3595 NE 207th St., North Miami Beach (phone: 933-8829).

Wolfie's A Miami Beach institution since 1947, it might be described as an overgrown deli. The eclectic, 500-item menu carries everything from knishes to chicken parmesan and mountainous desserts. Open daily 24 hours. No reservations. Major credit cards accepted. 2038 Collins Ave., Miami Beach (phone: 538-6626).

Ft. Lauderdale

For many Americans, the mention of Ft. Lauderdale still conjures up the 1960 movie *Where the Boys Are* (or its 1984 remake), which immortalized the seasonal migration of the nation's college students to this sunny city during spring break. That image, however, is out of date. Over the last decade, city leaders have discouraged that much-reported rite of spring in order to improve Ft. Lauderdale's overall appeal to adults and to expand family tourism. Their efforts have been successful—the annual undergraduate migration has diminished dramatically.

Today's collegians set their springtime compasses for Panama City and Daytona Beach while Mom, Dad, and the kids—along with increasing numbers of visitors from Europe and Latin America—populate Ft. Lauderdale's beaches. The players have changed, but the setting remains the same: Ft. Lauderdale still claims to receive 3,000 hours of sun a year—more than anywhere else in the continental US; the year-round average temperature remains in the comfortable mid-70s F; and—as the city's public relations people like to point out—Ft. Lauderdale has never, ever recorded a 100-degree temperature.

In addition to its benign climate, Ft. Lauderdale's proximity to the water has formed its character as a prime resort area. The city is virtually afloat. It (and surrounding Broward County areas) is bordered on the east by 23 miles of Atlantic Ocean coastline and beaches, on the west by that "river of grass," the Everglades. Between the two are 300 miles of the navigable Intracoastal Waterway and an intricate network of canals that is the source of Ft. Lauderdale's nickname, the "Venice of America."

While other resort areas count only their visitors, the Ft. Lauderdale area also counts boats. More than 42,000 are permanently registered, and 10,000 or so more join their ranks during the winter months, as the yachting crowd from as far away as Canada cruises down to the area's warm waters. (Author John D. MacDonald's readers will recognize the *Bahia Mar Marina* as the place where the laid-back sleuth Travis McGee moors his houseboat, the *Busted Flush*.) Moreover, thousands of smaller craft—sailboats and powerboats—knife through these waters throughout the year. In Ft. Lauderdale, even *Christmas* is celebrated in a nautical fashion. In mid-December, hundreds of elaborately decorated and lighted boats and yachts take to the Intracoastal Waterway for the unusual *Winterfest Boat Parade* from Port Everglades to Pompano Beach. Every available waterfront viewing point is packed as waving Santas navigate their water-sleighs past crowded bridges, backyards, and hotel balconies.

Ft. Lauderdale is named after Major William Lauderdale, who arrived in 1838 to quell the Seminole Indians and build a fort on the New River amid mosquito-infested, inhospitable mangrove swamps. Oddly, he was here only a few days and died not long afterward. The door for development first opened during the late 1890s, when entrepreneur Henry Flagler began extending his *Florida East Coast Railroad* south from Palm Beach. A swamp drainage and reclamation project was undertaken in 1906, and canals were dug to create "finger islands," thus maximizing the city's waterside real estate. Ft. Lauderdale was incorporated in 1911 and has welcomed millions of visitors since.

Today, Ft. Lauderdale is the largest of the 28 municipalities that constitute Broward County. Notably it's the second most populous—after Dade—of Florida's 67 counties. The county's permanent population of about 1.3 million (Ft. Lauderdale itself has 150,000 residents) swells each winter as more than five million tourists pour in. To these guests, Ft. Lauderdale and its vicinity offer a wide choice of places to stay and eat and things to do. Accommodations range from tiny motels to huge luxury hotels and sumptuous resorts; more than 28,000 rooms for visitors can be found in Greater Ft. Lauderdale, many of which are along the ocean. Even the most demanding diner will find satisfaction in one of the county's 2,500 restaurants, while its many nightclubs, discos, and theaters provide plenty of nighttime entertainment. In the sun-splashed daytime, those who tire of frolicking on the beach may work out on the approximately 76 golf courses and 550 tennis courts. Relaxed and informal, Ft. Lauderdale is best enjoyed in shorts and sandals during the day, with attire just a bit more dressy at night.

But Ft. Lauderdale is not just sunshine and surf. It's also a bustling commercial city, and its pride, Port Everglades, is the world's second-busiest cruise port. Near Port Everglades on the Intracoastal Waterway is the *Greater Ft. Lauderdale/Broward County Convention Center,* a nearly $50-million structure that opened in 1991. City leaders also have undertaken an ongoing $670-million refurbishment and expansion of Ft. Lauderdale's downtown core, and a number of high-rise office buildings have sprung up, attracting new businesses. Near those structures, on the New River, sits the impressive $50-million *Broward Center for the Performing Arts,* which anchors the city's arts and science district. Across the street is the new $30-million *Museum of Discovery and Science,* with everything from hands-on exhibits to a five-story, 3-D IMAX theater. *Riverwalk,* a landscaped path along the New River, goes past the *Broward Center for the Performing Arts,* restaurants, and historic buildings.

The cities that make up the greater Ft. Lauderdale area are a diverse lot. Davie, whose residents are fond of cowboy boots and hats, is considered the most "western" town this side of the Pecos; located 14 miles southwest of Ft. Lauderdale, it has dozens of farms, stables, saloons, country stores, and even a rodeo. In Hollywood, 7 miles south of Ft. Lauderdale, there's a Seminole Indian reservation, and the town's Broadwalk—an ocean promenade—has a strong French-Canadian flavor. Hallandale, 10 miles to the south, is the home of the well-known *Gulfstream Park* racetrack. Some 5¹/₂ miles to the south is Dania, whose name reflects its early Danish settlers; it's known for its antiques. Other Greater Ft. Lauderdale communities include: Sunrise, 10½ miles west; Plantation, 9½ miles west; Coconut Creek, 15 miles northwest; Pompano Beach, 8 miles north; Lauderdale-by-the-Sea, 4½ miles north; Oakland Park, 6 miles northwest; Pembroke Pines, 17 miles southwest; Deerfield Beach, 12 miles north; and Margate, 17 miles northwest.

As more and more people discover its enviable lifestyle, the Ft. Lauderdale area continues to grow and change. "The Strip," once party-central for the spring break crowd, has undergone a face-lift. Installed along the beachside are a promenade, a bicycle path, and a low, white, undulating sea wall with a neon-painted ribbon in ever-changing colors running along it. The wall has entryways from street to beach, flanked by spirals that look like sand castles. Though some T-shirt emporiums remain, hotels and shops are being remodeled and spruced up in sherbet colors.

Progress has its price, however, and ecologists and some governmental agencies are sounding alarms as developers draw closer and closer to the last available land in the region—the eastern fringe of the Everglades. The challenge that Greater Ft. Lauderdale now faces lies in controlling development while maintaining the many attractions that make the city appealing.

Ft. Lauderdale At-a-Glance

SEEING THE CITY

The most commanding view of this area is from the *Pier Top Lounge* of the 17-story *Hyatt Regency Pier 66* hotel (see *Checking In*). As the lounge makes one complete revolution every 66 minutes, it affords sweeping vistas of the Atlantic Ocean and its beaches to the east; Port Everglades and the *Greater Ft. Lauderdale/Hollywood International Airport* to the south; the city's many canals, sprawling suburbs, and the Everglades to the west; and more canals and the Intracoastal Waterway to the north.

SPECIAL PLACES

The best way to get around Ft. Lauderdale is by car. It's a sprawling city with a lot to see in all directions, but don't miss the unique water taxi service that cruises the Intracoastal Waterway, enabling passengers to hop on and off at various restaurants and attractions.

DOWNTOWN AREA

PORT EVERGLADES Because it has the deepest water of any port between Norfolk, Virginia, and New Orleans, Port Everglades is a magnet for cargo ships and the marine outfitting business, as well as for luxury cruise ships. In fact, it's the world's second-largest cruise port, after Miami. Thanks to the remodeling of former warehouses and new construction, the port today presents an attractive face, with some of its nine passenger terminals painted in a striking, bold design. An additional terminal under construction at press time should be operational this year. The *Greater Ft. Lauderdale/Broward County Convention Center* occupies the northern end of the grounds. The port presently has one restaurant, *Burt & Jack's,* co-owned by Burt Reynolds (see *Eating Out*). There are no organized tours, but visitors may catch a glimpse of the ships from their cars as they drive along Eisenhower Boulevard, if there's not too much commercial truck traffic. At times, naval vessels in port are open for free tours. State Rd. 84, east of US 1 (phone: 523-3404).

Business travelers and vacationers often combine an area visit with a cruise. More than 32 ships make Port Everglades their home port. Two offer day cruises (see *Day Cruises* in DIVERSIONS), while others embark on longer journeys, most often to the Bahamas and Caribbean Islands. Cruise lines that sail from Port Everglades on a variety of itineraries include *Celebrity Cruises* (phone: 800-437-3111); *Crystal Cruises* (phone: 800-446-6620); *Cunard Line* (phone: 800-221-4770); *Discovery Cruises* (phone: 525-7800; 800-937-4477); *Holland America Line* (phone: 800-426-0327); *Norwegian/NCL* (phone: 800-327-7030); *Princess Cruises* (phone: 800-421-0522); *Radisson Seven Seas Cruises* (phone: 800-285-1835); *Royal Olympic Cruises* (phone: 800-468-6400); *Seabourn Cruise Line* (phone: 800-929-9595); and *SeaEscape* (phone: 800-432-0900).

MUSEUM OF DISCOVERY AND SCIENCE One lure of Ft. Lauderdale's 85,000-square-foot museum is its five-story IMAX screen (one of the largest movie screens in the southeastern US), housed in a 300-seat theater. Among the delightful exhibits are a giant outdoor gravity clock whose winding balls captivate onlookers as they twist and turn through an oversized erector-set mechanism. Indoors, exhibits include walk-through simulated Florida ecological habitats with over 100 species of live animals and plants; two simulated space rides; interactive science displays for kids; and "Gizmo City," an area featuring hands-on activities like assembling gadgets and programming robots, as well as workstations that allow visitors to access the Internet and play virtual volleyball and hockey. There are Saturday classes for children (phone: 467-6637, ext. 315). A small restaurant and an excellent museum store are on the premises. Closed *Christmas Day*. Admission charge (additional charge for the theater, which screens up to 11 shows daily). 401 SW Second St., across from the *Broward Center for the Performing Arts* (phone: 467-6637 or 463-IMAX).

HUGH TAYLOR BIRCH STATE RECREATION AREA Just across the street from the beach is this lush, subtropical park. Its 180 acres, two nature trails, and two small playgrounds make it ideal for picnicking, ball playing, canoeing, biking, and hiking. It's a favorite with in-line skaters. A tunnel runs under the highway between the beach and the park. Open daily. Admission charge. 3109 E. Sunrise Blvd. (phone: 564-4521).

STRANAHAN HOUSE The restored 1901 home and Indian trading post of early settler Frank Stranahan, this is Broward County's oldest structure and one of the area's oldest museums. It's hard to imagine the Ft. Lauderdale of those days, but a tour of this house provides some idea of the hardships endured. Closed Mondays and Tuesdays. Admission charge. SE Sixth Ave. at Las Olas Blvd. and the New River Tunnel (phone: 524-4736).

BONNET HOUSE Built in the 1920s as a family retreat for artists Frederick and Evelyn Bartlett, this 36-acre private estate is one of the few remaining oceanfront wildlife areas in South Florida. The two-story house and grounds have been preserved and are on the National Register of Historic Places. Guided tours are offered Wednesdays through Sundays. Admission charge. 900 N. Birch Rd. (phone: 563-5393).

INTERNATIONAL SWIMMING HALL OF FAME Many of the world's top swimming and diving competitions are held at this renovated complex, but the Olympic-size pools are open to the public when there's no meet scheduled, and swimming lessons are offered year-round. The adjoining museum houses unusual aquatic memorabilia from more than 100 countries. Open daily. Admission charge. 1 Hall of Fame Dr., off Rte. A1A. (phone: 462-6536).

GREATER FT. LAUDERDALE

EVERGLADES HOLIDAY PARK Savor what the Everglades are all about while on a narrated airboat ride at this small park. You'll see some of the most beautiful birds Mother Nature has ever created (you might even spot an American bald eagle) as well as nesting alligators. (Your tour guide will give you a healthy respect for the power of alligator jaws, even those of the seemingly cute young ones.) There also are special tours offering insights into the lives of the Seminole Indians, a group of Native Americans whose history is little known outside this region. If you're feeling adventurous, rent a boat or an RV for a closer experience with nature. There's also a campground here. Open daily 24 hours. No admission charge to the park; a fee is charged for airboat rides. 21940 Griffin Rd., west of Hwy. 27 (phone: 434-8111). For more information, see *Tour 6: Cowboy and Indian Tour* in DIRECTIONS.

FLAMINGO GARDENS This 60-acre botanical garden has a flamingo exhibit, a tropical plant house, an Everglades wildlife sanctuary, orange groves, alligators, and river otters. A guided tram tour takes visitors through the groves, wetlands, and an indigenous hardwood hammock with stands of oak, gumbo-limbo, and fig trees. A screened-in aviary re-creates several native settings—including a mangrove swamp and a sawgrass prairie—for those who can't get out to the Everglades. Free-flying local birds, including cormorants and ospreys, can be seen throughout the groves. There's also a snack bar, a gift shop that sells nature books and crafts, a produce stall for purchasing and shipping citrus fruit, and a plant shop. Open daily. Admission charge. 3750 Flamingo Rd., Davie (phone: 473-2955).

LOXAHATCHEE EVERGLADES TOURS Just across the northern Broward County line, visitors can take an airboat trip through the Everglades without traveling great distances to the south. These airboats provide ramps that afford easy access to disabled passengers, and employ improved methods for muffling engine noises. Passengers skim over the "river of grass," spotting alligators and their babies in nests, plus myriad wild fowl such as gallinules. There's a small (and sparsely stocked) snack shop at the park. Open daily. No admission charge to the park, but there's a fee for airboat rides. From Rte. 441 take Loxahatchee Rd. (between Hillsboro Blvd. and Palmetto Park Rd.), then drive 6 miles west to the Everglades (phone: 407-482-0313; 800-683-5873).

HOLLYWOOD BROADWALK This 2¼-mile, 24-foot-wide, concrete ocean promenade is bordered by a bicycle path and lined with inexpensive outdoor cafés often featuring contemporary music. Bikes may be rented at various sites, and there's free music and dancing (the jitterbug and polka are favorites) at the Johnson Street bandstand Monday through Wednesday nights. This area has a strong Quebecois flavor and half the promenade signs are in French. Lifeguard stations are manned year-round. The Broadwalk extends south from *North Beach Park* (near Sheridan St.) to Harrison St. (phone: 921-3404 for information).

SAWGRASS MILLS MALL This 2.3 million-square-foot discount shopping complex, billed as the world's largest outlet mall, boasts such stores as *Saks Fifth Avenue, Neiman-Marcus, Brandsmart, JC Penney, Marshall's,* and *Spiegel,* and at least 270 specialty shops. It's so big that you can't see it all in one day; and it draws visitors from around the state (there's a separate entrance for tour buses). Among the temptations are an *Ann Taylor* clearance center, a *Joan & David* shoe outlet, and a newer wing featuring *J. Crew, Mikasa, Waterford,* and *Bernini* outlets. Many stores offer valid savings of 20% to 60%, but this mall is for savvy shoppers: It's important to know what things sell for elsewhere. Several restaurants and two food courts provide respite. An 18-screen movie theater, billed as the largest east of the Mississippi, completes the picture. Open daily. 12801 W. Sunrise Blvd., Sunrise (phone: 846-2350; 800-FL-MILLS).

SWAP SHOP The largest flea market in the South, it claims to be Florida's second-largest tourist attraction after *Walt Disney World.* With over 2,000 vendors, bargains range from electronic equipment to tomatoes. There's also daily entertainment. Open weekdays from 8 AM to 6 PM (outdoor stalls close an hour and a half earlier); on weekends, the complex is open from 7 AM to 7 PM (the outdoor stalls close at 6:30 PM). 3291 W. Sunrise Blvd. (phone: 791-SWAP). A second branch with 625 booths is open Tuesdays, Saturdays, and Sundays from 4:30 AM to 2 PM. 1000 State Rd. 7, Margate (phone: 971-SWAP).

BUTTERFLY WORLD Visitors can walk among the multicolored creatures fluttering freely in this three-acre, re-created jungle habitat. The butterflies are seen in all their stages of life, from larvae and pupae to cocoon and full adulthood. Certain species are attracted to light-colored clothing and certain scents; if you've spent a hot morning in traffic or sightseeing, you may find yourself converted into a temporary perch. There are butterflies from all over the world and a spectacular museum of mounted insects. Closed *Thanksgiving* and *Christmas Day.* Admission charge. Inside *Tradewinds Park,* 3600 W. Sample Rd., Coconut Creek (phone: 977-4400).

JOHN U. LLOYD BEACH STATE RECREATION AREA Many Ft. Lauderdale residents consider this *the* place for picnicking, swimming, fishing, canoeing, and other recreation. There are 244 acres of beach, dunes, mangrove swamp, and vegetation. Park rangers lead nature walks during winter months. Open daily. Admission charge. 6503 N. Ocean Dr., Dania (phone: 923-2833).

TOPEEKEEGEE YUGNEE PARK Locally called "T-Y Park" due to its difficult-to-pronounce Indian name, this is one of the area's more popular parks for families. Visitors can enjoy all kinds of activities—swimming, boating, canoeing, picnicking, barbecuing, hiking, and biking. Open daily. Admission charge on weekends and holidays. 3300 N. Park Rd., just off I-95, Hollywood (phone: 985-1980).

SEMINOLE INDIAN RESERVATION The reservation's *Native Village* includes a historical art exhibit, a gift shop with Indian arts and crafts, demonstrations of alligator wrestling, and snake and turtle shows. The exhibit offers an interesting glimpse into this little-known Native American group. The Seminole gave up their lands reluctantly and never did sign a treaty with the United States. Although bingo games for profit are not legal elsewhere in Florida, they're allowed here. The reservation's bingo hall and 24-hour casino holds up to 1,400 people and often is full; winners have pocketed as much as $110,000 for a single game. There's an admission charge for the village tour, and another for the bingo hall (includes bingo cards). Both are open daily. The village is at 3551 N. State Rd. 7, Hollywood (phone: 961-4519); the bingo hall is at 4150 N. State Rd. 7, Hollywood (phone: 961-3220). For more information, see *Tour 6: Cowboy and Indian Tour* in DIRECTIONS.

GOODYEAR BLIMP Though tourists may not go for a ride in the *Stars & Stripes* (it's only for corporate clients), they can see the 192-foot-long blimp up close at its hangar at varied times from November through May. Call in advance for schedule. No admission charge. 1500 NE Fifth Ave., Pompano Beach (phone: 946-8300).

GRAND PRIX RACE-O-RAMA A 1990s-style amusement park that's fun for the whole family (and a lifesaver on a rainy day), it features a 24-hour video arcade, five miniature golf courses, batting cages, bumper cars, go-karts, Nascarts, and Sky Coasters. Open daily; extended hours on weekends. Charges per game and attraction. 1500 NW First St., Dania (phone: 921-1411).

To experience fully the subtropical beauty and laid-back ambience that is Ft. Lauderdale, drive east on Las Olas Boulevard past its chic boutiques and palm-lined streets. Continue through the Isles of Las Olas area, which is laced with canals and filled with fancy homes nestled among royal palm trees. Large, luxurious boats are docked outside many of the homes. Look up and you may spot some of the colorful parrots that nest here. Proceed past the sailboat cove, where towering masts salute the blue sky, and cruise over the small bridge to Route A1A, along the Atlantic Ocean. Drive north, and at about 4 PM, stop at one of the sidewalk cafés or hotel patio bars facing the ocean to watch bicyclists, in-line skaters, joggers, and walkers along the promenade. The ocean will be filled with sailboats returning to safe harbor, and cruise and cargo ships steaming out to distant corners. Take off your shoes, walk along the sand at the water's edge—and let the images soak in.

Sources and Resources

TOURIST INFORMATION

The *Greater Ft. Lauderdale Convention and Visitors Bureau* is downtown (1850 Eller Dr.; Suite 303, Ft. Lauderdale, FL 33316; phone: 765-4466; 800-22-SUNNY; fax: 765-4467). Stop in or call for information on accommodations, activities, attractions, sports, dining, shopping, touring, and special events (closed weekends). Or call in advance for a free, information-filled book (phone: 800-22-SUNNY, ext. 711). There is also a 24-hour hotline that provides local travel directions in English, Spanish, French, German, and Portuguese (phone: 527-5600; cellular phone: #333). *The Broward County Arts and Entertainment Hotline* (phone: 357-5700) provides schedules of events and information about visitor attractions. Contact the *Florida Division of Tourism's Bureau of Visitor Services* (phone: 904-487-1462) for maps, calendars of events, and travel advisories.

LOCAL COVERAGE The *Sun-Sentinel,* a morning daily, carries listings on the following week's events in its "Showtime" section on Fridays; the *Miami Herald,* a morning daily, carries similar information in its "Weekend" section on Fridays. The free weekly alternative newspaper *XS* lists nightclubs, cultural events, and restaurants.

TELEVISION STATIONS WPBT Channel 2—public television; WTVJ Channel 6—NBC; WFOR Channel 4—CBS; WSVN Channel 7—Fox; and WPLG Channel 10—ABC.

RADIO STATIONS AM: WIOD 610 (news/talk); WINZ 940 (news/talk); WJNO 1230 (news/talk); WKAT 1360 (multilingual); WFTL 1400 (talk). FM: WKPX 88.5 (progressive/alternative rock); WAFG 90.3 (religious); WXEL

90.7 (public radio); WLRN 91.3 (public radio); WTMI 93.1 (classical); WLVE 93.9 (jazz); WZTA 94.9 (rock); WFLC 97.3 (adult contemporary); WKIS 99.9 (country); WHYI 100 (top 40); WLYF 101.5 (easy listening); WMXJ 102.7 (oldies rock); WSHE 103.5 (alternative rock); WHQT 105 (urban adult contemporary); and WRMA 106.7 (easy listening).

TELEPHONE The area code for Ft. Lauderdale is 954.

SALES TAX The city sales tax is 6%; there is also a 3% Broward County hotel tax.

GETTING AROUND

AIRPORT The *Greater Ft. Lauderdale/Hollywood International Airport* is 10 to 20 minutes by car from Downtown Ft. Lauderdale, depending on traffic conditions. *Broward County Mass Transit* (phone: 357-8400; TDD: 357-8302) provides bus service between the airport and the downtown bus terminal at Northwest First Avenue and Broward Boulevard; the one-way fare is $1. *Gray Line Airport Service* (phone: 800-244-8252 in Florida; 954-561-8888 elsewhere in the US) offers shared limousine service between the airport and points throughout Broward County for $6 to $20. *Tri-Rail* (phone: 728-8445; 800-TRI-RAIL) operates free shuttle buses between the airport and the airport station in Dania (about halfway between Hollywood and Ft. Lauderdale), where there are commuter trains to Ft. Lauderdale (see "Tri-Rail," below).

BUS *Broward County Transit* serves most of the area. Fares are $1; 15¢ for transfers. Weekly passes cost $8 and are available at selected hotels and motels. For information, call 357-8400.

CAR RENTAL Ft. Lauderdale is served by all the major national firms, one of which has its corporate headquarters in the city: *Alamo* (110 SE Sixth St.; phone: 525-2501; 800-327-9633). There are also several regional agencies; check the phone directory. For more information, see GETTING READY TO GO.

TAXI While you can hail a cab on the street, it's best to pick one up at a major hotel or restaurant or to call for one. The major cab company is *Checker/Yellow Cab* (phone: 565-5400). For information on cabs that accommodate wheelchairs, call 565-2800.

TRI-RAIL A double-decker train runs from West Palm Beach south through Ft. Lauderdale to Miami, and connects with Miami's *Metrorail/Metromover* and various county and shuttle bus lines. The train also connects the *Greater Ft. Lauderdale/Hollywood International Airport* with *Miami International* and *Palm Beach International Airports*. Extra trains and shuttles are scheduled for select games at Miami's *Joe Robbie* and *Orange Bowl Stadiums;* special events; and shopping trips to the *Swap Shop, Town Center Mall in Boca Raton,* and Miami's *Bayside Marketplace*. At times, special sightseeing package tours are available. The trains are accessible to the disabled. For information, call 728-8445 or 800-TRI-RAIL.

WATER TAXI Running from the 17th Street Causeway to Atlantic Boulevard in Pompano Beach, *Water Taxi* (651 Seabreeze Blvd.; phone: 467-6677) operates on demand daily and covers more than 100 landings. Some taxis are open-air boats; a couple of the vessels are larger and air conditioned. Vessels are also available for charter.

SIGHTSEEING TOURS

BOAT TOURS Dubbed the "Venice of America," Ft. Lauderdale is best seen by boat. The *Jungle Queen* (at the *Bahia Mar Marina,* 801 Seabreeze Blvd.; phone: 462-5596) offers three-hour sightseeing tours twice daily; it also takes riders down to Miami twice weekly for shopping sprees. The *Carrie B* (docked behind *Hyde Park* supermarket on Las Olas Blvd. at SE Fifth Ave.; phone: 768-9920) runs three one-and-a-half-hour daily trips on the New River down to Port Everglades year-round, and 90-minute sunset cruises daily from February through April. Large families and small business groups can charter the 120-foot *Sir Winston* (on the New River dock; phone: 462-7411), which transports groups along the waterways past millionaires' homes. Two-hour glass-bottom boat tours are conducted on *Pro Diver II,* sailing from the *Bahia Mar Marina* (phone: 467-6030) daily except Mondays.

HORSE-AND-CARRIAGE TOURS *Las Olas Horse & Carriage Inc.* (phone: 763-7393; 357-1950, beeper) offers horse-and-carriage tours of Las Olas Boulevard to *Colee Hammock Park* and back.

TRAM TOURS Another wonderful way to sightsee is aboard the open-air *South Florida Trolley,* which is available for group tours that can be arranged through a travel agent, tour operator, your hotel concierge, or by calling the company directly (phone: 429-3100). *Ellerworld Tours* picks up cruise ship passengers at the pier in Port Everglades, offering shopping excursions and a two-hour city tour (phone: 525-3381).

WALKING TOURS The *Ft. Lauderdale Historical Society* (phone: 463-4431) periodically conducts three-hour walking tours of the historical district from late October through mid-May. Participants learn about the Seminole Wars and early 19th-century farms and trading posts along the then-inhospitable New River.

SPECIAL EVENTS

The *Las Olas Art Fair* takes place on fashionable Las Olas Boulevard on two weekends in January and February, attracting more than 150,000 people (phone: 472-3755). The *Seminole Indian Tribal Fair,* usually held during the first two weeks in February on the reservation, is a showcase of Indian crafts, entertainment, and food (phone: 966-6300). The *Las Olas Art Festival,* hosted by the *Museum of Art,* takes place in early March. The festival attracts 300 artists, whose work is displayed in a juried show at

Bubier Park; many of these artists are not represented by galleries (phone: 525-5500). The *Honda Golf Classic,* one of the biggest *PGA* tournaments, is held in early March at the *Tournament Players Club at Eagle Trace* in Coral Springs; it attracts the *PGA*'s top players (phone: 346-4000). Also in March, the *Florida Derby Festival* hits town; activities such as the *Derby Ball* culminate in a thoroughbred race (with a purse of about $500,000) at *Gulfstream Park* (phone: 454-7000; 305-931-RACE). The other big March event in town is the annual *Ft. Lauderdale Festival of the Arts,* which brings three days of music to the *Broward Center for the Performing Arts,* with free outdoor concerts along the New River's *Riverwalk* (phone: 468-2687). At the end of February, cowboys kick up their heels at the *Westfest* in Davie, a ten-day affair featuring a rodeo, street fair, concerts, and carnival (phone: 581-0790; 800-962-2420).

In April, seafood is king at the *Ft. Lauderdale Seafood Festival* at *Bubier Park,* where 30 leading restaurants offer samples (phone: 463-4431). In late April, the *Pompano Beach Seafood Festival & Art Show* is held on the beach at East Atlantic Boulevard (phone: 941-2940). In May, anglers test their skill during the *Pompano Beach Fishing Rodeo,* where more than $250,000 in cash is awarded for the largest catches (phone: 942-4513).

September brings the *Las Olas Labor Day Art Fair,* which turns the entire boulevard into a pedestrian mall lined with art exhibits, street performers, and food booths (phone: 472-3755). *Oktoberfest* falls (naturally) in October and features lots of German food, drink, and music in *Bubier Park* (phone: 761-5360). The *Ft. Lauderdale Boat Show,* held in October at four area sites, is the world's largest in-water display of all types and sizes of watercraft (phone: 763-3661). In November, the *Promenade in the Park* features arts and crafts, food, and entertainment at *Holiday Park* (phone: 764-5973). Also held in November are the *Ft. Lauderdale International Film Festival,* with screenings of more than 100 independent films (phone: 563-0500), and the *Broward County Fair* in Hallandale (phone: 963-3247). The year's activities are capped by the December-long *Winterfest;* highlights include the *Ft. Lauderdale* and *Pompano Beach Boat Parades,* with as many as 100 boats festooned with colored lights and *Christmas* decorations plying the Intracoastal Waterway (phone: 767-0686), and a *Light up Lauderdale* laser show in *Bubier Park* on *New Year's Eve* (phone: 767-0686).

MUSEUMS

In addition to those described in *Special Places,* other Ft. Lauderdale area museums include the following:

FT. LAUDERDALE HISTORICAL SOCIETY Located in the historic district, the society headquarters hosts exhibits on Ft. Lauderdale and Broward County history. The society also conducts tours of Downtown Ft. Lauderdale. Closed Sunday mornings and Mondays. Admission charge. 219 SW Second Ave. (phone: 463-4431).

FT. LAUDERDALE MUSEUM OF ART Housed in a 63,800-square-foot building designed by Edward Larabee Barnes, the museum features 19th- and 20th-century European and American art, as well as West African, pre-Columbian, and American Indian works. There are more than 2,000 paintings and 5,000 prints in the collection. Traveling exhibits are housed in three galleries and there's a sculpture garden and auditorium. Open extended hours on Tuesdays; closed Sunday mornings and Mondays. Admission charge. 1 E. Las Olas Blvd. (phone: 525-5500).

GRAVES MUSEUM OF ARCHAEOLOGY AND NATURAL HISTORY This charming complex features some unusual exhibits such as a six-ton quartz crystal, a triceratops skull, and a diorama on the Tequesta Indians. Other highlights include an Egyptian room, African tribal art, marine archaeology, and pre-Columbian art. Closed Mondays. Admission charge. 481 S. Federal Hwy., Dania (phone: 925-7770).

YOUNG AT ART CHILDREN'S MUSEUM Primarily a hands-on museum, children can develop their artistic skills in this creative environment. Closed Sunday mornings and Mondays. No admission charge for children under two. 801 S. University Dr., Plantation (phone: 424-0085).

MAJOR COLLEGES AND UNIVERSITIES

Broward Community College has three campuses (central, 3501 SW Davie Rd., Davie; north, 1000 Coconut Creek Blvd., Coconut Creek; and south, 7200 Hollywood Pines Blvd., Pembroke Pines; phone for all: 475-6500). The *Nova Southeastern University* campus is in Davie (3301 College Ave.; phone: 800-541-NOVA). The *University Tower* in Ft. Lauderdale (220 SE Second Ave.; phone: 355-5200) is a facility for graduate classes shared by *Broward Community College, Florida Atlantic University,* and *Florida International University,* whose main campuses are in Broward, Palm Beach, and Dade Counties, respectively.

SHOPPING

For a break from the beach, visit one of the many shopping malls and stores in the Ft. Lauderdale area. For general shopping hours, see GETTING READY TO GO. The following places are in Ft. Lauderdale unless otherwise noted.

Broward Mall One of the South's largest shopping malls, with 130 specialty shops, this ultramodern mart's main stores are *Burdines, Sears, Mervyn's,* and *JC Penney.* Broward Blvd. and University Dr., Plantation (phone: 473-8100).

Fashion Mall at Plantation This center offers the county's only *Macy's,* plus *Lord & Taylor,* the *Sheraton Suites* hotel, and lots of specialty shops. 321 N. University Dr., Plantation (phone: 370-1884).

Fashion Row Also known as "Shmatte" (Yiddish for garments or rags) Row, it offers an array of discounts. One section of dress and handbag shops is located off Hallandale Beach Boulevard on Northeast First Avenue; the other is on Northeast Second Avenue between Northeast Third and Northeast Fourth Streets. Most Fashion Row shops are open daily from December through March; closed Sundays the rest of the year.

Festival Flea Market Mall At this 400,000-square-foot indoor flea-market-type mall in western Ft. Lauderdale, 650 vendors offer brand-new merchandise as well as antiques and collectibles. There are also eight movie theaters, an amusement arcade, a beauty salon, farmers' market, and an international food court. Many items are discounted. Closed Mondays year-round; closed Tuesdays June through September. Open on all holidays. 2900 W. Sample Rd., Pompano Beach (phone: 979-4555).

Galleria High-fashion clothes and home furnishings are sold at this three-story mall, featuring *Neiman Marcus, Saks Fifth Avenue, Dillard's, Lord & Taylor, Burdines,* and numerous smaller stores, including *Brooks Brothers* and *Cartier.* Valet parking available. 2414 E. Sunrise Blvd. (phone: 564-1015).

Las Olas Boulevard Between Southeast Sixth and 11th Avenues, this street is a window-shopper's delight. There are dozens of trendy specialty shops, galleries, restaurants, and lively sidewalk cafés. Our favorites include *Maus & Hoffman* (800 E. Las Olas Blvd.; phone: 463-1472) for upscale men's clothing; *Sophy Curson* (1508 E. Las Olas Blvd.; phone: 462-7770) for high-fashion women's clothing (open from late October through May only); and *Zola Keller* (818 E. Las Olas Blvd.; phone: 462-3222), with more fine fashions for women. Closed Sundays, except for *Zola Keller.*

Lord & Taylor Clearance Center Here you'll find clothing discounted up to 50% initially, with further reductions for special sales. 6820 N. University Dr. (McNab Rd. and University Dr.), Tamarac (phone: 720-1915).

Sawgrass Mills Mall This gigantic, 2.3-million-square-foot shopping center is billed as the world's largest outlet mall. 12801 W. Sunrise Blvd., Sunrise (phone: 846-2350; 800-FL-MILLS). For more information, see *Special Places.*

Swap Shop Indoor and outdoor booths beckon at this massive flea market—the largest in the South and a true bargain-hunter's heaven. 3291 W. Sunrise Blvd. (phone: 791-SWAP). A second branch has 625 booths. 1000 State Rd. 7, Margate (phone: 971-SWAP). For more information, see *Special Places.*

SPORTS AND FITNESS

BASEBALL The New York *Yankees* no longer hold spring training in Ft. Lauderdale, but their rivals, the Baltimore *Orioles,* brought their camp to *Ft. Lauderdale Stadium* (5301 NW 12th Ave.; phone: 938-4980) last year, with an option to return for the 1997 pre-season as well.

BOATING After the sunshine, the water is one of South Florida's greatest draws. The US Corps of Engineers maintains navigational aids, and private and public marinas provide virtually every type of boat for rent. For large charters, power-, or sailboats contact the *Heavy Hitter* at *Bahia Mar Marina* (801 Seabreeze Blvd.; phone: 523-5400) or *Club Nautico* (phone: 920-2796) with docks in Dania (at the *Harbourtowne Marina,* off US 1, 801 NE Third St.; phone: 926-0300); Ft. Lauderdale (2301 SE 17th St. Causeway, Slip A19; phone: 523-0033), and Deerfield Beach (*The Cove Marina,* 1755 SE Third Ct.; phone: 421-4628). Water bikes (jet skis) and power boats may be rented from *Sunrise Watersports* (2025 E. Sunrise Blvd.; phone: 462-8962).

FISHING As in Miami, there's just about every kind of angling you can think of here. For deep-sea adventure, numerous charter boats are available. There are plenty of listings under "Fishing" in the Ft. Lauderdale yellow pages, but we recommend the *Bahia Mar Marina* and *Club Nautico* (see *Boating,* above).

Landlubbers fish 24 hours a day from the 1,080-foot *Pompano Beach Fishing Pier* (two blocks north of East Atlantic Blvd.; phone: 943-1488) and *Anglin's Fishing Pier* (2 Commercial Blvd.; phone: 491-9403). There's an admission charge for each.

For seasons and regulations, see "Fishing" in *Miami,* THE CITIES.

FITNESS CENTERS *Nautilus Fitness Center* (1624 N. Federal Hwy.; phone: 566-2222), with certified instructors, offers all the standard Nautilus exercise equipment, plus freeweights and aerobics. It's open to the public for a fee.

GOLF Not surprisingly, Ft. Lauderdale boasts some great greens. Several resorts have excellent golf courses, and many that lack their own links provide access to other clubs. It's usually necessary to call ahead to reserve a tee time, especially during the winter season.

TOP TEE-OFF SPOTS

Bonaventure Two championship 18-hole courses lure golfers to this 500-room resort. The *East* course is considered one of Florida's top ten, and the waterfall hole is certainly challenging. There's also a driving range, putting green, and pro shop. Moonlight golf (for groups of 20 or more) adds to the standard tee-off times. Special packages combine spa and golf vacations (see *Sybaritic Spas* in DIVERSIONS). 200 Bonaventure Blvd. (phone: 389-2100; 800-327-8090; fax: 389-2124).

Palm-Aire Courses here have hosted the *Florida Open, US Open* qualifying matches, and the *Florida PGA* tournament. The 1,500-acre resort, which has a 140-room hotel and a residential development, offers four 18-hole championship golf courses (the *Palms, Oaks, Cypress,* and *Pines*) and a shorter 22-hole executive course (the *Sabals*). The *Cypress* will host the *Florida Open* through the year 2004. Instruction is available; combination spa and golf packages can be arranged. 2601 Palm-Aire Dr. N., Pompano Beach (phone: 978-1737; 800-272-5624; fax: 978-6066).

Other courses open to the public include *American Golfers Club* (3850 N. Federal Hwy.; phone: 564-8760); *Rolling Hills* (3501 W. Rolling Hills Cir., Davie; phone: 475-0400; 800-327-7735); *Grand Palms* (110 Grand Palm Dr., Pembroke Pines; phone: 437-3334); and *Jacaranda* (9200 W. Broward Blvd., Plantation; phone: 472-5836). For additional information, call the *Broward County Parks and Recreation Department* (phone: 357-8100).

HORSE AND DOG RACING There's thoroughbred horse racing at *Gulfstream Park* (Hallandale Beach Blvd. and US 1, Hallandale; phone: 454-7000) daily except Tuesdays from mid-January through March, and harness racing at *Pompano Harness Track* (1800 SW Third St., Pompano Beach; phone: 972-2000) from October through early September. Dogs race at *Hollywood Greyhound Track* (831 N. Federal Hwy., Hallandale; phone: 454-9400) from late December to late April. Call for racing dates.

HORSEBACK RIDING Cowboy country awaits in Davie, with many stables in the area offering trail rides and horse rentals. Among the larger ones are *Bar-B Ranch* (4601 SW 128th Ave., Davie; phone: 434-6175), which offers horse rentals, and *Myrland Stables* (5550 SW 73rd Ave., Davie; phone: 587-2285), which has trails and lessons. Both are open daily. On Saturdays and Sundays, Broward County also operates stables at *Tradewinds Park* (3600 W. Sample Rd., Coconut Creek; phone: 968-3880).

JAI ALAI This Basque import is the area's most fast-paced sport, with pari-mutuel betting adding spice. The season is year-round, except for two-and-a-half weeks in April and May. The action takes place at *Dania Jai-Alai* (301 E. Dania Beach Blvd., Dania; phone: 927-2841); it's closed Mondays and Wednesdays.

NATURE HIKES The *Broward County Parks and Recreation Department* sponsors a different nature walk each Friday and Saturday, October through May. Call for a schedule (phone: 357-8100).

PARASAILING Soar like a bird over Ft. Lauderdale with *Watersports Unlimited* (301 Seabreeze Blvd.; phone: 467-1316).

RODEO Cowboys compete in bronco riding, calf roping, and other activities at the *Rodeo Arena* in Davie, just behind the *Davie Town Hall* (6591 SW 45th St.; phone: 797-1166 or 797-1163. There's an admission charge. Also see *Tour 6: Cowboy and Indian Tour* in DIRECTIONS. The arena is also the site of country music concerts and "monster truck" shows, where people gather to watch enormous vehicles leap over one other.

SCUBA DIVING AND SNORKELING Stretching north from the Keys past Ft. Lauderdale, Florida's natural coral reef has suffered from overuse, damage from ships, and pollution. But diving remains popular in this part of Florida, partially due to the practice of sinking freighters and other large objects to create artificial reefs. The most famous sinking in recent years was the tanker *Mercedes,* which was swept by a storm onto socialite Mollie Wilmot's terrace before being scuttled in Ft. Lauderdale. More than 80 other sites also lure fish and coral to varying depths.

Dozens of dive shops offer half-day dive trips, basic resort courses that get neophytes into the water the same day, and certification and specialty courses. *Pro Dive* (*Bahia Mar Marina,* 801 Seabreeze Blvd.; phone: 761-3413; 800-772-DIVE outside Florida) has daily dives and a full range of courses. It also offers snorkeling trips Tuesdays through Sundays aboard the 60-foot glass-bottom boat *Pro Diver II.* Other dive shops offering certification are *Ocean Diving Schools* (750 E. Sample Rd., Pompano; phone: 943-3337) and *Force E* (2700 E. Atlantic Blvd.; phone: 943-3483). Many operators offer package deals with hotels.

SWIMMING The most crowded beach is along "The Strip" (otherwise known as "The Promenade") from Sunrise Boulevard to Bahia Mar. The quaint seaside village of Lauderdale-by-the-Sea is also popular; the beach is just north of Ft. Lauderdale. The Galt Ocean Mile is quieter, with an older crowd. Perhaps the quietest strand is the stretch between Galt Ocean Mile and Northeast 22nd Street, and you may find small pockets of peace in *John U. Lloyd Beach State Recreation Area* (see *Special Places*) or *North Beach Park* (Sheridan Rd. and Rte. A1A, Hollywood; phone: 926-2444). Deerfield Beach, from the border of Broward and Palm Beach Counties south to SE 10th Street, is a favorite of locals.

TENNIS Although most major hotels here have tennis courts, one is a true ace.

CHOICE COURT

Bonaventure The best tennis facilities in Ft. Lauderdale are found at this elegant resort, with its 24 tennis courts—seven clay and most nightlit. There are also five indoor air conditioned racquetball and squash courts, and a pro shop. Combination tennis and spa packages are available (see *Sybaritic Spas* in DIVERSIONS). 357 Racquet Club Rd. (phone: 389-8667; 800-327-8090; fax: 384-0563).

There are also numerous courts open to the public. Among them are *Holiday Park Tennis Center* (701 NE 12th Ave.; phone: 761-5378), where Chris Evert learned to play; *Dillon Tennis Courts* (4091 NE 5th Ave., Oakland Park; phone: 561-6180); *Pompano Beach Tennis Center* (900 NE 18th Ave.; phone: 786-4115); and *George W. English Park* (1101 Bayview Dr.; phone: 396-3620). For more information, contact the *Broward County Parks and*

Recreation Division (phone: 357-8100) or the *Ft. Lauderdale Parks and Recreation Department* (phone: 761-5346).

THEATER

Opened in 1991, the $55-million regional *Broward Center for the Performing Arts* (201 SW Fifth Ave.; phone: 462-0222; 522-5334, tickets) stages opera, theatre, ballet, and orchestra productions. The area's other major theaters are the *Parker Playhouse* (707 NE Eighth St.; phone: 763-2444), which features name actors in touring companies of Broadway productions, and *Sunrise Musical Theater* (5555 NW 95th Ave.; phone: 741-7300), which showcases plays, musicals, in-concert performances by musicians and comedians, and children's productions. *Bailey Concert Hall* at *Broward Community College* (3501 SW Davie Rd., Davie; phone: 475-6884) also stages children's theater, as well as plays and musical performances. The *Vinnette Carroll Theater* (503 SE Sixth St.; phone: 462-2424) presents multicultural productions in a converted church.

MUSIC

The *Philharmonic Orchestra of Florida* usually plays at the *Broward Center for the Performing Arts* (see *Theater;* phone: 561-2997; 800-226-1812). The center is also the site for performances by the *Symphony of the Americas* (phone: 561-5882) and the *Florida Grand Opera* (phone: 728-9700; 800-741-1010) during winter months; the latter often features visiting artists. Jazz, opera, and symphonic performances are staged throughout the year at *Broward Community College*'s *Bailey Concert Hall* (see *Theater*).

NIGHTCLUBS AND NIGHTLIFE

Most hotels and larger motels offer music and/or comedy acts nightly. The *Musician's Exchange Café* (729 W. Sunrise Blvd.; phone: 764-1912) is the place to go for jazz, blues, and rock. For dance and billiards, the young and wild go to *Baja Beach Club* (3200 N. Federal Hwy.; phone: 561-2432). *The Pier Top Lounge* at the *Hyatt Regency Pier 66* hotel attracts romantic couples of all ages (see *Checking In*). At *Squeeze* (2 S. New River Dr. W.; phone: 522-2151), there's dancing to progressive and alternative music. Cowboys and wannabes head to *Desperado's* (2520 S. Miami Rd.; phone: 463-2855), complete with line dancing, western clothing, and a mechanical bull. Jazz lovers flock to *O'Hara's Pub* (722 E. Las Olas Blvd.; phone: 524-1764), and the blues and beer group gathers at *Cheers* (941 E. Cypress Creek Rd.; phone: 771-6337). The hottest gay club remains *The Copa* (624 SE 28th St.; phone: 463-1507). A popular Ft. Lauderdale supper club is *Mario's East* (1313 E. Las Olas Blvd.; phone: 523-4990), which has live entertainment nightly; an elegant waterside spot is *Coconut's* (429 Seabreeze Blvd.; phone: 467-6788). And if you just want to sit at a sidewalk café, watch the waves and the people, and listen to good jazz, *Mistral* (see *Eating Out*) has just the thing every Friday and Saturday.

Best in Town

CHECKING IN

Ft. Lauderdale's busiest period is winter, when reservations should be made as far in advance as possible. During high season, a double room at a hotel in the very expensive category could run $200 to $300 per night; in the expensive category, $155 to $190; in the moderate category, $110 to $150; and in the inexpensive category, $65 to $100. In the summer, occupancy (and room) rates drop. Note that a 3% county tourist development tax and a 6% state sales tax are added to all hotel bills.

Most of Ft. Lauderdale's major hotels have complete facilities for the business traveler. Those hotels listed below as having "business services" usually offer such conveniences as meeting rooms, photocopiers, computers, translation services, and express checkout, among others. Call the hotel for additional information. Unless noted otherwise, hotel rooms have air conditioning, private baths, TV sets, and telephones.

In addition to the establishments listed here, the city has many smaller chain and family-operated hotels and motels. About 90 family-operated properties in the area have been designated "superior small lodgings" by the *Greater Ft. Lauderdale Convention and Visitors' Bureau* and *Nova Southeastern University*'s hospitality department, which conducts inspections of the facilities annually. For more information contact the *Greater Ft. Lauderdale Convention and Visitors Bureau* (see *Tourist Information*). All the hotels below are in Ft. Lauderdale and telephone and fax numbers are in the 954 area code unless otherwise indicated.

We begin with our favorite place, followed by recommended hotels, listed by price category.

A GRAND HOTEL

Marriott Harbor Beach Ft. Lauderdale's premier resort offers 16 acres of beachfront elegance. Guests think they're in a posh Caribbean retreat, what with the five restaurants (including the outstanding *Sheffield's;* see *Eating Out*), two lounges, a pool bar, five tennis courts, and exercise facilities. There's also a tropically landscaped free-form pool with a waterfall and 50 cabañas. The 624 rooms are undersized for the price; the 35 suites, however, are super. Free transportation to the *Galleria* mall and the shops along Las Olas Boulevard is an added plus; you also can get a ride to the *Bonaventure Country Club* if you're looking to play golf. This place is popular with families due to the year-round "Beach Buddies" supervised camp program for children ages five to 12. Business services are available. 3030 Holiday Dr. (phone: 525-4000; 800-222-6543; fax: 766-6152).

VERY EXPENSIVE

Bonaventure Although it's a long drive to the beach, this resort features one of the area's more popular spas and the best golfing and tennis facilities in town. Set in a lush 1,250-acre residential complex amid waterfalls, lakes, and manicured grounds are two championship 18-hole courses (see *Golf*); a racquet club with 24 tennis courts, five racquetball courts, and a squash court (see *Tennis*); five swimming pools; and a spa that offers a full range of health and nutrition programs in separate facilities for men and women (see *Sybaritic Spas* in DIVERSIONS). There are 500 rooms and suites, four restaurants, and two lounges. On weekends, the resort runs supervised activities programs for children ages three to 12. Business services are available. 250 Racquet Club Rd. (phone: 389-3300; 800-327-8090; fax: 984-0563).

Ft. Lauderdale Marina Marriott Located on the Intracoastal Waterway at the 17th Street Causeway, this property offers great views north and south from its 14-story tower and two low-rise sections. Most of the 580 rooms have balconies, and all have in-room safes and two telephones. The focal points here are the free-form pool, with its adjacent bar, and the marina, with slips for up to 35 yachts. There are four tennis courts, a health club, a sauna, an outdoor Jacuzzi, a gift shop, restaurants, lounges, and free shuttle service to the beach. Business services are available. 1881 SE 17th St. Causeway (phone: 463-4000; 800-228-9290; fax: 527-6705).

EXPENSIVE

Double Tree Next to the *Galleria* shopping mall and situated on the Intracoastal Waterway, this hotel's 231 modern suites are good values, with fully equipped kitchens, cable TV, 24-hour room service, and sleep sofas in the living rooms. Facilities include a pool, Jacuzzi, small exercise room, restaurant, lounge, and gameroom. The beach is within walking distance and airport transfers are complimentary. It's also accessible by water taxi. Business services are available. 2670 E. Sunrise Blvd. (phone: 565-3800; 800-222-8733; fax: 561-0387).

Embassy This conveniently located hotel offers 358 suites at prices equivalent to those for deluxe hotel rooms. There are a restaurant and lounge, a pool, a sauna, and a Jacuzzi on the premises. Lots of freebies are included in the room rate—daily full American breakfasts, beach shuttle service, parking, and airport transportation. Saluted by *Consumer Reports* magazine, the rooms are attractive and feature sleep sofas in the living rooms, wet bars with mini-fridges, dining tables, and kitchenettes with microwave ovens and coffee makers. Two children under the age of 12 may stay for free in their parents' suite. Business services are available. 1100 SE 17th St. Causeway (phone: 527-2700; 800-854-6146; fax: 760-7202).

Hyatt Regency Pier 66 Set on the Intracoastal Waterway with 388 rooms and suites in a 17-floor tower and two low-rise sections, this resort just completed a face-lift that has given it a sleek, contemporary look and has restored the property to its former position as one of Ft. Lauderdale's most prestigious hotels. Set on 22 acres, the resort offers a full-service 142-slip marina plus six restaurants and lounges, including the famous *Pier Top Lounge,* which revolves every 66 minutes, offering a 360-degree view of Ft. Lauderdale. Guests keep busy at the aquatics center, tennis courts, three pools, and the full-service *Spa LXVI* (see *Sybaritic Spas* in DIVERSIONS). Shopping is nearby, and there's transportation to the beach. Business services are available. 2301 SE 17th St. Causeway (phone: 525-6666; 800-327-3796; fax: 728-3541).

Lago Mar Built in 1952, this beachfront 10-acre complex has been expanded several times and attracts a crowd that has been returning for three generations. There are 32 guestrooms in addition to 138 one- and two-bedroom suites, which feature a tropical-style decor. Guests also enjoy four restaurants including an oceanside grill and bar, two pools, and four tennis courts. Business services are available. 1700 S. Ocean La. (phone: 523-6511; 800-255-5246).

Westin Cypress Creek The Westin group's first foray into Florida, this 14-story, 293-room, luxury property overlooks a five-acre lagoon that's spectacularly lighted at *Christmastime.* It features a health club, a large outdoor pool, and a lakeside pavilion; tennis and golf are a five-minute drive away. The *Cypress Room* restaurant is highly recommended; there is also a bar complex. Free parking and business services are available. 400 Corporate Dr., in the *Radice Corporate Center* (phone: 772-1331; 800-228-3000; fax: 491-6867).

MODERATE

Palm-Aire Home of Ft. Lauderdale's original spa, this resort is part of a residential complex of over 1,500 acres, with 160 rooms. Guests have the use of 37 tennis courts, one executive and four championship 18-hole golf courses (see *Golf*), three pools, a half-mile parcourse running track, two racquetball courts, a squash court, two restaurants, and a lounge. Special packages may be booked at the pricey spa, where health and beauty programs prevail (see *Sybaritic Spas* in DIVERSIONS). Business services are available. 2601 Palm-Aire Dr. N., Pompano Beach (phone: 972-3300; 800-272-5624; fax: 968-2711).

Radisson Bahia Mar This nautically oriented hotel, at the *Bahia Mar Marina* at the southern end of "The Strip," has 298 rooms, one restaurant (the *Bahia Mar Bar & Grill*), a free-form pool, a dive shop, glass-bottom boats for rent, four lighted tennis courts, and several boutiques. There are also 350 slips for fishing boats and pleasure yachts, and this is one of the sites of the country's largest in-water boat show (see *Special Events*). Business services are available. 801 Seabreeze Blvd. (phone: 764-2233; 800-327-8154; fax: 524-6912).

Ramada Plaza All 223 rooms (14 of which are suites) at this beachfront property have balconies, some with views of the Atlantic Ocean. The *Ocean Café* offers a mostly continental menu, and the *Polo Lounge* features live music and dancing nightly. Other features include a heated pool, a tiki bar for hors d'oeuvres and cocktails, sailboat rentals, and business services. 4060 Galt Ocean Dr. (phone: 565-6611; 800-678-9022; fax: 564-7730).

Sheraton Yankee Clipper "Moored" on the beach, the oldest building at this landmark resort looks like—what else?—a clipper ship. The four-building complex (some buildings are across the street and connected to the beach by an overpass) boasts 502 rooms. There are three heated swimming pools, a restaurant, a beachside bar, a lounge that offers entertainment, and an exercise room with weights and workout machines. Business services are available. 1140 Seabreeze Blvd. (phone: 524-5551; 800-325-3535; fax: 524-5376).

INEXPENSIVE

Bahia Cabana Small, unpretentious, and very Floridian, this informal place is nestled by the *Radisson Bahia Mar* resort. There are 116 rooms and apartments with kitchenettes located in five buildings (request the one most recently renovated). Also on the premises are three swimming pools, a 36-person Jacuzzi, saunas, an indoor sports bar, and an outdoor patio bar/restaurant overlooking the marina—a popular gathering spot for locals. While the standard rooms are reasonably priced, this hostelry is usually noisy, with a lot of young guests. 3001 Harbor Dr. (phone: 524-1555; 800-BEACHES; fax: 764-5951).

A Little Inn by the Sea This 30-room bed and breakfast hostelry on the beach is pleasant, homey, and down-to-earth, with a multilingual staff. Children under 10 stay for free in their parents' room. Nearby restaurants make for great dining. 4546 El Mar Dr., Lauderdale-by-the-Sea (phone: 772-2450; fax: 938-9354).

Riverside Offering 109 rooms and suites, this European-style hostelry has a convenient downtown location as well as a sedate ambience and a cozy lobby with a fireplace. Built in 1936, it is one of the city's oldest structures. There's a restaurant-lounge called *Indigo,* with a distinctive decor that features etched glass, and a swimming pool set amid tropical landscaping on the New River. Note that just a handful of rooms fall into the inexpensive category, and these have only one double bed. Business services are available. 620 E. Las Olas Blvd. (phone: 467-0671; 800-325-3280; fax: 462-2148).

EXTRA SPECIAL

Just 30 minutes north of Ft. Lauderdale, the elegant (and pricey) *Boca Raton Resort & Club* **is definitely worth a visit. Old World elegance per-**

meates the *Cloister,* the original 1926 hotel building masterminded by
Addison Mizner, a major Florida developer in the 1920s and 1930s. Richly
decorated contemporary rooms are found in the 27-story *Tower,* and soft
pastels dominate the spacious beachfront *Beach Club* rooms. The club's
site on a spit of land between the Intracoastal Waterway and the Atlantic
guarantees a watery vista from all but the *Cloister* rooms. Lanais are available for lounging, and there's direct access to the beach on the Atlantic
side. Guests also can use four pools, 34 tennis courts, two championship
golf courses, three fitness centers, and the myriad other amenities of the
sprawling 963-room resort, including several restaurants and lounges,
meeting space, and a concierge level. 501 E. Camino Real, Boca Raton
(phone: 407-395-3000; 800-327-0101; fax: 407-391-3183).

EATING OUT

There are some 2,800 restaurants in Broward County. Many of these are
well known, and most get quite crowded during the winter season, so it's
always a good idea to make reservations. In fact, restaurant dining is such
a part of the lifestyle that a *Restaurants & Institutions* magazine survey found
Ft. Lauderdale restaurants second only to New York City as the country's
busiest eating establishments. Casual dress is accepted at most restaurants,
though a few of the more expensive ones prefer that men wear jackets.
Expect to pay $100 or more for dinner for two at a restaurant in the very
expensive category; $55 to $100 in the expensive category; $30 to $55 in the
moderate category; and $30 or less in the inexpensive category. Prices do
not include wine, drinks, taxes, or tips. Unless otherwise noted, all restaurants are open for lunch and dinner and are located in Ft. Lauderdale. All
telephone numbers are in the 954 area code unless otherwise indicated.

We begin with our culinary favorites, followed by our recommendations
of cost and quality choices, listed by price category.

INCREDIBLE EDIBLES

By Word of Mouth This European café–style spot in the heart of Ft.
Lauderdale's commercial district serves some of the finest fare in
the area. The owner has not advertised since opening the restaurant more than a decade ago, but folks flock here to order abun-
dant salads, hand-size Portobello mushrooms stuffed with brie,
duckling soaked in apricot brandy, wild mushroom lasagna, out-
rageous lobster tarragon pie, and star-quality desserts (of the half-
dozen chocolate choices, our favorite is "brownie decadence,"
followed closely by white chocolate cheese cake with Key lime
curd). The menu changes daily. More homey than romantic, this
eatery is expensive, but a true treat for gastronomes. Closed

Sundays, Monday and Tuesday dinner, and Saturday lunch. Reservations advised. Major credit cards accepted. 3200 NE 12th Ave. (phone: 564-3663).

Darrel & Oliver's Café Maxx The decor is simple—the focus is on the great, albeit very pricey, food. The dishes created here are on the cutting edge of New American cooking; many of the highly praised recipes have appeared in well-known food magazines. This spot was created by restaurateur Dennis Max and chef Mark Militello, who now owns *Mark's Las Olas* (see below) and *Mark's Place* in North Miami Beach. The present owners are Darrel Brock and Oliver Saucy, who is also the executive chef. Each course is a carefully created visual masterpiece: Oysters are dipped in ground pistachios, fried, placed in their shells atop a bed of corn and tomato salsa, and surrounded by a mound of red and green curly lettuce, *enoki* mushrooms, lemongrass, and a nasturtium blossom. The Peking pork with a honey-sesame glaze and the white chocolate mousse pie with raspberry sauce and a white chocolate truffle are two other examples of the chef's melting-pot inventiveness. Open daily for dinner. Reservations necessary. Major credit cards accepted. 2601 E. Atlantic Blvd., Pompano Beach (phone: 782-0606).

La Vieille Maison The top romantic retreat in South Florida, this award-winning restaurant offers attentive service and classic French fare in a historic home styled by developer Addison Mizner and featuring courtyards, flowing fountains, gaslights, a profusion of fresh flowers, and Old World antiques. The $55-per-person prix-fixe winter menu includes an appetizer, sorbet, salad, entrée (the selection includes incomparable venison, sweetbreads with cumin, and filet of snapper in a black- and green-olive potato crust), baby vegetables, fruit and French cheese, and dessert. An à la carte menu is also available. The flawless *crêpe soufflé au citron* should not be missed. This elegant dining experience is our top choice for celebrating that special event with that special someone. Open daily for dinner. Reservations necessary. Major credit cards accepted. 770 E. Palmetto Park Rd., Boca Raton, a 20-minute drive from Ft. Lauderdale (phone: 421-7370 or 407-391-6701).

VERY EXPENSIVE

Burt & Jack's Owned by actor Burt Reynolds and his partner Jack Jackson, this beautiful Spanish-style villa offers first-rate lobsters and steaks. Reserve a window table so you can watch the cruise and cargo ships pass by. Jackets are required for men. Open daily for dinner. Reservations necessary. Major credit cards accepted. Berth 23, Port Everglades (phone: 522-5225).

Plum Room A harpist provides the background music at this spot, one of South Florida's more romantic, intimate dining rooms. The menu features beautifully presented continental food. There are classic dishes, including sole Véronique and beef Wellington, as well as such exotica as elk and tenderloin of buffalo. Don't miss the cream of mushroom soup, made with shiitake, *enoki*, and white mushrooms. There's also an extensive—and impressive—wine list. Open for dinner; closed Sundays. Reservations necessary. Major credit cards accepted. 3001 E. Oakland Park Blvd. (phone: 563-4168).

Sheffield's Located in the *Marriott Harbor Beach* resort, this posh dining room offers superb lobster bisque, chateaubriand, and Appalachian free-range chicken. Finish off your meal with one of the scrumptious desserts, especially the three-citrus cheesecake in a white chocolate collar, double chocolate macadamia mousse, and Marjolaine (thin layers of crisp hazelnut meringue separated by dark chocolate ganache with hazelnut and Chantilly cream fillings). Open daily for dinner. Reservations necessary. Major credit cards accepted. 3030 Holiday Dr. (phone: 766-6100).

EXPENSIVE

Armadillo Café The chef-owners serve large portions of Southwestern fare in a smoke-free eatery chock-full of cacti, cowboy hats, steer horns, and waiters with skinny bolo ties. The menu items range from flavorful to spicy; favorites include smoked duck quesadillas, Armadillo filet (butterflied beef tenderloin marinated in a special sauce and grilled), and yellowtail snapper seared with roast peppers and garlic. The tequila-grilled shrimp and roasted corn cakes with *chipotle* butter and tomato salsa are fabulous. Delicacies such as fresh rattlesnake, buffalo, and venison occasionally are offered. For dessert, try the deep-fried chocolate cinnamon fritters. Beverages choices include chile beer and excellent wines by the glass. Open daily for dinner; closed major holidays. Reservations necessary. Major credit cards accepted. 4630 SW 64th Ave. (corner of Griffin and Davie Rds.), Davie (phone: 791-4866).

Charley's Crab One of the best of Chuck Muer's seven South Florida restaurants, it has a wonderful location on the Intracoastal Waterway, with dining inside and out. The passing water show can range from a 110-foot Italian-designed yacht to a Labrador retriever, wearing a life vest and sunglasses, skimming along in a Seadoo. Specialties include an excellent Martha's Vineyard salad, a wide range of fresh fish prepared almost every way imaginable, and a terrific apple tart with homemade cinnamon ice cream. This spot can be reached by water taxi. Open daily; brunch served on Sundays. Reservations advised. Major credit cards accepted. 3000 NE 32nd Ave. (phone: 561-4800).

Chart House This branch of the chain offers the standard steaks and seafood with unlimited salad and fantastic mud pie for dessert. Its Downtown Ft.

Lauderdale location is a knockout. Housed in two homes (ca. 1904) on the New River, it has window tables that offer a passing parade of pleasure craft and working vessels. After dining, stroll along the 2 miles of the lushly landscaped *Riverwalk* to the *Broward Center for the Performing Arts,* or take a water taxi back to your hotel. Open daily for dinner. Reservations advised. Major credit cards accepted. 301 SW Third Ave. (phone: 523-0177).

La Coquille One of Ft. Lauderdale's best-kept secrets, this establishment has been entrancing diners for 14 years with meals that look—and taste—good enough to grace the cover of *Bon Appétit* magazine. The ambience is tropical, with mellow jazz adding to the mood; the fare is Provençal, and bilingual French waiters serve with warmth and humor. Menu highlights include tender and succulent lamb, shrimp grilled to perfection, and salmon with just the right amount of champagne sauce and leeks. Best of all, there's a four-course, $50 prix-fixe dinner for two that includes a bottle of French wine, allowing couples to celebrate in style without seriously damaging their wallets. Splurge on the Grand Marnier or chocolate soufflés, the latter served with fresh raspberry sauce—you won't regret it. Open Fridays for lunch, daily for dinner; closed August, and Mondays from May through October. Reservations advised. Major credit cards accepted. 1619 E. Sunrise Blvd. (phone: 467-3030).

Mai-Kai For four decades, this place has been a Ft. Lauderdale landmark, with its huge entranceway torches flanking a rattling plank-bridge entrance. Choose from the main dining room, where you can watch the nightly Polynesian show; smaller, lavishly decorated dining rooms; or outdoor seating by a waterfall. The gardens are lush, with authentic South Seas statuary. The food is interesting, with exotic drinks, such as the famous Mystery Drink (a show in itself), and Polynesian, American, and Cantonese dishes (a specialty is Peking duck). The *Molokai Bar* is filled with old-time nautical memorabilia. The Polynesian show (cover charge) is professional and highly entertaining. Open daily for dinner. Reservations advised. Major credit cards accepted. 3599 N. Federal Hwy. (phone: 563-3272).

Mark's Las Olas Chef Mark Militello's latest venture (his other is *Mark's Place* in North Miami Beach) serves New American cuisine with innovative flair. The menu changes daily, but generally the dishes are simpler here than at Militello's Dade County eatery, with an emphasis on lighter sauces and more grilling. Try the grilled chicken, fish, or beef dishes—they're all superb. Closed for lunch weekends. Reservations advised; a two-week wait isn't uncommon for weekend dates. Major credit cards accepted. 1032 E. Las Olas Blvd. (phone: 463-1000).

Martha's Located on the Intracoastal Waterway, where the passing boat scene provides its own entertainment, this eatery has a split personality—the glitzy downstairs serves dress-up types, while the second-floor deck is less formal, more tropical in flavor. The same courteous service and outstanding menu apply to both. Steaks, chops, and seafood are well prepared; fresh Florida snapper is offered eight different ways—the blackened version is perfectly cooked. Chicken gorgonzola with walnuts is also first-rate. Boat dockage available. Open daily; brunch served Sundays. Reservations necessary Saturday nights, advised the rest of the week. Major credit cards accepted. 6024 N. Ocean Dr., Hollywood (phone: 923-5444).

Silverado Café A bit of the Napa Valley has been transplanted to the *University Park Plaza* shopping center, where good cooking and California wines prevail. Dine amid Victorian decor or in a small room designed to look like the gondola of a hot-air balloon. Appetizers include Maryland crab cakes and escargots with mushrooms and anise-flavored liqueur, an outstanding black bean soup, and lobster ravioli. The fresh grilled fish and cashew chicken *à l'orange* are tops for main courses. Closed Mondays and for lunch weekends. Reservations advised. Major credit cards accepted. 3528 S. University Dr., Davie (phone: 474-9992).

MODERATE

Bimini Boatyard There's Bahamian decor and a view of the marina here—plus good food at reasonable prices and lots of singles action at the bar on Fridays. Specialties include conch fritters, pasta, pizza, blackened dolphinfish, and jerk ribs—along with wonderful Bimini bread. Open daily. Reservations accepted only for parties of eight or more. Major credit cards accepted. 1555 SE 17th St. Causeway (phone: 525-7400).

Brasserie Max The young and young at heart eat in casual comfort at this affordable spot created (but no longer owned) by noted restaurateur Dennis Max. Creative pizza and pasta dishes are favorites, but the restaurant hits its peak with oak-grilled specialties such as Caribbean pork chops served with homemade applesauce. Open daily. Reservations advised. Major credit cards accepted. In the *Fashion Mall at Plantation,* 321 N. University Dr., Plantation (phone: 424-8000).

Brazilian Tropicana Brazilian specialties are dished out here, along with a knockout show replete with soaring headdresses and skimpy outfits (on both the men and women!). Favorite dishes include *mariscada en molho verde* (clams, shrimp, scallops, mussels, and lobster in a garlic and white wine sauce), the all-you-can-eat *rodizio* (skewers of homemade sausage, chicken pork loin, and sirloin steak presented and sliced at your table), and shrimp casserole. Most dishes come with black beans, rice, and fried bananas. Open daily for dinner; shows presented Thursdays through Sundays (cover charge). Reservations necessary. Major credit cards accepted. 410 N. Federal Hwy., Pompano Beach (phone: 781-1113).

Gibby's This enormous eatery offers good value in a pretty setting of natural cedar, brick, and lush greenery. A humongous salad is included with basic steaks, fish dishes, and rack of lamb. Among the country's busiest restaurants, it serves about 1,500 dinners nightly in season. In summer, the lobster specials are unbeatable. Closed for lunch weekdays. Reservations advised. Major credit cards accepted. 2900 NE 12th Ter. (phone: 565-2929).

Mario's East On weekends, be prepared to wait at this ultramodern eatery where cheerful waiters often dance down the aisles. The ambience is loud, noisy, and fun, with a female singer who belts out pop songs. The consistently excellent fare is Italian, with an amazingly large selection of pasta, veal, chicken, and fresh seafood dishes as well as individual pizzas. Garlic lovers will be in heaven with the steamed clams and grilled portobello mushrooms. The veal Marsala, homemade ravioli, and shrimp marinara also receive rave reviews. There's a small dance floor and two popular bars. The average cost of a main course runs about $12, making this place a fabulous value. If you prefer a quieter meal come early or sit on the outdoor terrace, which is also great for people watching. Open daily. Reservations accepted only for parties of six or more. American Express accepted. 1313 E. Las Olas Blvd. (phone: 523-4990).

Sea Watch One of the few South Florida dining spots set on the Atlantic Ocean beach, this woodsy eatery has been here for almost 21 years. The fare is mostly fresh seafood, including those famous stone crabs; escargots with mushroom caps in garlic butter and Gulf garlic shrimp are also favorites. Open daily except *Christmas.* Reservations accepted only for parties of five or more. Major credit cards accepted. 6002 N. Ocean Blvd. (phone: 781-2200).

Victoria Park Set on a quiet side street, this tiny (only 11 tables) gem, built to resemble a house in St. Barts, produces outstanding French cookery with Caribbean overtones. The pork loin seasoned with Jamaican spices and sliced to resemble a castle is only excelled by the grilled duck breast with ginger cherry sauce. This spot can be reached by water taxi. Open for dinner; closed Sundays and Mondays. Reservations advised. Major credit cards accepted. 900 NE 20th Ave. (phone: 764-6868).

INEXPENSIVE

Brother's This popular place offers bagels and lox and corned beef on rye, as well as roasted chicken dinners and the like, to droves of locals. Save room for the seven-layer cake. Open daily for breakfast, lunch, and dinner. No reservations. Major credit cards accepted. 1325 S. Powerline Rd., Pompano Beach (phone: 968-5881).

Carlos & Pepe's The clientele at this popular hangout is eager and hungry; the setting is crowded but pleasant (light wood, green plants, and tile tables); and the menu is lighthearted Mexican (*fajitas, chimichangas,* and *chiles rellenos*). Open daily. No reservations. Major credit cards accepted. 1302 SE 17th St. (phone: 467-7192).

Ernie's Bar B Que A local institution for almost 40 years, it serves chicken, pork, and beef prepared in a special barbecue sauce that's famous throughout the area. For something different, try the fiery conch chowder. The decor has a rustic Key West style. Open daily. Reservations unnecessary. Master Card and Visa accepted. 1843 S. Federal Hwy. (phone: 523-8636).

Mistral This trendy sidewalk café on Ft. Lauderdale's "Strip" also boasts breeze-cooled indoor dining amid Mediterranean decor. People watching is an art form here. A wonderfully addictive black bean dip is served in place of butter. The *tapas* platter (with blackened fish, stuffed mussels, crawfish, and chick-pea dip) is excellent. Repeat diners (and there are plenty of them) come more for the ambience than the food, which tends to be spotty and overly seasoned. Jazz bands play every Friday and Saturday night. Open daily. Reservations accepted only for parties of six or more. Major credit cards accepted. 201 S. Atlantic Blvd./Rte. A1A (phone: 463-4900).

Shooter's Right at the edge of the Intracoastal Waterway, this is a great luncheon spot to watch the boats breeze by. The Friday night happy hour features a band, and hordes of locals stop in to see, be seen, and end the week with friends. Menu choices range from grilled tuna sandwiches to Mexican pizza to California-style salads. Casual, fun, and always hopping, this place has become a Florida institution. Open daily. No reservations. Major credit cards accepted. 3033 NE 32nd Ave., off Rte. A1A (phone: 566-2855).

Toojay's This upscale deli offers tasty interpretations of the usual fare, plus interesting sandwich combinations (try the turkey and chopped liver). Open daily. No reservations. Major credit cards accepted. 4401 Sheridan St., Hollywood (phone: 962-9909).

Diversions

Exceptional Pleasures and Treasures

Quintessential Miami

Most people think of Miami as a land of sun and fun, all pastel buildings and bronzed bodies tooling around in racy convertibles or on water bikes and Harley-Davidsons. But Miami offers much more. It is a city of varied cultures, home to Cubans, South Americans, Caribbean Islanders, Seminole Indians, and retired Northerners, and among its attractions are colorful neighborhoods, great seafood, Art Deco design, four professional sports franchises—and the beach. There are nightclubs for night owls, the nearby Everglades for those who are into gators and grasslands, and the Florida Keys for those looking for some respite from the mobs and some hints of Hemingway and Tennessee Williams. Below are some of the musts to put you in a Miami state of mind.

THE BEACH *The* reason most vacationers choose Miami. Back in the 1920s, developer Carl Fisher raised the land that's now Miami Beach five feet above sea level by loading it with sand that he then secured with rows of large palm trees. Ever since, visitors have been flocking to Dade County's 14 miles of beaches to enjoy the mild air, plentiful sun, and warm, aqua-colored sea. Numerous restoration projects replenishing the sands (the latest in 1988) have made the beach even more beautiful than it was when Betty Grable and Robert Cummings romped here in the 1941 movie *Moon Over Miami.* Over the years, the beach has retained its glamour; oceans of movies—including *Goldfinger,* starring Sean Connery as James Bond—have been filmed on its glistening white sands. The first modern on-screen incarnation of Miami Beach was TV's "Miami Vice," whose shots of the beach, the Art Deco District, and the posh hotels introduced the city to a new generation of sun worshipers. Miami continues to attract filmmakers, and visitors who just come here to soak up some rays are still apt to catch a glimpse of more than a few celebrities.

The water, especially in the summer, is comfortably warm and inviting; in winter, diehard surfers can pit themselves against some respectable waves. At most points, the beach is a 300-foot-wide swath of clean white sand reached by boardwalks; the approach is fringed with a 65-foot-wide band of beach grass and sea grapes that protects the dunes and the beach from erosion (thanks to the Dade County Beach Vegetation Project). Those not staying at beachfront hotels can enjoy the sand and surf at numerous public beaches. (All Dade County beaches are open to the public; however, parking is sometimes difficult.) Perhaps the best spot at which to capture a vintage Florida tan while sampling the true flavor of a Miami beach is at the *North Shore Open Space Park* (phone: 305-993-2032), a 40-acre state park that runs from 79th to 87th Streets in Miami Beach (entrances at 81st and 85th Sts., at Collins Ave.). For a nominal charge, sun lovers can bask and swim at a well-maintained, policed beach. Features include boardwalks, picnic tables and barbecue pits under palm trees, bicycle paths and bike rentals, bathrooms with lockers, outdoor showers, a playground area for tots, access ramps for the disabled, a concession stand (at 83rd St.), and metered parking. There's also a Vita Course—a trail with marked stops with workout equipment and instructions for specific exercises. Open year-round, it's definitely earned its place in the sun.

THE ART DECO DISTRICT This unique square-mile district, listed on the National Register of Historic Places, boasts the largest concentration of Art Deco resort architecture in the world. The Tropical Deco style of the buildings combines a warm peach, turquoise, lavender, and pink color scheme with stylized nautical motifs (mermaids, waves, and flying porpoises). Quintessential expressions of Miami, the eye-catching structures, with their porthole windows and metal railings, are juxtaposed against palm trees from the coconut plantation that once stood on the white strand.

The "art" in the Art Deco District extends far beyond the architecture, however; the human street scene is artwork in its own right. With a backdrop of wonderfully, whimsically restored buildings built between the 1920s and 1940s, a young man wearing bike shorts and sporting a live snake around his neck roller blades by; beautiful fashion models drape themselves in front of archways as cameras click away; tables chockablock with patrons line the wide sidewalks; and Japanese tourists stroll along, looking a bit perplexed. The photogenic potential of such contrasts appeals to scores of filmmakers, who opt for the realism of shooting here rather than on a Hollywood set; today the area is so much in demand for photo shoots for fashion magazines and catalogues that dozens of modeling agencies and production companies have sprung up here. Another growth industry is the music business; the Latin American labels of both Sony and Warner Brothers record companies are headquartered here.

The Art Deco District is Greater Miami's hot, "in" place, with world class restaurants and nightclubs that cater to the trendy and chic. With the world's most famous models and such celebrities as Madonna, Sylvester Stallone, and Cindy Crawford jetting here to make the scene (and often moving in), mere mortals shouldn't miss the chance to see what all the excitement's about. (For more information see *Tour 1: South Beach—The Art Deco District* in DIRECTIONS.)

LITTLE HAVANA This enclave of Cuban and Nicaraguan immigrants is the next best thing to traveling to Latin America. The neighborhood was primarily a Jewish community until about 36 years ago; after Castro took power in

Cuba, Cuban immigrants began arriving in droves, and the area became known as Little Havana. In recent years, other Hispanic groups have settled in the neighborhood—now more Nicaraguans than Cubans live here, and the area more often is called the Latin Quarter. A stroll down Calle Ocho (as SW Eighth St. is known in this part of town) is still a distinctly Latin experience. The sounds of merengue and rumba music can be heard wafting out of apartment windows and bars; the smells of *plátanos* (plantains), chicken and rice, black beans, and grilled pork strips commingle in the air; and street vendors sell vegetables and other wares. Mothers and their daughters attired in brightly colored, ruffled dresses shop at neighborhood bodegas for the evening meal. Men in *guayaberas* (embroidered shirts often worn in Latin American countries) gather in doorways or in *Máximo Gomez Park* (SW Eighth St. and SW 15th Ave.) to play dominoes or chess and smoke cigars (no cursing, gambling, or women allowed!). Eateries with grill-fronted windows that open onto the street dispense strong *café cubano* and guava *pastelitos;* stores sport signs in Spanish; and vendors in open-air markets hawk sugarcane stalks and green coconuts complete with straws for drinking the coconut milk. The air is alive with activity and the scene is splashed with the vibrant reds, yellows, and oranges of the Latin world.

For a taste of Cuba, try a Cuban sandwich (roast pork, ham, cheese, pickles, and mustard on crispy Cuban bread) at *Versailles* (3555 SW Eighth St.; phone: 305-445-7614) For a complete Latin meal, try *Centro Vasco* (see "Eating Out" in *Miami,* THE CITIES) for roast pork with rice and black beans, then flan (a custard covered with caramel syrup) for dessert.

The Hispanic fervor really erupts each year for *Carnaval Miami,* a nine-day celebration in early March featuring an 8-km run and folkloric entertainment; it culminates in *Calle Ocho: Open House,* the country's largest street festival. Begun in 1978 as a block party, this event now encompasses 23 blocks with 50 stages featuring 200 musical groups and nearly 400 vendors selling everything from hot dogs to paella—with plenty of samples. More than a million people participate. For information, contact the *Kiwanis Club of Little Havana* (phone: 305-644-8888). For those who really want to sample the flavor of Little Havana, *Miami River Inn* (see "Checking In" in *Miami,* THE CITIES) is a charming bed and breakfast establishment near Little Havana. But if it's the sultry sensuality of a Latin night that you seek, pick a dimly lit table for two at one of the local restaurants, order up some Cuban delicacy, make sure the salsa music is well within earshot, and then close your eyes—you might almost forget for a moment that you're in Miami!

FOOTBALL FEVER From September to January, both Miami and Ft. Lauderdale go nuts over football—collegiate and professional. The Miami *Dolphins* play at *Joe Robbie Stadium* in North Dade County. The *University of Miami Hurricanes,* the national college football power, toss the pigskin at *Orange Bowl Stadium.* Top-ranked collegiate teams go head-to-head in the *Carquest*

Auto Parts Bowl at *Joe Robbie Stadium* in late December. The world-famous *FedEx Orange Bowl Football Classic*—pitting the Big Eight collegiate conference champion against another nationally ranked team—traditionally played at *Orange Bowl Stadium* on the evening of *New Year's Day*—moves to *Joe Robbie Stadium* this year. It's preceded by the *Orange Bowl Parade,* a lavish procession downtown on Biscayne Boulevard on *New Year's Eve.* In response to this craziness, the *King Mango Strut Parade* winds its way through Coconut Grove a few days in advance—a socially satirical poke at much that is considered "holy" these days.

EARLY-BIRD SPECIALS AND OTHER DINING DEALS The classic joke is that Florida's state tree is the sabal palm and the state bird is the "early bird." To spread business over a longer dinnertime (especially in season, when long lines are frequently the norm), restaurateurs provide incentives to dine early by lowering prices before peak hours. As a result, bargain-hunting diners may have their evening meal as early as 4 PM; other eateries, however, offer their early-bird hours as late as 6 PM or so. Some early-bird deals to consider: At *Charley's Crab* (see "Eating Out" in *Ft. Lauderdale,* THE CITIES), those who sit down to dinner from 4 to 5:30 PM daily can choose from a menu that is limited but still features fresh fish and the noteworthy Martha's Vineyard salad—all for between $10 and $20—while enjoying the same waterfront entertainment as later diners. At the elegant *Dominique's* in the *Alexander* hotel (see "Checking In" in *Miami,* THE CITIES), you can savor an elegantly served four-course dinner for $21.95 between 6 and 7 PM. Be aware that early-bird meals sometimes are dubbed "sunset specials," "twilight dinners," or the like. If you don't mind eating early, be sure to ask restaurants if they offer such deals.

Better-kept secrets are summertime restaurant specials. Since business falls off when the "season" ends—usually in April or May—some restaurateurs have trouble retaining and paying their staffs over the summer. To drum up business, they offer specials such as two meals for the price of one. *Gibby's* (see "Eating Out" in *Ft. Lauderdale,* THE CITIES) features dinners with two Maine lobsters and all the fixings for the cost of a chicken meal during season—$19.95. Some upscale Broward County and Boca Raton restaurants, such as *La Reserve* (phone: 954-563-6644) overlooking the Intracoastal Waterway, offer an "elegant meal for two" from May through early December. Unlike the early-bird specials, these deals—fabulous four-course meals for two for less than $60, including a bottle of wine—are available all evening, although many restaurants do not offer them on Saturdays. Diners get to choose from four to five appetizers, five to six entrées, and four different desserts. Never mind the worm; here it's definitely the early bird that catches the inexpensive lobster, and the savvy tourist that savors the discounted dinner.

A Few of Our Favorite Things

Though Miami and Ft. Lauderdale boast plenty of fine hotels and restaurants and great places to play golf and tennis, we've singled out a few select spots that are guaranteed to delight pursuers of a variety of pleasures. Follow our lead; we promise you won't be disappointed.

Each place listed below is described in detail in the appropriate city chapter.

GRAND HOTELS AND A REGAL RESORT

The following are our special favorites for a stay in Miami and Ft. Lauderdale. One is a posh, Caribbean-style resort, the others offer European-style elegance and luxury, but each in its own way offers the highest caliber of service, food, and ambience. Complete information about our choices can be found on pages 56 to 58 of the *Miami–Miami Beach* chapter and pages 92 to 93 of the *Ft. Lauderdale* chapter in THE CITIES.

Miami

Grand Bay, Coconut Grove
Omni Colonnade, Coral Gables
Turnberry Isle, Turnberry Isle

Ft. Lauderdale

Marriott Harbor Beach, Ft. Lauderdale

INCREDIBLE EDIBLES

There are a number of factors that make dining in Miami and Ft. Lauderdale a special experience: the availability of the freshest seafood, the presence of some of the country's most innovative chefs, and a culinary language that incorporates Floridian, Cuban, and European accents. The following rank as our picks of the top restaurants in the region. Complete information about our choices can be found on pages 65 to 67 of the *Miami–Miami Beach* chapter and pages 96 to 97 of the *Ft. Lauderdale* chapter in THE CITIES.

Miami

Biltmore Café, Coral Gables
Chef Allen's, North Miami Beach
Fish Market, Miami
Grand Café, Coconut Grove
Mark's Place, North Miami Beach
Osteria del Teatro, Miami Beach
Yuca, Coral Gables and Miami Beach

Ft. Lauderdale
By Word of Mouth, Ft. Lauderdale
Darrel & Oliver's Café Maxx, Pompano Beach
La Vieille Maison, Boca Raton

TOP TEE-OFF SPOTS
The number of major golf tournaments that are held in the Miami/Ft. Lauderdale area are evidence enough of the region's exemplary greens (and predictably pleasant weather). The courses listed below—our particular favorites—are among the best in the world; any one of them will satisfy even the most demanding player. Complete information about our choices can be found on page 50 of the *Miami–Miami Beach* chapter and pages 88 to 89 of the *Ft. Lauderdale* chapter in THE CITIES.

Miami
Doral Golf Resort & Spa, Miami

Ft. Lauderdale
Bonaventure, Ft. Lauderdale
Palm-Aire, Pompano Beach

CHOICE COURTS
Florida's gentle sea breezes and warming sunshine offer a matchless setting for tennis buffs. The clubs below have all that an ace (or an amateur) could hope for—fine facilities, scenic backdrops, and all the extras. Complete information about our choices can be found on page 53 of the *Miami–Miami Beach* chapter and page 90 of the *Ft. Lauderdale* chapter in THE CITIES.

Miami
Doral Golf Resort & Spa, Miami
Fisher Island Club, Fisher Island
International Tennis Center, Key Biscayne
Turnberry Isle, Turnberry Isle

Ft. Lauderdale
Bonaventure, Ft. Lauderdale

Antiquing
Not everybody in Greater Miami lives among glass and Lucite. Many traditionalists prefer antiques, and lots of estate sales keep the suppliers going and customers coming.

Those who love to prowl among old things may find a bonanza at the *Coconut Grove Antique and Jewelry Show* (phone: 305-444-8454), held every month at the *Coconut Grove Convention Center* (2700 S. Bayshore Dr.;

phone: 305-579-3310). A biannual antiques show also is held at the *Broward County Convention Center* (1950 Eisenhower Blvd.; phone: 954-763-3661) in November and February, and once a year in late January at the *Coconut Grove Convention Center.*

"Antique Row" runs along the 100 block of Federal Highway (US 1) between North First Street and Dania Beach Boulevard in Dania, and spills into several of the side streets. The 150 stores and stalls deal in old china, furniture, books, jewelry, and assorted "chotchkes." Most are open Mondays through Saturdays from 10 AM to 5 PM. The following are worth a look:

English Accent Antiques (57 N. Federal Hwy., Dania; phone: 954-923-8383).

House of Hirsch Antiques (75 N. Federal Hwy., Dania; phone: 954-925-0818).

Kleinman Antiques (Antiques Gallery Mall, 60 N. Federal Hwy., Dania; phone: 954-920-2801).

Maxine's Antiques (10B N. Federal Hwy., Dania; phone: 954-920-0588).

Rose Antiques (17 N. Federal Hwy., Dania; phone: 954-921-0474).

RULES OF THE ROAD FOR AN ODYSSEY OF THE OLD

Buy for sheer pleasure, not for investment. Forget about the carrot of supposed retail values that dealers habitually dangle in front of amateur clients. If you love something, it will probably grace your home long after the moon over Miami stops shining.

Buy the finest example you can afford of any item, in as close to mint condition as possible. Chipped or broken "bargains" will haunt you later with their shabbiness. They also don't increase in value the way the mint stuff does.

Train your eye in museums and/or collections of things in the period that interests you. These are the best schools for the acquisitive senses, particularly as you begin to develop special passions. (Remember, Miami is prime Art Deco territory.)

Get advice from specialists when contemplating major acquisitions. Much antique and collectible furniture and many paintings have been restored several times. If you want to be absolutely certain that what you're buying is what you've been told it is, stick with the larger dealers. Some auction houses and even small museums have an evaluation office whose experts will make appraisals for a fee.

Don't be afraid to haggle—a little. Most dealers don't have fixed prices, so sharpen your negotiating skills and make an offer they can't refuse. A word of warning: While most larger dealers take credit cards, smaller shops do not.

When pricing an object, don't forget to figure the cost of shipping. Shipping home a large piece—furniture, sculpture, antique garden paraphernalia—can be a major expense. Be sure to add this into the cost of your purchase.

Historic Houses of Worship

Although Miami's history only goes as far back as the late 1800s (the city was incorporated in 1896, when the railroad came to town), there are a few historical churches of note. The oldest dates from the 12th century and was brought here from Spain. Most of the other noteworthy houses of worship fall into one of two basic architectural categories, either bearing the Spanish mark, with capped steeples, hand-carved wooden doors, and stone exteriors, or the Art Deco influence, with stucco exteriors, rounded corners, and spires. All welcome worshipers and wanderers alike.

CORAL GABLES CONGREGATIONAL CHURCH Dating from 1923, this church has a Spanish design, with a barrel-tile roof, pews carved from native cypress, and 16th-century furnishings. The bell tower is based on Spain's Giralda Tower. Guided tours are offered on Sundays at 11 AM or by appointment. Information: *Coral Gables Congregational Church*, 3010 DeSoto Blvd., Coral Gables (phone: 305-448-7421).

HISTORIC CONGREGATION BETH JACOB Miami's oldest synagogue, its two stucco buildings, both on the National Register of Historic Places, house a functioning Conservative congregation. The older building (311 Washington Ave.), dating from 1927, is Mediterranean-looking and features the original wooden front doors. The copper-domed building with stained glass windows (301 Washington Ave.) dates from 1936. It is also the site of the *Jewish Museum of Florida*, with exhibits detailing the contributions of Jews to the development of the state. Information: *Historic Congregation Beth Jacob*, 311 Washington Ave., Miami Beach (phone: 305-672-6150).

PLYMOUTH CONGREGATIONAL CHURCH This 1917 Spanish Mission–style coral rock structure boasts a 385-year-old hand-carved walnut and oak door from a Spanish monastery. While the grounds are open to the public, arrangements must be made in advance to view the interior of the church. Information: *Plymouth Congregational Church*, 3400 Devon Rd., Coconut Grove (phone: 305-444-6521).

ST. BERNARD DE CLAIRVAUX The Western Hemisphere's oldest building was not erected in Florida, but built in 1141 in Segovia, Spain. Publishing magnate William Randolph Hearst had it shipped in pieces to America in the 1920s. Twenty-five years later, Miami developers put it back together on this site, and it's still a functioning Episcopal church with beautiful stained glass windows and woodcarvings. There is also a small collection of ancient art and furnishings in the cloister. Open daily. Admission charge. Information: *St. Bernard de Clairvaux*, 16711 W. Dixie Hwy., North Miami Beach (phone: 305-945-1461).

TEMPLE EMANU-EL Built in 1946 (although the congregation dates from 1938), the temple is important for its size and its cultural activities. Guest performers and lecturers here have included the late Isaac Bashevis Singer, Norman Schwarzkopf, Henry Kissinger, and Itzhak Perlman. A white stucco structure with a silver dome over the sanctuary, the Conservative synagogue seats 1,800 and is the place of worship for 1,200 families. It's near the Art Deco District and the *Miami Beach Convention Center.* Information: *Temple Emanu-El,* 1701 Washington Ave., Miami Beach (phone: 305-538-2503).

TRINITY EPISCOPAL CATHEDRAL Home of Miami's oldest congregation (dating from 1896), this white neo-Romanesque church was built in 1925. Known for its beautiful rose window, the church is the seat of the Diocese of Southeast Florida. Information: *Trinity Episcopal Cathedral,* 1545 N. Bayshore Dr., Miami (phone: 305-374-3372).

Sybaritic Spas

With several resorts featuring health and fitness spas, there is an abundance of opportunities to be pampered and pummeled throughout Miami and Ft. Lauderdale. Although sun worshiping with abandon is no longer in vogue, these spots provide new ways to care for your health and appearance. In addition to skin-care programs, massages, and facials, diet and stress-management plans help visitors to better care for their bodies—and their minds.

Many clients of these spas are show-business and *Fortune* 500 executive—types who slip down to Florida for stays lasting from a day to a few weeks. Many facilities are at the high end of the price scale—and can make a major dent in the pocketbook. But remember, even the more costly spas include all meals and most activities in their rates. So when you next feel the need to really shape up or slow down, go ahead and book a stay at one of the following houses of revitalization.

BILTMORE Located in the hotel of the same name, this spa's facilities include a 15,000-square-foot gym filled with free weights and state-of-the-art exercise and cardiovascular equipment, including treadmills, Stairmasters, stationary bicycles, and rowing machines. There's a modern exercise room where aerobics, yoga, and tai chi classes are held. Aquacise sessions take place in the enormous pool. Fitness and rejuvenation are both stressed, with pampering facials, massages, body wraps, loofah baths, hydro-massage, and reflexology offered alongside the more traditional beauty treatments such as manicures and pedicures. Refreshments are available poolside and low-calorie dishes are featured in the hotel's restaurants. Five different beauty, fitness, and pampering day-at-the-spa specials are offered. Information: *Biltmore Spa and Fitness Center,* 1200 Anastasia Ave., Coral Gables (phone: 305-445-1926; 800-727-1926; fax: 305-448-9976).

BONAVENTURE Frequently judged among the country's best, this spa's attractions include hot and cold plunge pools, aerobic and water aerobic exercise classes, massage options (Swedish, shiatsu, and reflexology), aromatherapy, herbal and sea kelp body wraps, thermal back treatments, and nutrition consultation. The executive wellness program is run in conjunction with the *Miami Heart Institute.* The resort's beautiful grounds feature five swimming pools, 24 tennis courts, two 18-hole championship golf courses, horseback riding, racquetball, and squash courts. The spa dining room has a varied menu; smoking is prohibited. Information: *Bonaventure Resort and Spa,* 250 Racquet Club Rd., Ft. Lauderdale (phone: 954-389-3300; 800-327-8090; fax: 954-384-0480).

EDEN ROC The crowning touch of a $30-million restoration and redesign completed in 1995, the *Spa of Eden* at this resort was promptly named one of the top 15 spas in the US by *Fitness* magazine and *USA Today.* There's a 10,000-square-foot indoor complex with a full-size basketball court, three international squash courts, and a racquetball court, as well as the only rock climbing wall in Florida. The only oceanfront spa in the country, it offers both state-of-the-art fitness facilities and traditional pampering. For example, the Dead Sea mud wrap, administered on the beach, is followed by a refreshing dip in the ocean, and cold "valerian" gel treatments (similar to aloe) provide soothing relief to sunburned skin. Information: *Eden Roc Resort & Spa,* 4525 Collins Ave., Miami Beach (phone: 305-531-0000; 800-327-8337; fax: 305-531-6955).

FONTAINEBLEAU HILTON RESORT & TOWERS The hotel's *Spa Pavilion* enticements include massage therapy, mineral baths, whirlpool baths, Cybex machines, free weights, aerobics classes, cellulite treatments, and a cardiovascular room. More than 100 classes are conducted weekly, including water aerobics and yoga. There are some spa items on hotel menus. Information: *Fontainebleau Hilton,* 4441 Collins Ave., Miami Beach (phone: 305-538-2000; 800-548-8886 in Florida; 800-HILTONS elsewhere in the US; fax: 305-532-8145).

HYATT REGENCY PIER 66 The full-service *Spa LXVI* at this Intracoastal resort offers Nautilus machines; saunas and steamrooms; facials; loofah baths; herbal wraps; and Swedish, deep-tissue, aromatherapy, and "stress-buster" massages. There are two swimming pools, indoor and outdoor Jacuzzis, two lighted tennis courts, and a beauty salon. Information: *Hyatt Regency Pier 66,* 2301 SE 17th St. Causeway, Ft. Lauderdale (phone: 954-525-6666; 800-327-3796; fax: 954-728-3541).

PALM-AIRE Stars such as Elizabeth Taylor, Billy Joel, and Liza Minnelli have shaped up here. Spa offerings include aerobics and water exercise classes, outdoor and private indoor whirlpool baths, saunas, massage choices (Swedish, shiatsu, and reflexology), aromatherapy, thalassotherapy, facials, herbal wraps, and a solarium. The spa dining room features delicious calorie-controlled meals, along with demonstrations, lectures, books, and instruction to help you take the spa experience home. Information: *Palm-Aire Resort and Spa,* 2601 Palm-Aire Dr. N., Pompano Beach (phone: 954-972-3300; 800-272-5624; fax: 954-968-2711).

PIER HOUSE Key West is home to one of the state's best spas. Located in a separate section of the *Pier House Resort,* with 22 guestrooms, it has a small gym equipped with free weights and Stairmasters, a Jacuzzi, steamrooms, and saunas, as well as a beauty salon. Programs and treatments include fitness classes, facials, massages, reflexology, and loofah salt rubs. Information: *Pier House Resort,* 1 Duval St., Key West (phone: 305-296-4600; 800-327-8340; fax: 305-296-7569).

SPA AT DORAL This complex lures those interested in health and fitness, diet control, and stress management. Judged the top North American spa by "Lifestyles of the Rich and Famous," it attracts a list of international guests who consider it the country's most beautiful and luxurious. Fabulous facilities include four exercise studios (with 30 daily exercise classes), a weight room with cardiovascular equipment, a large outdoor pool with a hot tub, an outdoor lap pool, an indoor exercise pool, hydrotherapy tubs, saunas, an indoor track for walking and jogging, and an outdoor quarter-mile parcourse running track and exercise stations. There are personalized assessments, tai chi and dance classes, cellulite-reduction programs, collagen-repair facials, personal trainers, a beauty salon, cooking demonstrations, and take-home programs. Meals are elegantly served in the restaurant, with surprisingly sumptuous choices—even a glass of wine. Guests also may use facilities at the adjoining *Doral Golf Resort & Spa* (see "Checking In" in *Miami,* THE CITIES). Information: *Spa at Doral, Doral Golf Resort & Spa,* 8755 NW 36th St., Miami (phone: 305-593-6030; 800-331-7768; fax: 305-591-9268).

SPA AT PGA The renowned *Professional Golfers Association of America (PGA)* resort, with five championship 18-hole golf courses, 19 tennis courts, and three indoor racquetball courts, also has a state-of-the-art spa with fitness classes, beauty sessions, and salon treatments, including Swedish and shiatsu massage and hydrotherapy. The highlight here is the "Relaxing Waters of the World," a complex of six outdoor therapy pools, including two with imported mineral salts. Spa guests also have access to the fitness center, aerobics classes, five-lane lap pool, and the *Health Bar* restaurant at the nearby *Health & Racquet Club.* Accommodations are in the main hotel. Information: *Spa at PGA National Resort,* 400 Ave. of the Champions, Palm Beach Gardens (phone: 561-627-2000; 800-633-9150; fax: 561-622-0261).

SPA INTERNAZIONALE With its Spanish-style architecture, the *Spa Internazionale* on fabulous Fisher Island offers several programs for beauty, fitness, and relaxation: aromatherapy, hydromassage, Swedish massage, Vichy Shower body polishes, herbal wraps, facials, computerized fitness assessments, and personal training. Other facilities include an indoor lap pool with retractable roof, a Jacuzzi with cold plunge pool, an outdoor Roman waterfall, aerobics classes, and a beauty salon. Information: *Spa Internazionale, Inn at Fisher Island,* 1 Fisher Island Dr., Fisher Island (phone: 305-535-6030; 800-537-3708; fax: 305-535-6032).

TURNBERRY ISLE This marina/golf/tennis complex also offers a health- and beauty-oriented spa with deep-sea mud treatments for the face and body, Finnish saunas, Turkish steamrooms, a cold plunge pool, indoor and outdoor whirlpool baths, Nautilus equipment, eight Cybex training machines, racquetball courts, aerobics classes, and more. Diet plans are supervised by a staff physician; spa dishes are available on both dining room menus, including "Cuisine Salud" at the highly regarded *Veranda* restaurant. Resort options include two championship Robert Trent Jones Jr. golf courses and 24 tennis courts. Information: *Turnberry Isle Resort & Club,* 19999 W. Country Club Dr., Aventura, Turnberry Isle (phone: 305-932-6200; 800-327-7028; fax: 305-937-0528).

Day Cruises

A favorite activity of vacationers and Floridians alike is the cruise, which can last anywhere from a one- to three-day sail. A short ocean jaunt provides an introduction to the sea for novices, but is popular among many frequent cruisers as well. These brief getaways allow passengers to enjoy a taste of the Bahamas or indulge in a little gambling without changing their home base. Cruises may be booked in advance directly through a cruise company or through a travel agent, though there is a no-refund policy as long as the ship sails, so those who book ahead risk losing the price of the cruise. It's also possible to wait until the chosen day—arrive early and be willing to stand in line for a vacant spot. Prices, as on longer cruises, include meals on board, activities, nightclub entertainment (tips and alcoholic drinks are extra), and access to casinos, which don't open until ships pass the 20-mile limit. High rollers are frequently seen queuing up outside closed casino doors. Kids under 11 usually sail free; inquire when making reservations.

DISCOVERY This is the largest day cruise liner hereabouts, debarking from Port Everglades, Ft. Lauderdale. It offers daytime and evening "cruises to nowhere" and trips to Freeport on Grand Bahama Island. Buffet dining and a cabaret show are included; à la carte dining is an additional charge. A casino, pool, and disco are on board. Information: *Discovery Cruises,* 1850 Eller Dr., Ft. Lauderdale (phone: 954-525-7800; 800-937-4477).

SCANDINAVIAN DAWN The *SeaEscape* sails from Port Everglades, Ft. Lauderdale. It has daytime and evening "cruises to nowhere" and excursions to Freeport on Grand Bahama Island. There's buffet or à la carte dining. Information:

SeaEscape Cruises, 140 S. Federal Hwy., Dania (phone: 954-925-9700; 800-327-2005).

A Shutterbug's View

With all its pastels, seascapes, and picturesque neighborhoods, Miami is a very photogenic city. There is architectural variety: Art Deco is juxtaposed with modern, ornate with ordinary, and a skyline bristling with the temples of modern commerce with the seashore reaching to meet it. There is also natural variety: Flowers embroider a park footpath, a palm tree waves in the breeze, and a sunrise sparks the horizon over the ocean. There's human variety as well: Immigrants exchange the latest news from the Old Country in Spanish, ruddy fishermen return with their catch, and beachcombers flaunt their tans on the boardwalk. The thriving city, the shimmering sea, the parks, the people, and traces of rich history make Miami a fertile stomping ground for shutterbugs. With backdrops like these, even a beginner can achieve remarkable results with a surprisingly basic set of lenses and filters. Equipment is, in fact, only as valuable as the imagination that puts it into use.

LANDSCAPES, SEASCAPES, AND CITYSCAPES Miami's populated beaches and historic buildings are visiting photographers' favorite subjects. But the city's green spaces and waterways provide numerous photo possibilities as well. In addition to the historic hotels, churches, and the Art Deco District, be sure to look for natural beauty such as the *Fairchild Tropical Gardens,* the well-manicured plots of flowers in the public parks, and the rolling waves of the Atlantic.

Although a standard 50mm to 55mm lens may work well in some landscape situations, most will benefit from a 20mm to 28mm wide-angle. The Ft. Lauderdale skyline from the top of the *Hyatt Regency Pier 66* resort, for example, is the type of panorama that fits beautifully into a wide-angle format, allowing not only the overview, but the opportunity to include people or other points of interest in the foreground. A fruit stand, for instance, may be used to set off a view of a street in Little Havana; or people can provide a sense of perspective in a shot of a café in the Art Deco District.

To isolate specific elements of any scene, use your telephoto lens. Perhaps there's a particular architectural detail in an Art Deco building or an interplay of light and shadow on the façade of an old Spanish church that would make a lovely shot. The successful use of a telephoto means developing your eye for detail.

PEOPLE As with taking pictures of people anywhere, there are going to be times in Miami when a camera is an intrusion. Your approach is the key: Consider your own reaction under similar circumstances, and you have an idea as to what would make others comfortable enough to be willing subjects. People are often sensitive to having a camera suddenly pointed at them, and a polite request, while getting you a share of refusals, also will provide a chance to shoot some wonderful portraits that capture the spirit of the area as surely as the scenery does. For candid shots, an excellent lens is a zoom telephoto in the 70mm to 210mm range; it allows you to remain unobtrusive while the telephoto lens draws the subject closer. And for portraits, a telephoto can be used effectively as close as seven feet.

For authenticity and variety, select a place likely to produce interesting subjects. The *Bayside Marketplace* is an obvious spot for visitors, but if it's local color you're after, visit the Broadwalk in Hollywood, or Little Havana, South Beach, and Coconut Grove. Aim for shots that tell what's different about South Florida. In portraiture, there are several factors to keep in mind. Morning or afternoon light will add richness to skin tones, emphasizing tans. To avoid the harsh facial shadows cast by direct sunlight, shoot in the shade or in an area where the light is diffused.

SUNSETS While the sun doesn't set over the ocean in Miami, there are days when the last golden rays reflect off a lone sailboat, or when a fiery light hits the *Adrian* hotel's pink and turquoise façade, crowning it with magical clouds of pink and lavender, purple and red.

When shooting sunsets, keep in mind that the brightness will distort meter readings. When composing a shot directly into the sun, frame the picture in the viewfinder so that only half of the sun is included. Read the meter, set, and shoot. Whenever there is this kind of unusual lighting, shoot a few frames in half-step increments, both over and under the meter reading. Bracketing, as this is called, can provide a range of images, the best of which may well be other than the one shot at the meter's recommended setting.

Use any lens for sunsets. A wide-angle is good when the sky is filled with color-streaked clouds, when the sun is partially hidden, or when you're close to an object that silhouettes dramatically against the sky.

Telephotos also produce wonderful silhouettes, either with the sun as a backdrop or against the palette of a brilliant sunset sky. Bracket again here. For the best silhouettes, wait 10 to 15 minutes after sunset. Unless you are using a very fast film, a tripod is recommended.

Orange, magenta, and split filters often are used to accentuate a sunset's picture potential. Orange will help turn even a gray sky into something approaching a photogenic finale to the day, and can provide particularly beautiful shots linking the sky with the sun reflected on the ocean. If the sunset is already bold in hue, however, the orange will overwhelm the natural colors—as will a red filter—but will produce dramatic, highly unrealistic results.

NIGHT If you think that picture possibilities end at sunset, you're presuming that night photography is the exclusive domain of the professional. If you've got a tripod, all you'll need is a cable release to attach to your camera to assure a steady exposure (which is often timed in minutes rather than fractions of a second).

For situations such as evening concerts or nighttime harbor cruises, a strobe does the trick, but beware: Flash units are often used improperly. You can't take a view of the skyline with a flash. It may reach out as far as 30 feet, but that's it. On the other hand, a flash used too close to a subject may result in overexposure, resulting in a "blown out" effect. With most cameras, strobes will work with a maximum shutter speed of 1/125 or 1/250 of a second. If you set the exposure properly and shoot within range, you should come up with pretty sharp results.

CLOSE-UPS Whether of people or of objects such as Art Deco spires, close-ups can add another dimension to your photography. There are a number of shooting options, one of which is to use a 70mm or a 210mm lens at its closest focusable distance. Unless you're working in bright sunlight, a tripod will be worthwhile. If you are very near your subject and there is a good deal of reflective light, it may pay to underexpose a bit in relation to the meter reading.

If you do not have a telephoto lens, you still can shoot close-ups using a set of magnification filters. Filter packs of one-, two-, and three-time magnification are available, converting your lens into a close-up lens. Even better is a special macro lens designed for close-up photography.

It's tough to get broad perspectives in Miami, where the highest elevations are bridges—there's not a hill in sight. But there are still plenty of picturesque places to shoot—as evidenced by all the professional photographers toting heavy equipment around.

A SHORT PHOTOGRAPHIC TOUR

Here are a few of the most photogenic places in Miami and Ft. Lauderdale.

THE BEACHES There are good views of the sand and surf everywhere on Miami Beach, but the boardwalk that runs between 21st and 46th Streets affords a bit of elevation and a better perspective.

SOUTH BEACH Stroll along the ocean side of Ocean Drive rather than trying to snap pictures from a moving car in the Art Deco District. The intersection of Ocean Drive and 13th Street is particularly colorful—on the south corner you'll see the *Carlyle* hotel with its buff and mauve exterior and green-trimmed "eyebrows"; on the north corner is the *Cardozo,* bedecked in white and lilac with purple "eyebrows." Though not open to the public, the hotels have accessible and photogenic exteriors. At Eighth Street you can shoot the pink and turquoise *Adrian* and include in the picture the *Tudor* (down the street at Collins Ave.), with its rounded entry and neon-lighted finial. Approaching from the west by car, you may be able to capture the unique towers of the district's three signature tall hotels—from north to south, the *Ritz Plaza,* the *Delano,* and the *National*—in one shot taken around 17th Street.

CRUISE SHIPS For a fantastic view of a half-dozen cruise ships with Miami sky-scrapers in the background, drive across MacArthur Causeway (A1A) between Miami and Miami Beach and pull in at the sign for *Chalk's International Airlines*. You will find the most ships docked on Saturdays and Sundays. Catch them pulling out in the late afternoon, decks lined with smiling and waving passengers. Just remember not to shoot directly into the sun.

DOWNTOWN For terrific views of Downtown Miami, including *Bayside Marketplace,* visit the fifth-floor pool area or jogging track of the *Inter-Continental* hotel (100 Chopin Plaza; phone: 305-577-1000; 800-327-3005). *Metrorail* or *Metromover* stations also offer bird's-eye views.

FT. LAUDERDALE The best view of Ft. Lauderdale is from the *Pier Top Lounge* atop the *Hyatt Regency Pier 66* resort (2301 SE 17th St., Ft. Lauderdale; phone: 954-525-6666). The tower's top revolves once every 66 minutes, pro-viding wonderful vistas of the ocean, Intracoastal Waterway, and canals.

Directions

Introduction

To most tourists, Miami means miles and miles of beach, splendid swaths of white sand that seem to go on from here to tomorrow. But for those who can pry themselves away from the shore, there's a whole other Miami just waiting to be discovered. Parts of this other Miami—small neighborhoods, historic churches and landmarks, and picturesque cafés and shops—are best explored on foot; other sections cover a broader area and require a car. (Whether you're walking or driving, pay careful attention to street names; it makes a big difference whether the "20th" you're seeking is a street or an avenue.) Our first tour begins in South Beach, the Art Deco District at the southern tip of Miami Beach. From there we proceed west, back to the mainland, then to South Miami and over to Key Biscayne. We continue south to Coconut Grove, Miami's oldest and most bohemian neighborhood, and then tour the lovely suburb of Coral Gables, before heading to the Latinized area of Calle Ocho. Just for fun, we've thrown in a cowboy and Indian tour in Ft. Lauderdale before moving north to luxurious Palm Beach for a glimpse at the lifestyles of its rich, often famous, and sometimes notorious residents.

For those who'd like to journey farther, we've also included tours of the secluded, but oh-so-beautiful, Florida Keys and the almost otherworldly, farthermost reaches of the Everglades. As we said, Miami is much more than just another pretty beach.

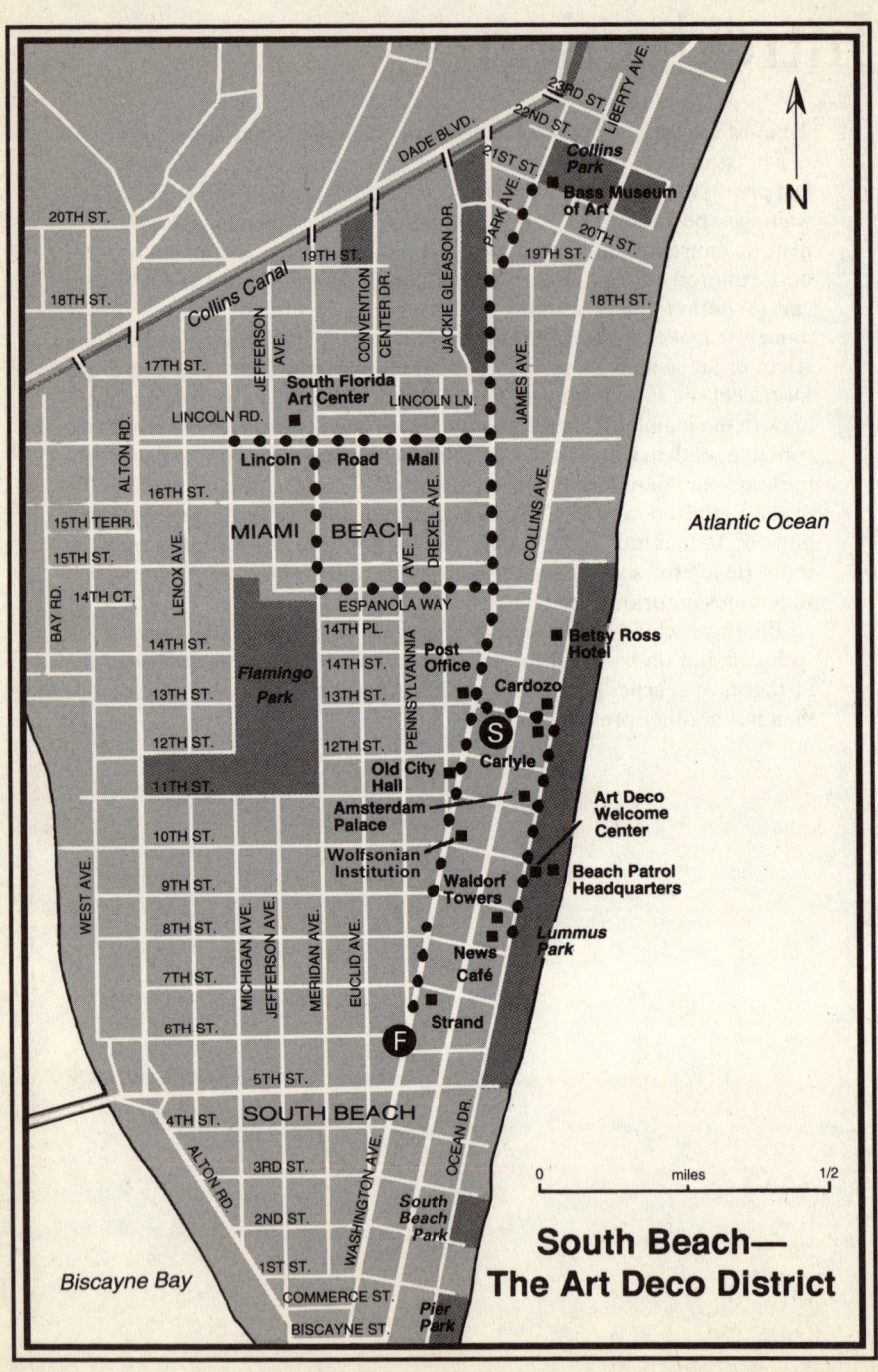

South Beach—
The Art Deco District

Tour 1: South Beach— The Art Deco District

One of the oldest Miami Beach neighborhoods, the Art Deco District— known the world over as South Beach and sometimes as SoBe—is again in the limelight. After years of decline, in the past 15 years it has become one of the country's trendiest places to sun and schmooze, to see and be seen.

The district, along with the rest of Miami Beach, originally was developed as a coconut plantation, and although the enterprise failed, many beachfront coconut palms remain. In the 1920s, Carl Fisher began developing the beach as a vacation area for well-heeled sun worshipers. He dredged the mosquito-ridden mangrove swamps and built the first bridge to the mainland.

In the 1920s and 1930s, hotel guests and residents in the southern part of Miami Beach were largely Jews, who were restricted to living south of 15th Street and east of Washington Avenue. Beyond those boundaries, developer Carl Fisher enforced the "Caucasian Clause" of his predecessors' real-estate contracts and denied Jews and blacks the opportunity to stay in his hotels or to buy real estate. (He made some notable exceptions, however, permitting Bernard Gimbel, the department store founder, to stay at his *Flamingo* hotel, and John Hertz, founder of the Yellow Cab Company, to buy land.) The district was then developed by the Lummus brothers, who admitted Jews but prohibited blacks.

Most of the construction in this area occurred just after World War I. But Miami's initial building boom went bust; the hurricane of 1926 struck, destroying what had been built, and the Depression followed. Undaunted, Miami developers tried again in the late 1930s—and this time, for a while at least, succeeded. This era of development saw two major periods of Art Deco construction and design. The first, the Classical Art Deco period, was inspired by the French Arts Décoratifs movement. The style was characterized by elaborately designed fountains and rich surface ornamentation, but used tropical themes—palm trees, flowers, dolphins, flamingos—and soft pastels to adorn and reflect its resort setting. The second, the Art Moderne period, was influenced by industrial design. Its architectural style was characterized by minimal ornamentation, rounded corners, and cantilevered window shades called "eyebrows." Adapting the sleek designs of cars and planes from the Art Moderne period, Miami developed a tropical version of the design movement, employing transportation motifs. Also during this period, a number of buildings in the Spanish-Mediterranean Revival style, with arches, barrel-tile roofs, and a Moorish look, were constructed in Miami Beach.

World War II brought all frivolous construction to a halt, and when Miami got back to building after the war, the softer, more decorative, Classical Art Deco motifs prevailed. Like most of the country, Miami Beach shared in the postwar prosperity of the 1950s. It was not until the 1970s that the South Beach area fell into decline, and the former hotels became homes for the elderly living on Social Security.

In the late 1970s, however, the Art Deco District began a dramatic period of revival. Thanks to the efforts of preservationists, spearheaded by the late Barbara Baer Capitman (who founded the *Miami Design Preservation League*), many buildings were saved from demolition. The area was officially designated as the Art Deco District in 1979 and placed on the National Register of Historic Places. With about 650 important buildings within the square mile bordered by the ocean on the east and *Flamingo Park* on the west, and running from Fifth to 23rd Streets, the district has the greatest concentration of Art Deco architecture in the country. During the 1980s, many of the buildings—most of which were originally painted white, with warm pink and yellow trim—were daubed with ice-cream-soda colors of raspberry pink, banana yellow, and blueberry blue. This imaginative coloration soon spread throughout South Florida.

But the Art Deco District is more than just a collection of historic buildings. The recently refurbished hotels have become fashionable, restaurants are receiving critical acclaim, and nightspots stay open until the wee hours. (On the down side for hotel guests who aren't night owls, the street noise often continues until about 4 AM.) Groups of fashion models and photographers fly in from New York, Paris, and Frankfurt to do photo shoots for magazines and clothing catalogues. There's a sense of cutting-edge excitement here that draws celebrities, jet setters, artists, musicians, and the like from all over the world.

There are few metered spots here, so streetside parking is always a problem (although several garages are slated to open in the next few years). Head directly to the municipal parking lot on 13th Street between Ocean Drive and Collins Avenue. (Most major restaurants along Ocean Drive offer valet parking as well.)

On Collins Avenue, across the street from the parking garage, you'll see the Spanish-Mediterranean Revival *Alamac* apartment building with its barrel-tile roof. One block west, at the northwest corner of 13th Street and Washington Avenue, sits the still-functioning 1937 main *Post Office,* with a lantern finial crowning its dome. Climb the pink marble steps and enter through the brass doors for a peek into the impressive rotunda lobby.

Retrace your steps east on 13th toward the ocean. At the corner of 13th Street and Ocean Drive stand two Art Deco landmarks: On the south side is the closed *Carlyle* hotel, painted buff and mauve with green-trimmed "eyebrows"; on the north side is the white and lilac *Cardozo,* with aqua "eyebrows" and a terrific-looking lobby (the 1959 Frank Sinatra movie *Hole in the Head* was filmed here). Most of the 15 or so restaurants along this stretch of Ocean Drive are popular among locals who sit either at tables on the broad sidewalk or in the slightly more formal indoor dining rooms. Despite the pleasant ambience, the culinary creations are sometimes pedestrian. For more first class fare, try *Max's South Beach* (see "Eating Out" in *Miami,* THE CITIES).

Walk south on Ocean Drive, where the majority of the district's hotels line the street facing palm-studded *Lummus Park* and the beach. Building after building, it's an Art Deco–phile's delight. Virtually every structure has been turned into a chic hotel or stylish eatery. There are also a few shops selling funky clothes and beach articles; note that here and elsewhere in the Art Deco District, clothing shops may not open until late morning (11 AM), but remain open into the evening (until 9 or 10 PM). Plan to have breakfast or lunch at one of the popular outdoor places such as the *News Café* (see "Eating Out" in *Miami,* THE CITIES) or *Lario's on the Beach* (820 Ocean Dr.; phone: 305-532-9577), the Cuban eatery owned by Gloria and Emilio Estefan.

The *Amsterdam Palace* (1116 Ocean Dr.) was bought by Italian designer Gianni Versace, who converted the one-time apartment building into a home. It looks a bit out of place architecturally, with its arched entrance and windows, barrel-tile roof, and wrought-iron balconies. In fact, it was built in 1930 in the Spanish-Mediterranean Revival style, modeled after the colonial *Alcázar de Colón,* home of Diego Columbus (Christopher's brother), in the Dominican Republic. Although the building is not open to the public, its exterior is well worth noting.

At 10th Street, stop by the *Art Deco Welcome Center* (*Ocean Front Auditorium,* 1001 Ocean Dr.; phone: 305-672-2014), which is open daily. Here you can join the 90-minute Saturday morning walking tour. Also, there's the two-hour Sunday morning bicycle tour leaving from *Miami Beach Bicycle Center* (601 Fifth St., Miami Beach; phone: 305-673-2055); bikes are available for rent. Both tours are led by local historians, with colorful anecdotes spicing up the history. (There's a fee for each tour.)

If you choose to proceed on your own, remember that Miami Beach streets progress logically, with numbered streets running east-west; street addresses reflect the closest numbered cross street to the south. And don't forget to look up to spot the area buildings' characteristic parapets and finials.

If you've resisted strolling over to the beach until now, detour to the *Beach Patrol Headquarters* behind the auditorium at 10th Street. The building resembles a ship, typical of the Nautical Moderne style. Its seaside face, with porthole windows and metal ship railings, recalls the *Normandie,* the Art Deco *French Line* cruise ship. Inside, lectures and films are often presented; outside, in-line skaters perfect their skills.

Notice the vertical neon sign and racing stripes of the *Breakwater* (940 Ocean Dr.). A pool links this hotel and the *Edison* (960 Ocean Dr.), which reflects a Spanish-Mediterranean Revival influence. At 860 Ocean Drive, the 1937 *Waldorf Towers* sports Art Deco "eyebrows" to shield it from the sun, and a unique rooftop tower.

For an interesting detour on your way back to the parking garage, cut over to Collins Avenue and walk north. At 12th Street is the *Marlin* hotel; its interior decor—considered by locals to be anything from weird to wonderful—is worth a look (also see "Checking In" in *Miami,* THE CITIES).

At this point, you can walk or drive north to *Lincoln Road Mall Parking,* at Washington Avenue and 17th Street, near the *Jackie Gleason Theater of the Performing Arts (TOPA).* Just south of the parking area is *Lincoln Road Mall,* a trendy pedestrian shopping street between 16th and 17th Streets.

Before you explore Lincoln Road, a detour to the *Bass Museum of Art* (2121 Park Ave.; phone: 305-673-7533) is recommended. Go north on Washington past the *Jackie Gleason Theater of the Performing Arts* and the *Miami Beach Convention Center* until you come to 19th Street. Turn right, and make an immediate left onto Park Avenue. At the corner of 21st Street and Park is the museum, built in 1930 of Key stone (oolitic limestone). Outside adornments include carved seagulls on the roof and bas-relief panels with nautical themes over doorways. Housed here are two enormous 17th-century Flemish tapestries, along with works by Botticelli, Ghirlandaio, and Rubens. The museum is closed Sunday mornings and Mondays; there's no admission charge for children under 12. For additional details, see "Special Places" in *Miami,* THE CITIES.

Return to Washington Avenue, and retrace your steps south. At Lincoln Road, turn right (west). Built by Carl Fisher as an artery to the island's first commercial area, Lincoln Road is still lined with many Art Deco buildings. In 1960, the city hired Morris Lapidus, the architect who designed the *Fontainebleau* hotel, to design new landscaping for *Lincoln Road Mall,* a pedestrians-only shopping street that was fashionable in the 1970s. The stores of that era now are gone, but much of the street is enjoying a retail revival, and the city in 1995 launched a multimillion-dollar renovation project. Walk west to the *Miami Beach Community Church* (500 Lincoln Rd.); built in 1921, it is one of the city's oldest churches. Pass the headquarters for the *New World Symphony* (541 Lincoln Rd.; phone: 305-673-3331) to Meridian Avenue (the 800 block). Between this block and Lenox Avenue, about 100 artists work in studios and galleries. The *South Florida Art Center* (810 Lincoln Rd.; phone: 305-674-8278) owns three buildings housing a gallery and rotating exhibits, and leases studio space to artists. Also here are the home of the *Miami City Ballet* (905 Lincoln Rd.; phone: 305-532-7713); a branch of *Books & Books* (933 Lincoln Rd.; phone: 305-532-3222), selling (what else?) books and offering a film series; plus about 10 restaurants, from fine Italian dining spots to casual cafés. Try *Pacific Time* for a great meal (see "Eating Out" in *Miami,* THE CITIES).

Go south on Meridian Avenue; between 15th and 14th Streets is Española Way. Turn east (left) and stroll to the block between Drexel and Washington Avenues, known as the Spanish Colony. This block has been refurbished, bringing to life the coral-painted Spanish-Mediterranean Revival–style buildings with their iron balconies, red tile roofs, and gas streetlamps. The alleged birthplace of the US rumba craze (legend has it that Desi Arnaz launched it here), today this area is home to art galleries and vintage clothing and furniture stores. Continue east on Española Way and turn right (south) onto Washington; in a block you'll come to the *Clay Hotel and Miami Beach International Youth Hostel* (1438 Washington Ave.; phone: 305-534-2988), where young travelers can often find lodging. At 1445 Washington Avenue, the 1938 *Cameo* theater hosts all manner of performers (305-532-0922).

Continue south on Washington Avenue. On the west side (at No. 1130) sits the nine-story *Old City Hall,* dating from 1927. The Spanish-Mediterranean Revival–style building boasts barrel-tile roofs and Corinthian columns. Peek inside to see the lobby's moldings and old brass fixtures.

On the east side of Washington, at the corner of 11th Street, is the *11th Street Diner.* Transplanted from Wilkes-Barre, Pennsylvania, the vintage steel diner (ca. 1948) serves standard old-fashioned meals along with more contemporary fare (see "Eating Out" in *Miami,* THE CITIES).

At the corner of 10th Street stands the Washington Storage Building. Built in 1927 for summer storage serving winter visitors, it features ornate carved relief bands in the Spanish Baroque style. It now houses the *Wolfsonian Museum* (1001 Washington Ave., phone: 305-531-1001), with changing exhibits documenting American and European cultural history of the late-19th to mid-20th centuries. Reservations necessary; admission charge. (Also see "Museums" in *Miami,* THE CITIES.)

On the corner of Seventh Street is a rounded building that originally housed a bakery. The 1934 building—which has appeared on the cover of *Progressive Architecture*—looks like a wedding cake, with stepped back "layers" and a parapet for the bride and groom. Painted tan, with blue and green trim, it's now home to the *Washington Tavern* restaurant, a good stop for pizza, pasta, or burgers (phone: 305-534-1684).

Walk south on Washington past the *Strand* restaurant (No. 671; phone: 305-532-2340), formerly the *Famous,* featuring a ziggurat (jagged) parapet, pelican capitals, and American fare.

Return to your car to follow *Tour 2: South Miami by Car.*

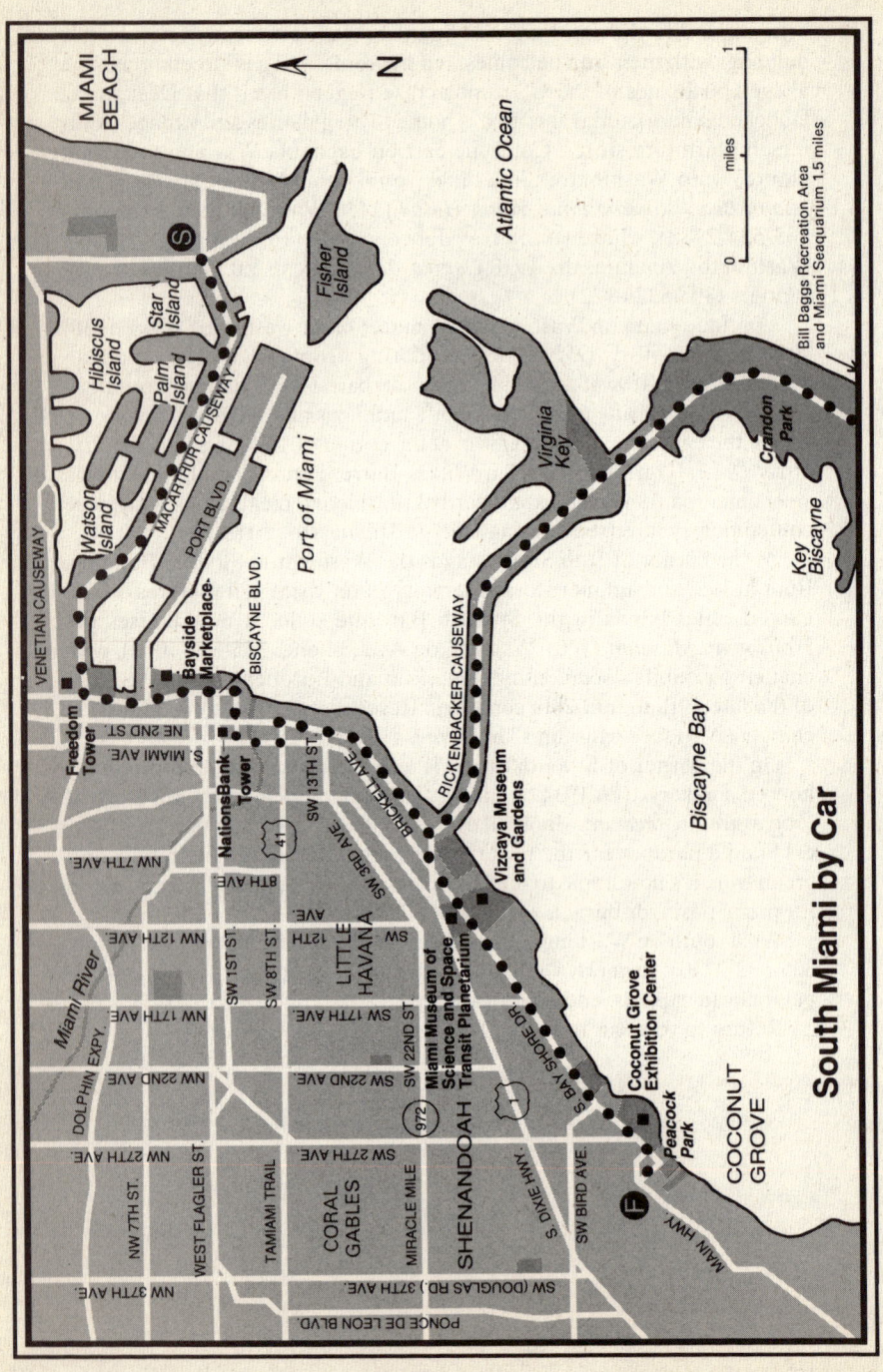

South Miami by Car

MIAMI BEACH

Atlantic Ocean

Fisher Island

Hibiscus Island

Palm Island

Star Island

Watson Island

MACARTHUR CAUSEWAY

PORT BLVD.

VENETIAN CAUSEWAY

Port of Miami

BISCAYNE BLVD.

Bayside Marketplace

Freedom Tower

NE 2ND ST.

S. MIAMI AVE.

NationsBank Tower

SW 13TH ST.

BRICKELL AVE.

SW 3RD AVE.

8TH AVE.

NW 7TH AVE.

41

Miami River

SW 1ST ST.

SW 8TH ST.

LITTLE HAVANA

12TH AVE.

SW 17TH AVE.

SW 22ND AVE.

SW 22ND ST

SW 27TH AVE.

NW 12TH AVE.

NW 17TH AVE.

NW 22ND AVE.

DOLPHIN EXPY.

NW 27TH AVE.

NW 37TH AVE.

NW 7TH ST.

WEST FLAGLER ST.

TAMIAMI TRAIL

CORAL GABLES

MIRACLE MILE

972

SHENANDOAH

Miami Museum of Science and Space Transit Planetarium

S. DIXIE HWY.

SW BIRD AVE.

SW (DOUGLAS RD.) 37TH AVE.

PONCE DE LEON BLVD.

S. BAY SHORE DR.

Vizcaya Museum and Gardens

RICKENBACKER CAUSEWAY

Virginia Key

Crandon Park

Key Biscayne

Biscayne Bay

Coconut Grove Exhibition Center

Peacock Park

COCONUT GROVE

MAIN HWY.

Bill Baggs Recreation Area and Miami Seaquarium 1.5 miles

N

0   miles   1

S

F

Tour 2: South Miami by Car

From Miami's South Beach, drive across MacArthur Causeway (Rte. 395). To the right, on the turquoise waters of Biscayne Bay, sit the private islands of Star, Hibiscus, and Palm, with their spectacular private homes and equally spectacular yachts. Most of us can't get past the guardhouses, but as you drive across Watson Island on the causeway, you can get a pretty good view. On the left, you'll pass the ferry to the plush Fisher Island resort. Also on the left, note the string of cruise ships lined up at the Port of Miami, the world's busiest cruise port. Pull over at the sign to *Chalk's International Airlines* (a seaplane company), and park the car. As you relax beneath the trees you can watch the huge cruise ships maneuver in and out of port. (For more information see "Special Places" in *Miami,* THE CITIES.) You can't turn left coming out of *Chalk's,* so go east on the causeway and make a U-turn at Palm Island.

Continue west to Route 1 (Biscayne Blvd.) and go south through Downtown Miami. Notice the peach *Freedom Tower* (No. 600) on the right, a Spanish Renaissance–style building dating from 1925 and replicating Spain's Giralda Tower. Built for the *Miami News,* it received its nickname when it was used as the Cuban Refugee Emergency Center in 1962. Rescued from the wrecker's ball, it briefly housed offices and is once again abandoned.

On the left is *Bayside Marketplace* (401 Biscayne Blvd.), where shoppers and diners can spend several hours. The Rouse-developed complex harbors 150 shops and eateries—most are branches of the national and international chains that you would expect to find in an upscale urban marketplace. But pushcart vendors sell everything from crafts to ethnic clothing, and the food is definitely more Latin in flavor than in most other US shopping centers. (For more information, see "Special Places" in *Miami,* THE CITIES.)

Continue south on Biscayne, and follow the signs to US 1 South (Brickell Ave.). Note the downtown commercial area to the right, and the *Metromover* skyway automated cars, which afford the best views of the city. Notice in particular *NationsBank Tower,* formerly *Centrust Tower* (100 SE Second Ave.), three graduated ellipses of glass that, when lit at night, look like a glowing waterfall; and the marble-clad *Inter-Continental Miami* hotel, which boasts a double helix monument to the martyred *Challenger* astronauts (also see "Checking In" in *Miami,* THE CITIES). Circle around to the right. On your left is the *First Union Financial Center* (200 Biscayne Blvd.), at 55 stories the tallest building in Florida. Turn left on Northwest Second Avenue to cross the Miami River at the Brickell Avenue bridge. The bridge, completed in late 1995, features a bronze spire that reaches 70 feet into the air. The spire is a monument to the Tequesta Indians, who were the first settlers on this part of the river. Passing over the bridge, look to the right for the *Metrorail* track adorned by the *Miami Line,* a 300-foot, multicolored neon public sculpture by Rockne Krebs; it's particularly striking at night, but visible only from I-95 farther east.

Brickell Avenue from Southeast 15th Street to Southeast Fifth Street is like Wall Street with palm trees; more than two dozen imaginatively designed buildings house several US, European, and Latin American international bank headquarters. Unlike Wall Street, however, these sparkle with marble and mirrors; some even have palm trees poking their tufted tops through the atria.

Continue south on Brickell past the pricey condominiums on the left, many boasting striking architecture. *Villa Regina* (1581 Brickell Ave.), an Isamu Noguchi–designed condominium building, has a rainbow-hued exterior decorated by Israeli artist Yaacov Agam. Another eye-catching structure is the *Atlantis* (2025 S. Brickell Ave.), which was seen in opening shots of "Miami Vice." Designed by the progressive architecture firm Arquitectonica, it has a square-shaped hole in the middle of the building, a five-story-high central courtyard housing a curved red staircase, a full-size palm tree, and a hot tub.

If you're visiting anytime from mid-May through June, detour a block west of Brickell to South Miami Avenue, between Southwest 15th Street and Southwest 25th Street. The four-lane, malled street here is lined with huge royal poinciana trees, which, during that time of year, form a canopy of huge orange-colored blossoms. To pinpoint the best blooming periods, call the *Fairchild Tropical Garden* (phone: 305-667-1651).

At the end of Brickell, there are two options: You can go left across the Rickenbacker Causeway to Key Biscayne to visit the *Miami Seaquarium* (see route below) or follow the signs to South Miami Avenue, which passes *Vizcaya Museum and Gardens* (3251 S. Miami Ave.; phone: 305-250-9133) on the left. The opulent 1916 Italian Renaissance–style villa was the winter home of International Harvester Company's James Deering. Fronting on the bay, it rivals any mansion in Newport, Rhode Island. It's closed *Christmas Day;* admission charge (for details, see "Special Places" in *Miami,* THE CITIES).

On the right is the *Museum of Science and Space Transit Planetarium* (3280 S. Miami Ave., Coconut Grove; phone: 305-854-4247), which offers live demonstrations of scientific phenomena, 150 hands-on exhibits, and multimedia laser shows. It's closed *Thanksgiving* and *Christmas Day;* admission charge (also see "Special Places" in *Miami,* THE CITIES).

Continue south—South Miami Avenue changes to South Bayshore Drive—past a high-rent condominium area. On the right, note *The Windward,* the large red sculpture by Alexander Leiberman, resting in front of the *Grand Bay* hotel (at 27th Ave.). On the left, with colorful nautical flags painted on its exterior, is the *Coconut Grove Convention Center* (2700 S. Bayshore Dr.; phone: 305-579-3310). Here sailboat masts seem to sprout like trees in a forest; the bay plays a major role in life hereabouts. Stop in at *Monty's Stone Crab* (see "Eating Out" in *Miami,* THE CITIES) for a casual lunch on the deck, and stroll the dock at the marina to see the boats. Soon the road curves in front of *Peacock Park* (named for early settlers Charles and Isabella Peacock, who built the first hotel on South Florida's mainland), a small park with assorted ball courts. Continue to the next traffic light and make a hard left onto Main Highway, the heart of Coconut Grove (see *Tour 3: Coconut Grove* in this section).

FARTHER SOUTH: KEY BISCAYNE

From the southern end of Brickell Avenue, or from the Southeast 26th Road exit of US Route 1, follow the signs eastbound to Rickenbacker Causeway to Key Biscayne (a "key" is a low island, or reef). Key Biscayne is a large island—once a coconut plantation—that's the winter home of the rich and famous; it's the site of two large public parks, as well as a major tennis competition.

Cross the first bridge (look to your left for a first-rate view of Downtown Miami, Miami Beach, and the Port of Miami) to a small island known as Windsurfer Beach. Aficionados bring their own gear or rent on the spot from *Sailboards Miami* (on Rickenbacker Causeway, just beyond the toll booths; phone: 305-361-SAIL). There are picnic facilities, public bathrooms, and parking. The beach isn't much by Miami standards, but in addition to windsurfers it also attracts fisherfolk, who cast their lines from the old bridge that parallels the new span.

Continue across William Powell Bridge to Virginia Key. On the right is the *Miami Seaquarium* (4400 Rickenbacker Causeway; phone: 305-361-5705). Fifteen daily shows feature dolphins, manatees, sea lions, sharks, and even a killer whale. It's open daily; admission charge (for more information see "Special Places" in *Miami,* THE CITIES).

From here, drive over the next bridge onto Key Biscayne; you'll be on Crandon Boulevard. Pass the *Crandon Marina,* with charter sailboats and motorboats available for half or full days (phone: 305-361-1281). Plan on lunch or cocktails at *Sundays on the Bay,* a delightful spot adjacent to the marina with a dockside deck where diners can watch the boating scene while enjoying anything from a snack to first-rate continental fare (phone: 305-361-6777).

The road continues through a natural area of palmettos, palms, and sea grapes; this is *Crandon Park,* with public beaches and picnic areas. Past the park and about 1½ miles from the *Seaquarium,* the *International Tennis Center* is on the right. The Dade County facility offers 26 courts (two grass, 16 hard, and eight clay), a pro shop, and lessons; it's open daily (see "Tennis" in *Miami,* THE CITIES). The center is also the site of the annual *Lipton*

Championships, which draw almost 200,000 fans and top-ranked tennis players from around the world each March (phone: 305-446-2200 for tournament information).

Pass through the center of Key Biscayne and turn right at the next traffic light onto Harbor Drive. Drive about 1½ miles onto Mashta Island. Developed by Dr. William J. Matheson in 1902, the island was named by Matheson's daughter—"mashta" is an Egyptian word meaning "home on the resting spot by the sea." Circle around to the right to see the stunning residences, especially those on the northwest side; located right on Biscayne Bay, they enjoy a magnificent view of Downtown Miami. Richard Nixon's "winter White House" was in this neighborhood until it was torn down in the 1980s.

Continue to the end of Key Biscayne to get to the 400-acre *Bill Baggs Cape Florida State Recreation Area,* with its 1¼-mile-long public beach, four boardwalks, restrooms, picnic areas, pavilions, and changing areas. The area was devastated by Hurricane Andrew in 1992, but replanting efforts have begun to take root. The exotic Australian pines were replaced with sea grapes, gumbo limbos, and other native plants, which are slow-growing but more authentic. The lighthouse, built in 1825, has just been completely restored. Stop at the adjacent *Lighthouse Café* (1200 S. Crandon Blvd., phone: 305-361-8487) for shrimp, chicken wings, or a burger; here you can also rent umbrellas, lounge chairs, rafts, bicycles, ocean kayaks, and Roller Blades. The recreation area is open daily; admission charge (also see "Special Places" in *Miami,* THE CITIES).

To leave Key Biscayne, exit the park and follow Crandon Boulevard north. Before crossing the causeway from Key Biscayne to the mainland, you'll find beaches off to the right. Most have jet ski rentals, and all afford a fabulous view of Downtown Miami's skyline, Brickell Avenue's colorful condos, and Dodge Island, with its large ships. If the night sky cooperates, you may even get a different perspective on that moon over Miami.

Tour 3: Coconut Grove

Coconut Grove is Miami's answer to New York City's Greenwich Village, complete with shops selling high fashion and funky duds, elegant restaurants, and droves of casual eateries with tables spilling out onto the sidewalks. It's fun to stop at an outdoor café, nurse an ice-cream cone or a beer, and watch the passing parade. Kids with punk hairdos flit by on skateboards, and seniors shop for antiques and paintings. The arty and intellectual types, hippies, and descendants of early Bahamian settlers have largely been pushed out by luxury condominiums that are home to wealthy Europeans, Latin Americans, and Miami professionals. But in the center of the Grove, at almost any time of the day or night, it's a great place to people watch, participate in an impromptu sing-along, or listen to the musicians who perform on the streets.

The *King Mango Strut Parade,* Coconut Grove's funky, not to mention funny, answer to the *Orange Bowl Parade,* takes place each December. A decidedly tongue-in-cheek event, it may include strutting marching groups decked out as characters off the label of Fruit of the Loom underwear, and there's always someone offering a spoof of the current president or mayor.

Art lovers gather here in February, when the *Coconut Grove Arts Festival* draws hundreds of thousands to its juried outdoor exhibits. For information on the festival, call the festival office (phone: 305-447-0401).

Begin your Coconut Grove tour at the intersection of Grand Avenue, Main Highway, and McFarlane Road, across from the *CocoWalk* entertainment complex. Stroll along Main Highway on the left side of the street, past boutiques, art galleries, and outdoor cafés. Just outside the *Ouch Boutique* (3415 Main Hwy.; phone: 305-443-6824) is the Grove's only remaining street mural. Stop inside *Ouch* to see one-of-a-kind outfits designed by owner Chris Di Pietro—several have been bought by Sylvester Stallone and Madonna.

Continue on to *La Boulangerie* (3425 Main Hwy.; phone: 305-443-0776), a French bakery and outdoor café with mouth-watering chocolate croissants, breakfast and luncheon specials, and café au lait. Stay on the left side of the street; you'll pass *St. Stephen's Episcopal Day School* before coming to *The Barnacle,* a state historic site and park that contains the original home of the first Grove settler, Commodore Ralph Munroe. The two-story house, built in 1891, sits on the coastal ridge overlooking Biscayne Bay. Tours of the house are offered; it's open Fridays, Saturdays, and Sundays (phone: 305-448-9445). Turn left down the side street just past *The Barnacle* to see Millionaires' Row, where multimillion-dollar mansions line the bay.

Across the street from *The Barnacle,* at the corner of Main Highway and Charles Avenue, is the *Coconut Grove Playhouse* (3500 Main Hwy.; phone: 305-444-7814). *Waiting for Godot* had its US premiere here in 1956, only one of this small, not-for-profit state theater's triumphs. The theater often

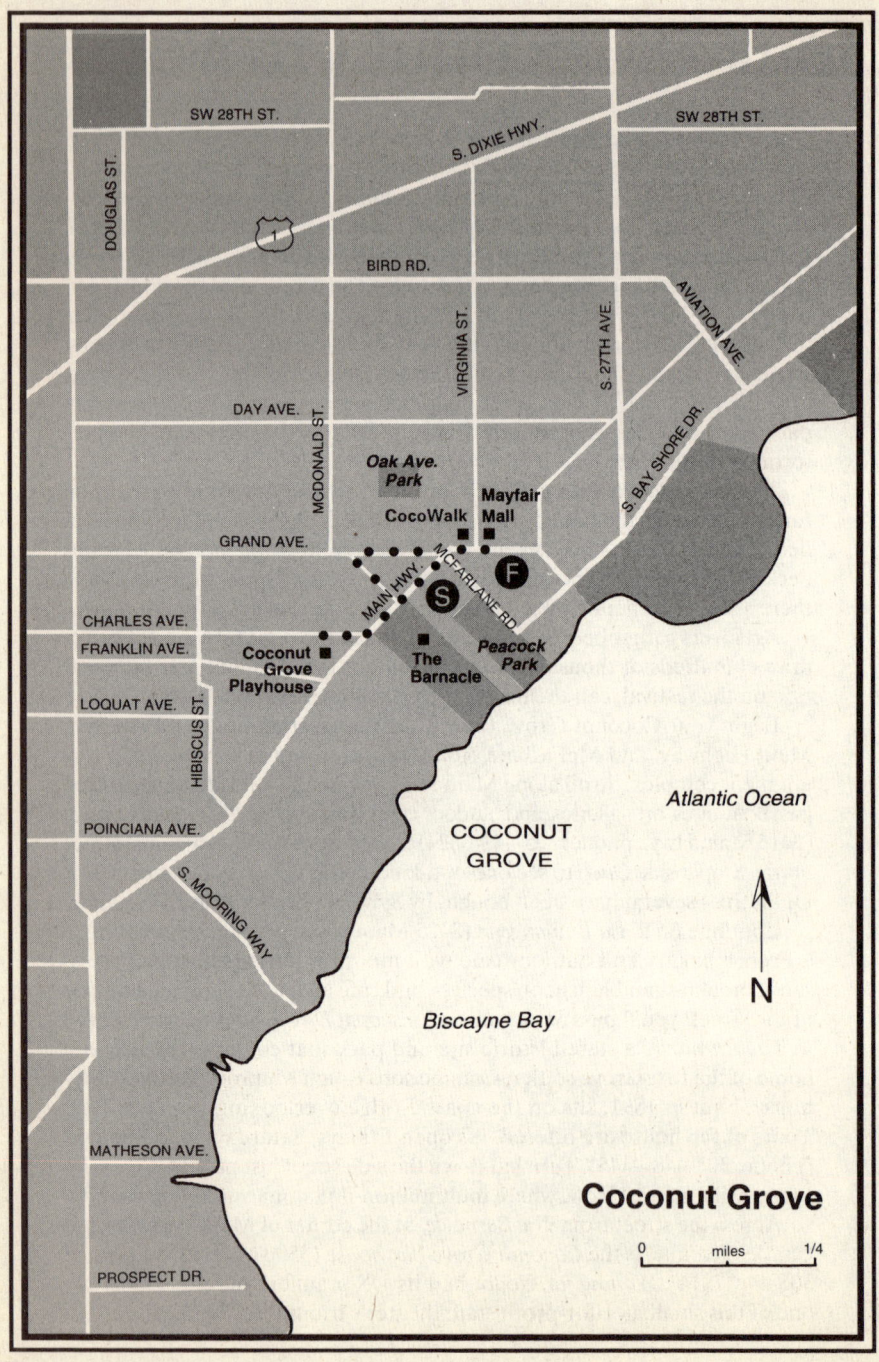

SW 28TH ST.

S. DIXIE HWY.

SW 28TH ST.

DOUGLAS ST.

BIRD RD.

VIRGINIA ST.

S. 27TH AVE.

AVIATION AVE.

DAY AVE.

MCDONALD ST.

S. BAY SHORE DR.

Oak Ave. Park

CocoWalk

Mayfair Mall

GRAND AVE.

MCFARLANE RD.

MAIN HWY.

S

F

CHARLES AVE.

FRANKLIN AVE.

Coconut Grove Playhouse

The Barnacle

Peacock Park

LOQUAT AVE.

HIBISCUS ST.

Atlantic Ocean

POINCIANA AVE.

COCONUT GROVE

S. MOORING WAY

N

Biscayne Bay

MATHESON AVE.

Coconut Grove

0   miles   1/4

PROSPECT DR.

plays host to pre-Broadway tryouts and performs two cabaret shows each season.

Peek down Charles Avenue to see the original wood-frame houses built by the black Bahamians who emigrated here to work in the nearby coconut groves late in the last century. Homes in this area, the site of Miami's first black settlement, date from 1889. Walk back along Main Highway the way you came, passing *Spokes Bicycle Shops* (3488 Main Hwy.; phone: 305-529-1688), where you can rent bicycles or in-line skates. One block farther down is the *Green Street Café* (3468 Main Hwy.; phone: 305-567-0662), a good place to sit and people watch.

Turn left onto Commodore Plaza, lined with bistros such as *Café Europe Bistro* (3159 Commodore Plaza; phone: 305-448-5723) and *Kaleidoscope* (3112 Commodore Plaza; phone: 305-446-5010), and upscale boutiques such as the *Carlos Art Gallery* (3162 Commodore Plaza; phone: 305-445-3020), selling bright Haitian paintings, and *Salo Design by Yvonne* (3141 Commodore Plaza; phone: 305-443-1861), selling one-of-a-kind mobiles, stained glass, modern furniture, painted silk, ceramics, and ethnic jewelry.

Turn right onto Grand Avenue. About halfway up the block on the left is *The Last Carrot* (3133 Grand Ave.; phone: 305-445-0805), serving fresh-squeezed juices, smoothies, and pita bread sandwiches. Nearby is *TAFA* boutique (3111 Grand Ave.; phone: 305-461-1717), which specializes in West African handicrafts. There are also several art galleries here featuring unusual artwork and paintings. On the right side of the street about a block and a half farther is *Maya Hatcha* (3058 Grand Ave.; phone: 305-443-9040), with a huge selection of imported goods from the Far East, Central America, Africa, and the Middle East, and *Condomania* (3066 Grand Ave.; phone: 305-445-7729), an unusual shop that specializes in condoms.

At the intersection continue straight on Grand Street to *CocoWalk* mall, a three-story upscale shopping center with a Spanish–Mediterranean decor. Here you find more boutiques and restaurants, a movie theater complex, *Dan Marino's American Sports Bar & Grill,* and *Café Tu-Tu Tango* (for details on both restaurants see "Eating Out" in *Miami,* THE CITIES).

Across the street from *CocoWalk* are three fast-food eateries, including *Johnny Rockets* (Grand Ave. and McFarlane Rd.; phone: 305-444-1000), a 1950s-style hamburger joint. Continue one block to Virginia Street and look up to see the butterfly-wings sculpture flanking the top three floors of the *Mayfair Mall,* a city-block-long shopping, restaurant, and hotel complex with a multiscreen movie theater and a fabulous open-air atrium. In the mall (but accessible from the street) is *Oakfeed* (2911 Grand Ave.; phone: 305-448-7595), the Grove's largest health food store; there's also an adjacent restaurant with a health-oriented menu.

For those who want to continue sightseeing, the elegant community of Coral Gables is a 15-minute drive northwest of Coconut Grove (see *Tour 4: Cruising through Coral Gables*).

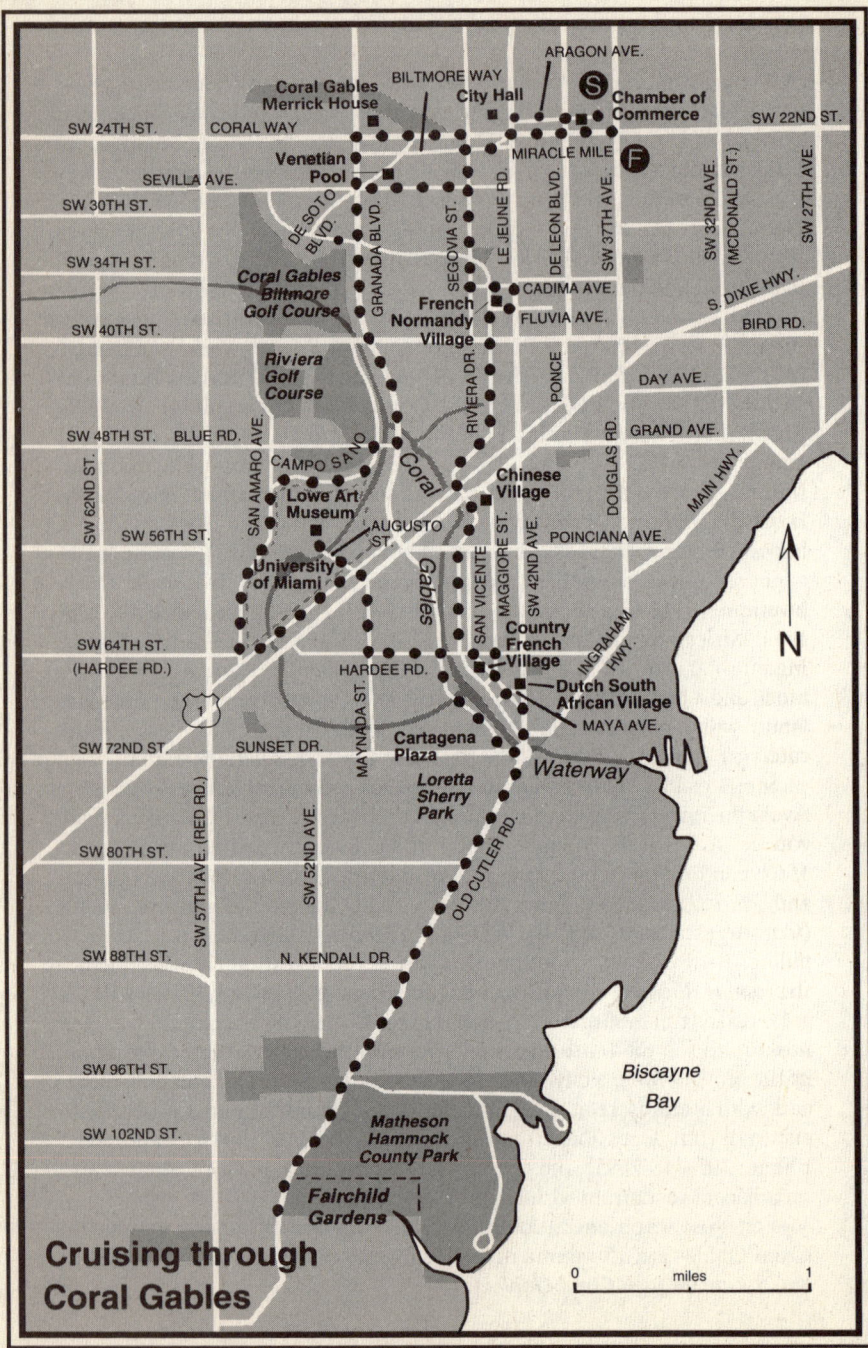

Cruising through Coral Gables

Tour 4: Cruising through Coral Gables

George Merrick developed this prime residential area in the 1920s as part of his scheme to create a perfectly designed city. Patterning it on ancient communities, Merrick gave Coral Gables curving boulevards (which make it very easy to get lost here) and four grand entrances flanked by Spanish-style spiral pillars. Merrick built more than 600 homes and donated land for the city's first church, library, and what would become the *University of Miami.* Unfortunately, inflated land values wreaked financial havoc, and Merrick and other investors lost everything. The hurricane of 1926 dealt another stunning blow to the area. Eventually, however, the city took over Merrick's debts and sold off his many building projects. After World War II, Coral Gables prospered as a residential area, just as George Merrick had hoped it would.

Today, the 12-square-mile city remains an area of great beauty, with lovely homes set among spacious gardens. Canals leading to Biscayne Bay run through residential neighborhoods, and docked boats bob in the water. Many of the original buildings remain, and ongoing restoration projects are returning many to their former grandeur. Coral Gables also is home to a number of multinational business offices, as well as numerous sophisticated restaurants.

Start this driving tour at the *Chamber of Commerce* building (50 Aragon Ave.—look for the US flag flying from the top; phone: 305-446-1657), where you can pick up maps and brochures. Make a left turn out of the *Chamber of Commerce* parking lot onto Aragon Avenue, continue for three blocks, and turn left again onto Le Jeune Road. Go one block to the Miracle Mile (Coral Way), make a half-turn right onto Biltmore Way, and immediately pull into one of the metered parking spaces on your right. (Don't look for street signs at eye level or above in most of the Gables; look down—most are discreetly placed in whitewashed cornerstones on the ground.) You are now in front of *City Hall* (405 Biltmore Way; phone: 305-446-6800), built in 1928 of Key stone (oolitic limestone native to the area). Note its colonnaded façade, then peek inside to see some of the original fixtures, furnishings, and paintings. (It's closed weekends.)

Continue west on Biltmore Way to the second traffic light (two blocks) and turn left onto Segovia Street. Now drive three blocks to Sevilla Avenue and turn right; proceed four blocks and make a sharp right turn by the fountain onto De Soto Boulevard. At No. 2701 stop at the *Venetian Pool,* the only swimming pool listed in the National Register of Historic Places. Originally a rock quarry, this large, free-form lagoon once attracted movie stars such as Esther Williams. It's now open to the swimming public (closed Mondays from *Labor Day* through May); there's an admission charge (phone: 305-460-5356). For additional details, see "Special Places" in *Miami,* THE CITIES.

Turn right around the *Venetian Pool,* make a right onto Toledo Street and an immediate left onto Sevilla; then go three blocks to Segovia Street. At Segovia, turn right and continue south nine blocks to the traffic light at University Drive and turn left; immediately bear right into Cadima Avenue. Notice the deep setbacks and unobtrusive low metal street lamps throughout the area and the few lovely large banyan and Indian fig trees. Proceed two blocks and turn right onto Le Jeune Road.

In this area, developer George Merrick created a residential district featuring tiny one- to three-block "villages," each with a distinct architectural style. Drive two short blocks and turn right onto Viscaya Court, where there are several occupied remains of Merrick's experiment. Here is the French Normandy Village built in a French rural architectural style, with white stucco townhouses sporting steep roofs, wooden crossbeams, and flower boxes beneath multi-paned windows. Circle back to Le Jeune and turn right; go two short blocks south to Fluvia Avenue and turn right; proceed one block to Riviera Drive and turn left. Follow Riviera for 15 blocks (about a mile) and cross US 1 (South Dixie Hwy.) to Menendez Avenue, the next street on the left. Bear immediately to your right onto Sansovino Street and stop. Here is the Chinese Village, the most bizarre of Merrick's communities, with blue-and-yellow tile upturned roofs, doorways painted red and yellow, and Chinese dragons adorning entranceways. Drive to the end of the block and turn right. Go a block and turn right again onto Castania Street; after another block turn left onto Riviera Drive and continue for about five blocks (a little more than half a mile) to Hardee Road, then turn left. Drive one block to San Vicente Street and slow down. Continue on Hardee, looking on both your right and left to see examples of the Country French Village manor homes, with red tile roofs, stucco façades, wooden beams, and chimneys. Continue one block to Maggiore Street and turn right, then go two blocks to San Vicente and turn left. At the third corner on the left, at Maya Avenue, stands the Dutch South African Village, with homes of white stucco and curlicued gables.

Circle around the block, returning to Le Jeune Road; turn right onto Le Jeune. Proceed two to three blocks, passing over the canal. Stop at the wood benches that denote the tiny *Loretta Sherry Park* on the right. Here are some lovely, large canalfront homes (several with equally lavish yachts) typical of this upscale residential area. Continue around the circle (Cartagena Plaza) to Old Cutler Road. Drive south a little less than 2 miles. On the left is the entrance to the *Matheson Hammock County Park & Marina.* Park and walk along its winding trails through native forest to a manmade lagoon overlooking Biscayne Bay, where you can take a dip. Although the buildings were destroyed by Hurricane Andrew in 1992, the park has reopened.

Facilities include a beach, a marina, a picnic area, changing areas, portable bathrooms, and showers. The park is open daily; there's an admission charge (phone: 305-665-5474 or 305-666-6979).

About a half-mile farther south on Old Cutler Road, on the left side, is *Fairchild Tropical Garden,* where something's always in bloom. The 83-acre grounds, said to be the largest tropical botanical garden in the continental US, afford visitors hours of beauty and tranquillity. Along with the world's largest collections of palms, there's a rain forest, a rare-plant house, and a one-acre Hurricane Andrew exhibit. Guided walking and tram tours are available at no extra charge. The garden is open daily except *Christmas;* admission charge (phone: 305-667-1651). Also see "Special Places" in *Miami,* THE CITIES.

Drive back a little over 2 miles on Old Cutler Road to Cartagena Plaza. Circle it to the third right, which is Sunset Drive, and take the first right after that, on to Granada Boulevard. Follow it for about a half-mile to Hardee Road. Turn left on Hardee and go about a third of a mile west, passing a section between Cellini and Leonardo Streets where a new French-looking community mimics Merrick's older experiment. Proceed a block farther to Maynada Street and turn right. Continue for another third of a mile to Augusto Street. Follow Augusto across US 1 and Ponce de León Boulevard. About a block farther on the right, behind a free-form sculpture, is the *Lowe Art Museum,* on the *University of Miami* campus (1301 Stanford Dr.; phone: 305-284-3535). The museum, which features a permanent Renaissance art collection and changing exhibits, is closed Sunday mornings and Mondays; there's an admission charge.

In addition to the museum, the *University of Miami* campus is home to a large undergraduate population, graduate schools in law and marine and atmospheric science, and the highly regarded *University of Miami/Jackson Memorial Medical Center*—not to mention the famed *Hurricanes* football team. Return to Ponce de León Boulevard, turn right, and proceed to the fourth traffic light. Turn right onto San Amaro Drive, locally known as Hurricane Drive because it passes behind the stadium where the football team practices. Drive a little less than a mile down San Amaro, keeping your eyes peeled for one of those famous *Hurricanes,* and then bear right onto Campo Sano. Proceed east for a half-mile to University Drive. Go left (north) and, at the next corner, turn right on Blue Road. Cross the canal and turn left at the first light onto Granada Boulevard.

Continue north for 1 mile to Anastasia Avenue and turn left. One block down on your left is the *Biltmore* hotel, a 1926 replica of Giralda Tower in Seville, Spain. Built as a luxury hotel as part of George Merrick's grand plan for Coral Gables, it hosted notables such as Bing Crosby and Judy Garland until the federal government acquired it in the 1940s and converted it into a veteran's hospital, covering the marble floors with linoleum and painting over the mosaic tile ceiling. It stood vacant for years, was renovated, opened as a hotel, closed, and in 1991 opened once again. Nearly

$70 million has been spent restoring it to its former glory. Stroll around the lobby, noting the 20-foot-high columns, arched vaulted ceiling, and restored Spanish woodwork. The 315-foot tower is a landmark for miles around, and the *Biltmore* still boasts the largest hotel swimming pool in the world, with 600,000 gallons of water. (Also see "Checking In" in *Miami,* THE CITIES.)

Leaving the *Biltmore,* return east on Anastasia and turn left onto Granada Boulevard. At the traffic light, turn right on Coral Way. In the first block, on your left, is the *Coral Gables Merrick House* (907 Coral Way; phone: 305-460-5361), built of oolitic limestone in 1907 as the Merrick family home. The interior still retains many of its original furnishings from the 1920s. Other pieces reflect the varied history of the city. The house is only open Sunday and Wednesday afternoons or by appointment; there's an admission charge.

Continue east on Coral Way, then turn right at Segovia Street (the next traffic light). Take the next left on Biltmore Way, and then bear left again onto Coral Way and cross over Le Jeune Road. The area between Le Jeune Road and Douglas Road is known as the Miracle Mile. The name derives from the fact that the stretch is exactly a half-mile long—the developer, looking to hype the center, decided that it was a "miracle" mile round-trip. Today it's an attractive pedestrian thoroughfare with 160 shops and eateries. One noteworthy emporium is *Books & Books,* around the corner (296 Aragon Ave.; phone: 305-442-4408). Owner Mitch Kaplan regularly mounts photographic exhibits and schedules readings and lectures by well-known writers. North of Aragon Avenue are several fine restaurants including *St. Michel* (162 Alcazar Ave.; phone: 305-446-6572), a bistro in a charming 1926 bed and breakfast establishment. Also in the area is *Yuca,* a lively modern eatery offering innovative Cuban dishes along with entertainment on weekends, and *Las Puertas*, which puts a new twist on Mexican dishes (see "Eating Out" in *Miami,* THE CITIES for both).

Tour 5: Little Havana

This Miami neighborhood has an interesting ethnic background. Earlier called Shenandoah, Little Havana was mainly a middle class Jewish neighborhood until the 1950s, although a large Hispanic group had settled here even before Fidel Castro took power in Cuba. With the arrival of refugees from Castro's reign, however, the area took on a distinctively Cuban character. The Jewish shops gradually became Hispanic, although some of the older signs still are visible (a kosher butcher shop is now a grocery selling pork). In recent years, the neighborhood continued to evolve. Many of the original middle class Cuban residents have moved on to more affluent neighborhoods, and other Hispanic groups have settled here. Now more Nicaraguans than Cubans live in Little Havana, and the area increasingly is called the Latin Quarter.

To get to Little Havana from Downtown Miami, drive south on Biscayne Boulevard, following signs around to Brickell Avenue (Rte. 1). Cross the Miami River and continue to Southeast Seventh Street. Turn right and proceed to Southwest 13th Avenue and park. Walk a block south to the corner of Southwest 13th Avenue and Southwest Eighth Street (the heart of Little Havana, the street is known by its Spanish name, Calle Ocho, here). This is the site of the *Brigade 2506 Memorial,* a monument to those who died in the unsuccessful 1961 Bay of Pigs invasion of Cuba. The monument symbolizes the political outlook of many who settled here in the 1950s. (For a thorough background, read Joan Didion's *Miami* or David Rieff's *Exile.*) Just south of the monument is a pleasant park with other memorials to *la causa* (the "cause" being the fight against Castro), including a sculpture by Tony Lopes of a brigade soldier with an assault rifle, a bust of patriot Jose Martí, and a cast-bronze map of Cuba.

From the monument, walk west along the south side of Calle Ocho. Here is a collection of furniture stores, clothing shops, beauty parlors, meat markets, record stores blasting music, mom-and-pop grocery stores, and restaurants that dispense Cuban goodies, proving that franchises haven't yet taken over all of America. At the corner of Southwest 14th Avenue is *Calle Ocho Marketplace,* which combines a coin laundry, dry cleaner, fruit and vegetable stand, and diner in a testament to the Cuban entrepreneurial spirit. A colorful mural depicts Varadero, a favorite beachfront haunt in the Cuba of days past. As you stroll, look down and notice the red-brick sidewalk, dubbed the *Hispanic Walkway of Stars.* Squares are dedicated to various Hispanic stars, including Gloria Estefan, María Conchita Alonso, Celia Cruz, and Julio Iglesias.

Across 14th Avenue, note the *McDonald's* restaurant. Because new buildings must adhere to the Spanish architectural style, this one has a red-

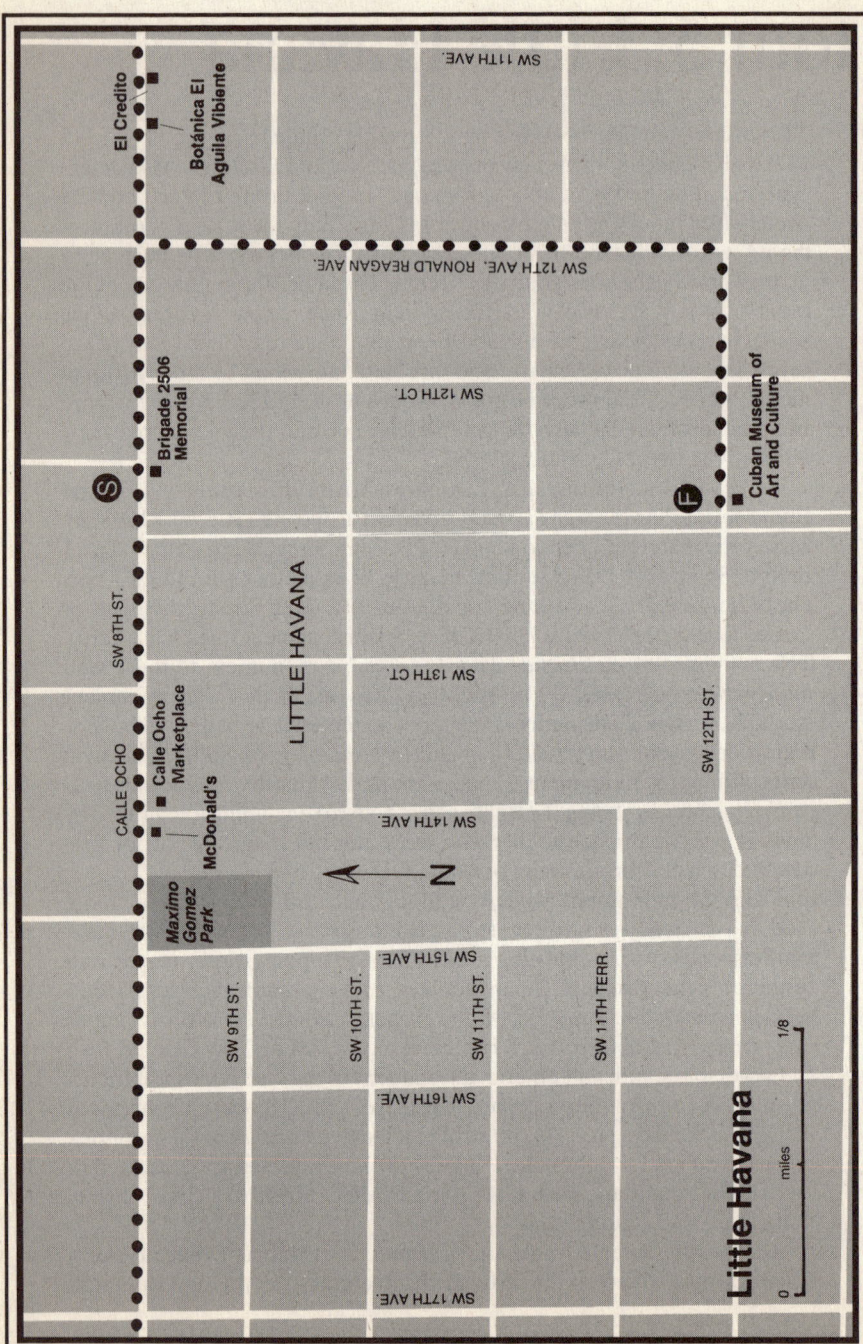

Little Havana

Little Havana

El Credito

Botánica El Aguila Vibiente

SW 11TH AVE.

SW 12TH AVE., RONALD REAGAN AVE.

Brigade 2506 Memorial

SW 12TH CT.

Ⓢ

SW 8TH ST.

Cuban Museum of Art and Culture

Ⓕ

LITTLE HAVANA

Calle Ocho Marketplace

SW 13TH CT.

CALLE OCHO

McDonald's

SW 14TH AVE.

N

SW 12TH ST.

Maximo Gomez Park

SW 9TH ST.

SW 15TH AVE.

SW 10TH ST.

SW 11TH ST.

SW 11TH TERR.

SW 16TH AVE.

SW 17TH AVE.

0   1/8

miles

tile roof and blue tiles on its stuccoed exterior. It may be the only *McDonald's* that serves *café con leche.*

At the corner of Southwest 15th Avenue is *Máximo Gomez Park,* where elderly men in *guayaberas* sit at outdoor tables under roofed areas playing dominoes and chess. Hispanic music fills the air. Although this is a city park, it is open only to those with a membership card and they must be males above age 55. A mural on the wall inside the park honors the 33 Latin American and Caribbean presidents who attended the historic Summit of the Americas in Miami in December 1994.

Farther along Calle Ocho, between Southwest 17th and 18th Avenues, is a wonderland of piñatas at *La Casa de Las Piñatas* (1756 SW Eighth St., Second Floor; phone: 305-649-4711). The standard Mexican paper donkeys are available, but hanging throughout the store are fantastic creations such as a tableau of a beauty pageant, complete with beauty queen, emcee, and television cameraman. Unlike Mexican piñatas, which are smashed with a stick by blindfolded partygoers, the Cuban ones have ribbons attached to a cardboard bottom and can be reused. Celebrants pull on the ribbons until the candy and small toys inside spill out—a tradition at children's parties, especially at *quinces,* the often lavish parties thrown for 15-year-old girls (akin to a "Sweet 16" party). Prices range from $25 to as high as $500. The store is closed on *Christmas Day.*

Now cross the street and retrace the route on the opposite side of Calle Ocho. The *Dunkin Donuts* at 16th was the first in the country to serve *café cubano* (espresso served in thimble-sized cups and fondly referred to as "rocket fuel"). It also bakes guava doughnuts. *España Importers* (1615 SW Eighth St.; phone: 305-856-4844) is a shop crammed with life-size religious statues, conga drums, flamenco dolls, and domino games.

La Casa de Los Trucos (1343 SW Eighth St.; phone: 305-858-5029), between 14th and 13th Avenues, does big business in satin and sequined costumes—especially at *Halloween*—but there are magic tricks, wacky souvenirs, and other fun gifts for children, too.

Between 10th and 11th Streets you'll spot signs of Little Havana's transformation into a refuge for the Hispanics of Central America. Storefronts announce they will mail packages to El Salvador, Honduras, Guatemala, Nicaragua, and Costa Rica. Stop in at the *Nicaragua Bakery* (1169 SW Eighth St.; phone: 305-285-0239) for a sweet.

Between 12th and 11th Avenues cross back over to the south side of the street to see the *Botánica el Aguila Vibiente* (1122 SW Eighth St.; phone: 305-854-4086), where candles, herbs, roots, and oils are sold, many for use in the controversial Santería rituals. Santería, which originated in Cuba, is a religion that combines elements of Catholicism and the native religion of West Africa's Yoruba people.

At 11th Avenue, don't be fooled by the unassuming storefront that hides *El Crédito* (1106 SW Eighth St.; phone: 305-858-4162), Miami's largest hand-rolled cigar factory. Stop in to watch cigars being made. The business began in Havana in 1907, and opened here in 1969. Today the tobacco is imported mainly from the Dominican Republic and Mexico. It's closed Sundays.

Little Havana's biggest festival is the *Carnaval Miami,* held every March. During the celebration Calle Ocho, Southwest Eighth Street becomes a pedestrian mall from Fourth to 27th Avenues; Latino bands play salsa on the flat rooftops, conga lines form up and down the streets, the smells of Cuban and other Hispanic foods beckon the hungry, and the merriment continues until the wee hours.

For a typical Cuban meal—roasted pork, paella, or *arroz con pollo,* and flan for dessert—plus fiery flamenco shows every weekend, go to *Málaga,* on Calle Ocho between Southwest Seventh and Southwest Eighth Avenues. Every weekend there's live jazz, dancing, and entertainment (sometimes flamenco shows) at *Centro Vasco,* which serves Spanish-Basque dishes and *tapas* late into the night. It's located on Calle Ocho at Southwest 22nd Avenue. (For additional details on both restaurants, see "Eating Out" in *Miami,* THE CITIES). As befits a Latin quarter, most restaurants don't get crowded until after 10 PM, and the entertainment gets livelier as the evening progresses.

For an inexpensive lunch, pop into *Versailles* (3555 SW Eighth St.; phone: 305-445-7614). Pick up a shot glass of Cuban coffee at the window (there's one line for both coffee and lottery tickets) or be seated at an inside table. Try a Cuban sandwich consisting of ham, cheese, pickles, and mustard on crusty Cuban bread.

Tour 6: Cowboy and Indian Tour

For a change from the sun and surf of South Florida, head to the land of cowboys and Indians—just southwest of Ft. Lauderdale. Here the Seminole Tribe of Hollywood (Florida) have a reservation. The tribe is a fairly recent arrival historically, having relocated here in the early part of the 18th century. An amalgamation of the Creek, Oconee, and other tribes, the confederation took the name "is-te-seminole," meaning separatists, to differentiate themselves from other Florida Indians who had become tolerant of white settlers. Today, they too have intermarried with other area residents.

Many of the Seminole tribe members have developed enterprises aimed at tourists, such as the *Native Village* and *Seminole Bingo and Casino* hall (see below). Some seem very commercial, but despite the kitsch, some offer insights into earlier lifestyles.

The year's major event at the reservation is the *Seminole Indian Tribal Fair* (held in mid-February), featuring Native American food, art, and tribal dancing from all over North America; there's also a rodeo. For information, call 954-584-0400.

From US 1 or I-95, drive west on Sheridan Street (State Rd. 822) in Hollywood to US 441 (also called State Rd. 7) and turn right (north). After about 10 blocks, be on the lookout for the *Native Village* (3551 N. State Rd. 7; phone: 954-961-4519), a commercial enterprise on the right; it's run by Bobbie Billie, the chief's wife. After passing through the gift shop, wander around a jungle-like setting of small lakes, waterfalls, and dripping foliage. Tropical birds call out, roars blast from the three caged Florida panthers (a protected, endangered species), and in the snake pit, a trainer approaches a rattlesnake—very carefully. The man describes the various venomous snakes slithering about, and then provokes a nonvenomous type to bite him. But the most excitement is generated at the alligator wrestling exhibit. The trainer enters the pit, describing the native animal's characteristics, and then pries its mouth open to reveal 80 large teeth. The trainer's hand darts in and out of the huge mouth and the animal snaps its jaws shut— usually *after* the trainer's hand has been withdrawn. The *Native Village* is closed Sundays; there's an admission charge.

On the west side of the street is the *Seminole Bingo and Casino* hall (4150 N. State Rd. 7; phone: 954-961-3220), with one of the largest bingo halls in Florida (and arguably in the US). Although high-stakes bingo is illegal elsewhere in Florida, it's permitted here because the land is a federally protected Indian reservation. The enclosed hall, seating 1,400, attracts play-

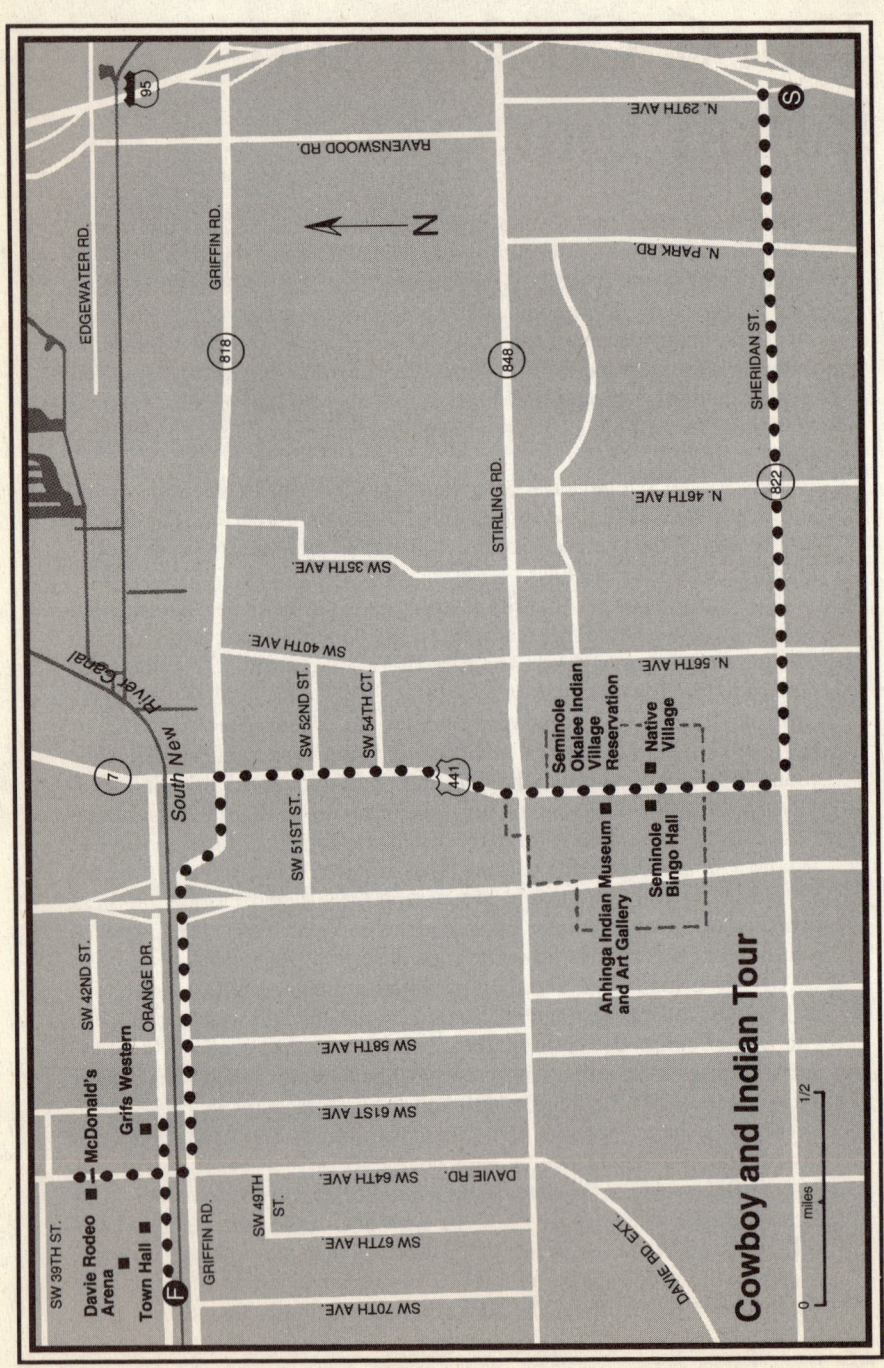

Cowboy and Indian Tour

N

95

EDGEWATER RD.

RAVENSWOOD RD.

GRIFFIN RD.

818

River Canal

South New

7

SW 39TH ST.

Davie Rodeo Arena

McDonald's

Grifs Western

Town Hall

SW 42ND ST.

ORANGE DR.

GRIFFIN RD.

SW 49TH ST.

DAVIE RD.

SW 70TH AVE.

SW 67TH AVE.

SW 64TH AVE.

SW 61ST AVE.

SW 58TH AVE.

SW 51ST ST.

SW 52ND ST.

SW 54TH CT.

SW 40TH AVE.

SW 35TH AVE.

STIRLING RD.

848

441

Seminole Okalee Indian Village Reservation

Native Village

Anhinga Indian Museum and Art Gallery

Seminole Bingo Hall

N. 56TH AVE.

N. 46TH AVE.

SHERIDAN ST.

N. PARK RD.

N. 29TH AVE.

822

S

DAVIE RD. EXT.

0   1/2   miles

ers hoping to win the $10,000 jackpots. Often these jackpots climb to $50,000 and even $100,000. A 24-hour casino area offers 290 video slot machines and 36 poker tables. The hall is open daily; there's an admission charge.

A few blocks north is a complex of *chickee* huts (open-air, native thatch structures), including a haircutting salon. Stop in at the *Anhinga Indian Museum and Art Gallery* (5791 S. State Rd. 7; phone: 954-581-0416) for nicely crafted pottery, colorful appliquéd Indian skirts and jackets, and beaded jewelry. It's open daily; no admission charge.

Continue north to Griffin Road and turn left (west). Drive along the South New River Canal to Davie Road (SW 64th Ave.) and you're in cowboy territory. When the area was developed in the early part of the 20th century, it was dotted with orange plantations, sugarcane fields, dairy farms, and ranches. The cattle herders evolved into cowboys, and others who love horsing around followed suit.

Today, visitors can still spot some equestrians, often clad in cowboy-cut jeans and Stetson hats, riding their steeds through the streets. Shops advertise boot and saddle repairs, and shopping centers are designed to look like porches at a ranch; many even feature hitching posts for visitors arriving by horseback. Nearby is *Boot Barn* (7138 Stirling Rd.; phone: 954-435-BOOT), which carries such brands as Tony Lama, with handmade boots made of snake, alligator, lizard, buffalo, and elk (closed Sunday mornings). Ranches where horses are boarded abound, and riders can rent mounts by the hour or by the day. The region's heritage leaps to life during the annual *Orange Blossom Festival* held in late March, a week-long celebration featuring rodeos, food, and music.

Turn right on Davie Road, cross over the canal, and immediately turn right on Orange Drive (SW 45th St.). Stop at *Grifs Western* (6211 SW 45th St.; phone: 954-587-9000), a 20,000-square-foot emporium featuring saddles, hats, western shirts, and seemingly miles of boots, priced from $80 to $600.

Return to Davie Road and turn right. On the left, at Southwest 41st Street, stands a two-story, saloon-style *McDonald's.* Out back, riders can park their horses at hitching posts in the Golden Arches' corral.

Retrace the path on Davie to Orange Drive and turn right. On the right is the *Town Hall* (6591 SW 45th St.; phone: 954-797-1000), a western-style complex of rough-hewn cedar. (The fire and police stations down the road bear similar façades.) In back of *Town Hall* is the covered *Davie Rodeo Arena,* where up to 5,000 folks can watch bareback riding, calf roping, steer wrestling, tie-down roping, bull riding, and barrel racing every Wednesday night and occasionally at other times. For information, contact the *Davie Arena Event Line* (phone: 954-797-1166). The *Five Star Pro Rodeo* monthly series features professional rodeo cowboys from around the country, and points for the events go toward the *National Finals Rodeo* in Las Vegas. The *Florida State Championship Rodeo* takes place here each November.

If you can't wait to get in the saddle yourself, mosey up to one of the area stables. You can rent horses at the *Bar-B Ranch* (4601 SW 128th Ave., Davie; phone: 954-434-6175) or join a supervised ride at the *Myrland Stables* (5550 SW 73rd Ave., Davie; phone: 954-587-2285); both are open daily.

Those in the area at dinnertime who wish to sample authentic Southwestern food (not the standard Tex-Mex, fast-food variety) should stop in at Davie's *Armadillo Café* (see "Eating Out" in *Ft. Lauderdale,* THE CITIES).

For an experience unique to South Florida, a quick and easy visit to the Everglades awaits. Continue west on Griffin Road about 25 miles to US 27 (it's 18 miles west of I-95, a half-hour drive from 441) and the *Everglades Holiday Park* (21940 Griffin Rd.; phone: 954-434-8111). A narrated airboat ride skims guests over the sawgrass through America's only subtropical wet-lands. Visitors will probably spot snoozing live alligators (sometimes a nest of babies) and flocks of tropical birds such as red-legged gallinules. In addi-tion to the visual experience, passengers will learn about local Native American history, food, and clothing. There's also an alligator wrestling show and wildlife exhibit, and Seminole crafts are sold in a straw hut. The park is open for wandering, fishing, and one-hour airboat tours. There's a fee for the tours.

Another alternative is 12 miles north of the *Everglades Holiday Park:* the *Sawgrass Recreation Park* (5400 US Rte. 27; phone: 954-389-0202 or 800-457-0788), where the admission price includes a thrilling airboat tour through the Everglades; a narrated tour of an 18th-century Indian village; and a fascinating, educational, and hands-on (for those who want to) exhibit featuring alligators, crocodiles, and caymans, as well as nonvenomous snakes. Fishing boats can be rented; guided full-day fishing trips also are offered. Facilities include a well-stocked market and gift store, restrooms, showers, and picnic areas. Both RV and tent campsites are available. The park is open daily. Also see *Tour 9: Everglades National Park.*

Tour 7: Palm Beach

Palm Beach, where the rich, the famous, and the infamous "winter," makes for an interesting day's excursion. It's a two-and-a-half- to three-hour drive north from Miami and an hour and a half from Ft. Lauderdale, and there are several interesting sights along the way.

Take I-95 North (just be sure to avoid it during rush hours; those in the western region of South Florida may prefer to take Florida's Turnpike, which is less heavily trafficked). For a short—or long—diversion, get off at Palmetto Park Road (Exit 38) and go east for 2 miles to Federal Highway (Rte. 1). Turn left and pass one traffic light. On the right, turn into *Mizner Park,* a stunning complex of pink buildings with orange barrel-tile roofs, green balconies, brick roads, and splashing fountains. This multi-use center offers outdoor cafés to linger at and boutiques to browse through. Particularly interesting is *Liberties* (309 Plaza Real; phone: 561-368-1300), a giant book and music store that features frequent readings by celebrity authors.

Return to I-95 North and continue to Southern Boulevard, State Road 80 (Exit 50). Those traveling with children, or who simply love animals, should head west 18 miles to *Lion Country Safari* (Southern Blvd. W., West Palm Beach; phone: 561-793-1084). Visitors remain in their cars and drive through the 500-acre park, passing prides of lions, herds of antelope, and African elephant families that live in re-creations of African areas such as the Serengeti Plains and Skukuza Veldt. If you stop, a rhinoceros may lumber alongside your car. Paddleboat and kiddie rides plus a snack bar are also on the premises. Plan to spend several hours. The park is open daily; admission charge.

After the safari, return to Southern Boulevard and go east for a little more than 19 miles. Follow the Southern Boulevard Bridge across the Intracoastal Waterway; note the winter waterfront mansions on the left. The closest one, with a pink 75-foot Moorish tower, is *Mar-A-Lago,* the estate currently owned by Donald Trump, but originally built for the late Marjorie Merriweather Post, heiress to the Post cereal fortune. Trump recently turned the 118-room mansion at the corner of Southern and South Ocean Boulevards into a private club (with an initiation fee of $25,000). The building is listed on the National Register of Historic Places. You're now on the island of Palm Beach, one of the barrier beaches along South Florida's east coast.

Proceed around the traffic circle, turn left on A1A (S. Ocean Blvd.), and continue north past the *Mar-A-Lago* estate. The ocean is on the right. On the left, the boulevard is dotted with elegant mansions owned by such people as members of European royalty or giants of American industry. The Beatles' John Lennon briefly owned the seven-bedroom home at 720

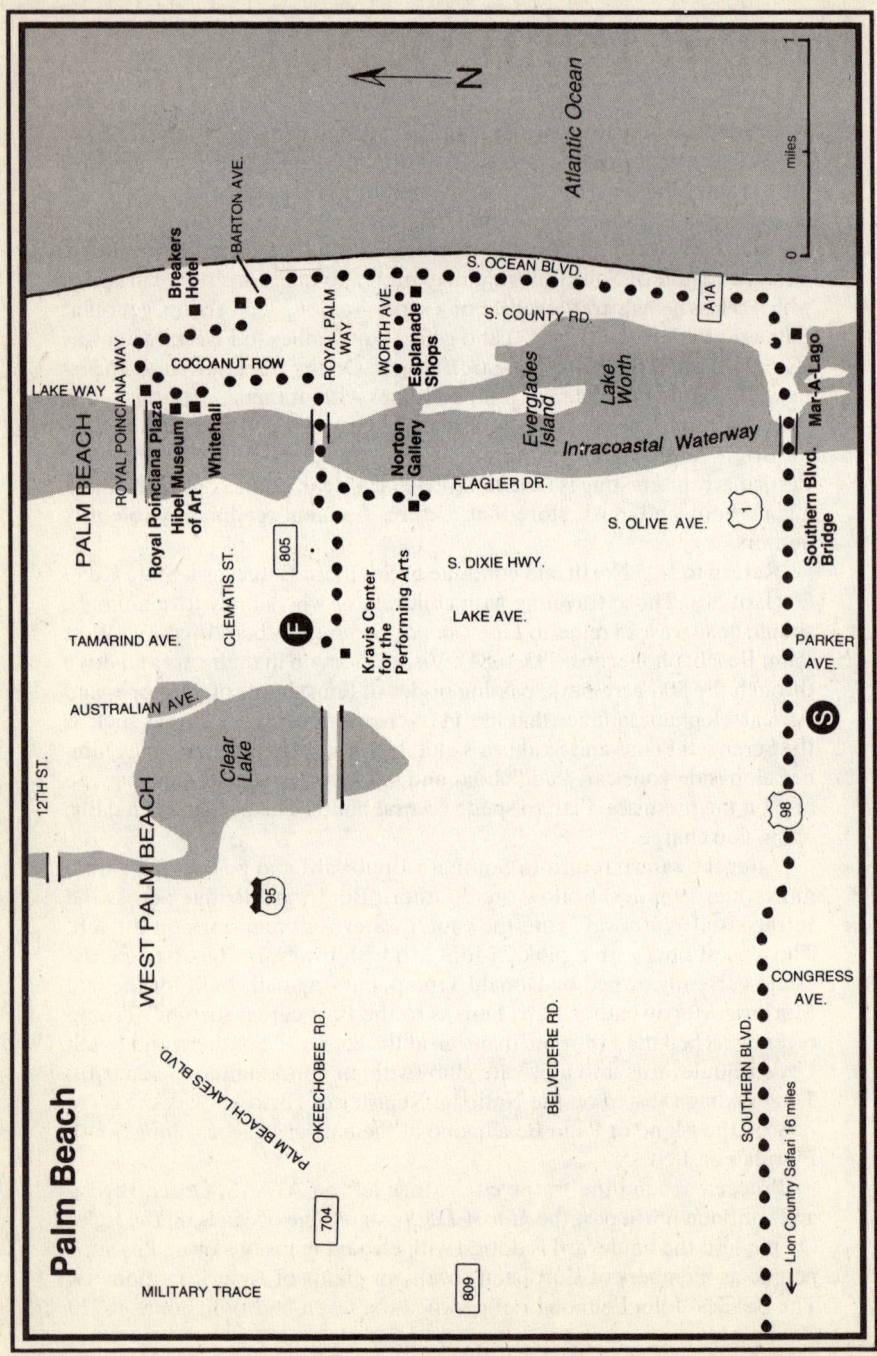

Palm Beach

N

Atlantic Ocean

1 miles
0

S. OCEAN BLVD.

Breakers Hotel
BARTON AVE.

ROYAL POINCIANA WAY
LAKE WAY
COCOANUT ROW
ROYAL PALM WAY
WORTH AVE.
Esplanade Shops
S. COUNTY RD.
A1A

Royal Poinciana Plaza
Hibel Museum of Art
Whitehall

Norton Gallery

FLAGLER DR.

Everglades Island
Lake Worth
Intracoastal Waterway
Mar-A-Lago
Southern Blvd. Bridge

PALM BEACH

CLEMATIS ST.

805

S. OLIVE AVE.

1

S. DIXIE HWY.

LAKE AVE.

TAMARIND AVE.

F

PARKER AVE.

Kravis Center for the Performing Arts

S

AUSTRALIAN AVE.

WEST PALM BEACH

Clear Lake

98

12TH ST.

95

OKEECHOBEE RD.

CONGRESS AVE.

PALM BEACH LAKES BLVD.

BELVEDERE RD.

704

SOUTHERN BLVD.

809

MILITARY TRACE

Lion Country Safari 16 miles

South Ocean Boulevard. The Spanish, French, and Italian architecture of the mansions on this street recalls the landscape along the Riviera.

About a mile and a half from the traffic circle, look to the left for the street sign marked Worth Avenue. This famed street is well worth a visit. If there are no vacant parking meters, there's a parking lot (with valet parking) at the *Esplanade Shops* about half a block down on the left, just east of *Saks Fifth Avenue.* Or try the outdoor lot a few blocks away on Peruvian Avenue.

Whether you're a world class shopper or just the window shopping type, these few blocks along Worth Avenue should not be missed. The 200 glamorous stores—and the elegantly dressed shoppers who frequent them—are reminiscent of Beverly Hills's Rodeo Drive (actually, the Palm Beach version has been around a lot longer). One recent visitor from Beverly Hills noticed more Rolls-Royces here in a day than he ever spotted back home.

In addition to its pricey shops, Worth Avenue offers striking architectural beauty. The four-block-long street is lined with one- and two-story shops built by 1920s architect Addison Mizner in the Spanish-Mediterranean Revival style he thought the region's history and climate demanded. (Mizner was responsible as well for many grand homes throughout the area for families such as the Vanderbilts and the Phippses.) Worth Avenue's buildings are white stucco with orange barrel-tile roofs, and they drip with cerise bougainvillea. Arched galleries face miniature royal palm trees, and everything is spotless and subdued.

At the eastern end of the avenue, the two-story *Esplanade Shops* complex, with its Spanish tiles and water fountains, adds further charm to the scene. On the second floor of the complex is one of Palm Beach's top restaurants for a fashionable lunch or dinner, the award-winning *Café L'Europe* (150 Worth Ave.; phone: 561-655-4020). It specializes in French and continental fare served in an elegant setting of rich woods, leaded glass, heavy lace curtains, and crystal. There is a champagne and caviar bar that offers five varieties of the fishy delicacy.

Don't miss the "vias"—charming side courtyards off the street with gurgling fountains, lush flower beds, and additional shops and eateries.

Worth Avenue's high-fashion shops include *Martha* (No. 230; phone: 561-655-0833), *Valentino Boutique* (No. 204; phone: 561-659-7533), *Salvatore Ferragamo* (No. 200; phone: 561-659-0602), and *Saks Fifth Avenue* (No. 172; phone: 561-833-2551). Leather goods are at *Gucci* (No. 256; phone: 561-655-6955), *Hermès* (No. 255; phone: 561-655-6655), and *Louis Vuitton* (No. 251; phone: 561-833-4671); and jewelry can be purchased at *Tiffany* (No. 259; phone: 561-659-6090), *Cartier* (No. 214; phone: 561-655-5913), and *Van Cleef & Arpels* (No. 249; phone: 561-655-6767). Fragrances and ready-to-wear fashions are at *Chanel* (No. 247; phone: 561-655-1550). *Wally Findlay Galleries* (No. 165; phone: 561-655-2090) is among Worth Avenue's art galleries.

From Worth Avenue, take the boulevard north as far as it goes in this part of town (Barton Avenue). Ahead at the curve is a white-pillared house that belongs to cosmetics magnate Estée Lauder (126 S. Ocean Blvd.). Local lore has it that if the guards stand at the doorway, she's in residence. (Don't expect to approach any of these well-guarded private homes.)

Follow Barton left to South County Road (the first traffic light) and turn right. At the second light (Breakers Row), turn right into the *Breakers* hotel (1 S. County Rd.; phone: 561-655-6611) and park near the fountain. This 528-room stucco hotel, built in 1926 (after two former wooden incarnations burned down), is reminiscent of a European palace with its Italian Renaissance–style antique furniture and hand-painted ceilings. Notice the 15th-century tapestries in the lobby. If your visit coincides with the "season," you may spot one or several of the many movie stars and heads of government who stay here. Have lunch in the *Beach Club,* overlooking the ocean, or in the *Fairways Club,* overlooking the golf course. You may want to return later for dinner in the elegant *Florentine* dining room, which serves continental fare, and where diners sit beneath 25-foot frescoed, beamed ceilings patterned after those at the Palazzo Davante in Florence. Sample the famed wine list and dance to live orchestra music. Men are requested to wear jackets (phone: 561-659-8480).

Once refreshed, continue north on South County Road, which becomes North County Road at Royal Poinciana Way. On your left at the intersection of North County Road and Royal Poinciana is *St. Edward's Roman Catholic Church,* where Rose Kennedy once worshiped. Follow North County Road as it curves into ocean-hugging North Ocean Boulevard. You'll see more impressive homes up here. *Palm Beach Country Club* will be on your right soon. Farther north, the former Kennedy compound is at 1095 North Ocean Boulevard, but it isn't visible from the street. The road ends at East Inlet Drive, so turn around and head back down North County Road, noting the sights you missed on the way up.

Turn right on Royal Poinciana Way. At the next light (Cocoanut Row), turn left. On the right is *Royal Poinciana Plaza,* a low-key complex housing the *Royal Poinciana Playhouse,* stores, and restaurants. Also in the plaza is the "famous-for-all-the-wrong-reasons" *Au Bar* (336 Royal Poinciana Way; phone: 561-832-4800), the rendezvous spot for the hip, young crowd. For a quick snack, stop at *Too-Jay's* (313 *Royal Poinciana Plaza;* phone: 561-659-7232) for New York–style delicatessen sandwiches, unusual salads, and fantastic desserts, including a killer chocolate cake. Also at *Royal Poinciana Plaza* is the *Hibel Museum of Art* (No. 150; phone: 561-833-6870), which mounts the original oils, lithographs, bronze sculptures, and collectible plates of 77-year-old artist Edna Hibel. The first female artist to be awarded the medal of honor by Pope John Paul II, Hibel also has been honored with a fellowship to the World Academy of Art and Science. The museum is closed Sunday mornings and Mondays; no admission charge.

Proceed south on Cocoanut Row; less than two blocks ahead on the right is the *Henry Morrison Flagler Museum.* The museum is located in a 73-room mansion called *Whitehall,* which was the home of Flagler, a cofounder of the Standard Oil Company who brought what is now the *Florida East Coast Railroad* south through the state to Key West. (He subsequently opened resorts throughout Florida, and is credited with establishing Palm Beach and aiding the development of Miami Beach and Key West.) Flagler built this home in 1901 for his third wife, who was 38 years his junior. (One of his other tokens of affection was a pearl necklace with a clasp enhanced by a 12-carat diamond.)

A vacation home like those in Newport, Rhode Island, *Whitehall* cost $2.5 million to build and $1.5 million to furnish. (In 1996 dollars, that would run over $70 million to build and over $42 million to furnish.) Its 110-foot-long foyer is decorated in seven kinds of marble. Features include gilded moldings, ceiling murals, museum-quality furnishings, enormous Baccarat crystal chandeliers, columns, fireplaces, and artwork. Children will enjoy the antique doll collection. There also are costume collections dating from 1895 to 1915, and lace, silver, and other collections. Allow about an hour and a half for a tour. The museum is closed Mondays, *Christmas Day,* and *New Year's Day;* there's an admission charge (phone: 561-655-2833).

Continue south on Cocoanut Row and turn right on Royal Palm Way (towering royal palms line both sides of this especially striking street). Drive over Royal Palm Bridge and turn left onto Flagler Drive. Proceed about a third of a mile to the *Diana Place* complex on the right, site of the one-story, buff-colored *Norton Gallery* (1451 S. Olive Ave.; phone: 561-833-2133, museum; 561-832-5194, information), which displays a permanent collection of French Impressionist, Chinese, and American art, plus traveling exhibitions. The gallery is closed Mondays; donation requested.

Retracing your route on Flagler, return to the bridge (Lake View Ave.) and turn left. Stay on the right side as you cross Dixie Highway (US 1), and follow the road as it curves right and then continues straight as Jessamine Street. Continue west across the railroad tracks. Straight ahead (after the third light from the bridge) is the $52-million *Kravis Center for the Performing Arts* (701 Okeechobee Blvd.; phone: 561-832-SHOW; 800-572-8471). It stages opera and ballet performances plus national productions of Broadway shows. Drive straight into the parking garage on Tamarind Avenue, if you like, or continue on.

At this point, Jessamine Street has turned into Okeechobee Boulevard. From the corner of Okeechobee and Tamarind Avenue, continue west on Okeechobee for 1 mile, until you see the signs for I-95 southbound, which will bring you back to your starting point.

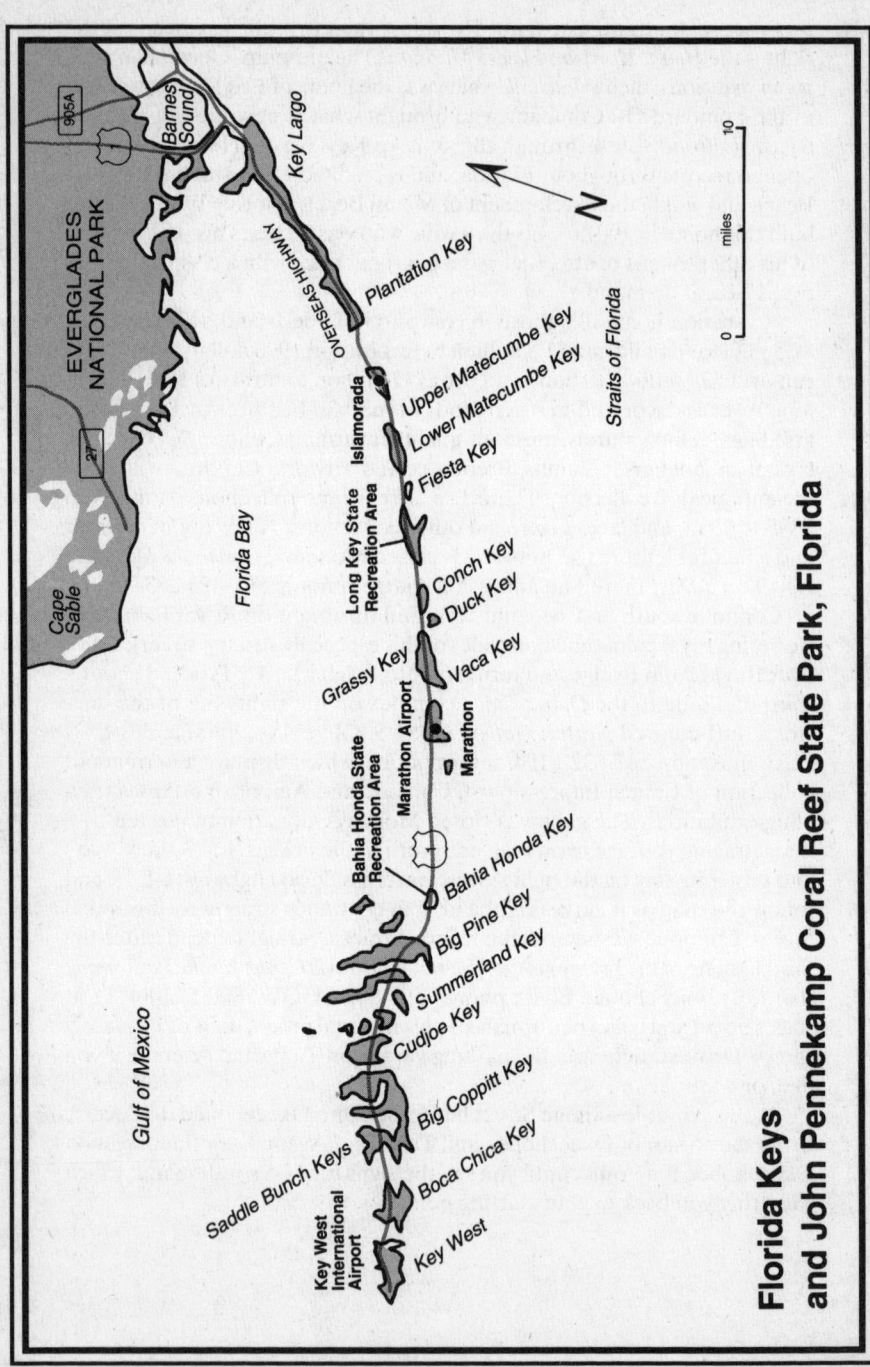

Florida Keys
and John Pennekamp Coral Reef State Park, Florida

Tour 8: Florida Keys and John Pennekamp Coral Reef State Park

Curving 150 miles out into the Gulf of Mexico from the southern tip of mainland Florida, the Florida Keys dot the waters like an ellipsis following a phrase. And in many ways this archipelago is an afterthought to that great landmass above, centered on Miami, with its glittering nightlife and crowded swimming beaches. The 45 principal islands (a "key" is a low island, or reef) that make up the Keys are generally tucked soundly away by 11 PM, have very few sandy beaches despite miles of coastline, and few glamorous resorts. A seven-story hotel—a midget by Miami standards—is a skyscraper hereabouts.

What the Keys do have, however, are some of the finest seascapes anywhere in the world—the blue waters of the Atlantic to the east and south and the green seas of the Gulf of Mexico on the northwestern side. As you drive along the Overseas Highway (US 1), a toll-free road that spans the islands with 43 bridges (some only 100 feet long, one stretching more than 7 miles), you are surrounded by sea and sky on all sides. Even on the Keys themselves, many of which are only a few hundred yards wide, you can see through the mangroves, Caribbean pine, and silver palmetto to the water, which is the overwhelming presence here. And though you can't see it from a car, the view is even more dramatic below the ocean surface.

Depending on which island you're visiting, a trip to the Florida Keys can be an easy day's excursion. The drive from Miami to Key West via the Overseas Highway (US 1) takes about three hours; Key Largo is just an hour away. Try to avoid traveling the highway on the weekends when it's jammed with Miami day-trippers. An accident on US 1 can shut down traffic for hours.

The Keys are bordered by an offshore coral reef averaging 5 to 8 miles offshore. The *Florida Keys National Marine Sanctuary,* measuring 2,800 square nautical miles, extends from Dade County west to the Dry Tortugas (it's actually the same reef that continues northward past Ft. Lauderdale, with some gaps along the way). All along the route, there are dive shops (most indicated by the red-and-white-striped "divers down" flag), which arrange private or group snorkeling expeditions to nearby reefs. The best section of the reef that can be seen close up is at the *John Pennekamp Coral Reef State Park* in Key Largo. It is a slightly hallucinogenic underwater scene, as bright blue and green tropical fish move in and out of the sculptured reefs of white, pink, and orange coral. No boat is needed if you just plan to snorkel; though the sights offshore are even more marvelous.

The story of the Overseas Highway is interesting. During the late 1880s, Henry Flagler, an associate of John D. Rockefeller, aimed to establish a "land" route to Cuba by extending the *Florida East Coast Railroad* line to Key West. From there he planned a ferry shuttle for the final 90 miles to Havana. He invested some $20 million in the construction of tracks, but the line never showed a profit and the *Labor Day* hurricane of 1935 wiped out the tracks and roadbed. At that point, the government stepped in and began building the Overseas Highway along the same route. In 1982, 37 bridges were replaced with wider, heavier spans. Many of the old bridges remain open for pedestrians and fisherfolk, among them the well-known Seven-Mile Bridge at Marathon (featured in the 1995 Arnold Schwarzenegger film *True Lies*).

Of the 45 Keys linked by the highway, several are major islands with accommodations, restaurants, shops, and their own unique character. Much of this local flavor has to do with the natives of the area. They're Floridians, but they call themselves "Conchs" (pronounced *konks*). Descended from London Cockneys who settled in the Bahamas, the Conchs also have Cuban, Yankee sailor, and Virginia merchant blood. Not surprisingly, Conchs always have been people of the sea—fishermen, boatmen, sponge divers, and underwater salvagers.

Fishing is king in these parts, with over 300 varieties of fish in the surrounding waters. Besides attracting anglers, the abundance of fresh fish has stimulated Keys chefs to dream up such creations as conch fritters alongside their land-bound flights of fancy such as Key lime pie. (Made from limes native to the Keys, the pie must be yellow, not green, to be genuine.)

Key Largo is the first of the Keys and the longest, but what is most interesting here is under water. Running parallel to the Key for 21 miles is *John Pennekamp Coral Reef State Park* (PO Box 487, Key Largo, FL 33037; phone: 305-451-1202; 305-451-1621, concession and equipment rental information), the country's first underwater state park, and the largest living coral reef in the continental US. The park is a snorkeler's and scuba diver's heaven, encompassing 165 square miles of the Atlantic Ocean, hundreds of species of tropical fish, and 55 different varieties of coral. Laws forbid taking any coral, tropical fish, lobsters, or conch shells from the water, so the area will be preserved for others to see.

To get an overview of the reef and surrounding ocean, take the glass-bottom boat tour operated by the park. The tour, offered three times a day, weather permitting, provides valuable insights into the ecological balance of the reef. The boat journeys several miles out onto the high seas to the reef's most spectacular section, where you'll see beautifully colored coral formations and other marine life, including barracuda, giant sea turtles, and sharks.

You also can venture into the water for snorkeling and scuba diving tours of the reef. The park offers snorkeling and scuba excursions and rents equipment; gear and tours are also available at Key Largo's many dive shops. If you dive, be sure to see the nine-foot-tall bronze statue *Christ of the Deep,* situated 20 feet beneath the sea in the *National Marine Sanctuary.* The statue, which was dedicated in 1966, symbolizes peace for mankind.

The park has a beach with a roped-off swimming area that is good for a dip or some casual snorkeling. For those who want to stay above water, there are trails for canoeing in the mangrove hammock. The water is so crystal clear that you can look down from your canoe and see spectacularly colored fish darting in and out of the mangrove roots. In addition, the park offers 47 campsites, all with tables, charcoal grills, electrical hookups, and water. Reservations for the sites should be made up to 60 days in advance—this is a very popular destination. (Private campgrounds are scattered throughout the Keys if you can't get into *Pennekamp.*) Be warned if you camp in a tent: The ground is usually rocky or gravel-covered. The park is open daily; there's an admission charge. Stop by the visitors' center for information on the reef and park programs. Information on Key Largo may be obtained by calling the *Key Largo Chamber of Commerce* (phone: 800-822-1088).

The next island is Upper Matecumbe Key, site of Islamorada, a sport fishing center in an area that's famous for fishing. Its many coral reefs in the surrounding shallow waters attract scuba and skin divers as well. The *Underwater Coral Gardens,* which feature two colorful coral deposits and the wreck of a Spanish galleon, are good for underwater exploration and photography and can be reached by charter boat. For information on Islamorada and also Long Key (see below), call the *Islamorada Chamber of Commerce* (phone: 800-322-5397).

Farther down is Long Key, where you can go for some underwater hunting for Florida lobster—crustaceans without the pincers. However, the season is limited—it can be held anytime between August and February, and its length varies each year based on how many lobsters are in the water. The *Long Key State Recreation Area* (mile marker 67.5; phone: 305-664-4815) features 60 beachfront campsites on a sandy shore, picnic areas with tables, barbecue grills, fresh water, and nature trails through the mangrove swamps. Part of Long Key is a mangrove forest so dense it's reminiscent of the Black Forest. As you hike through it, imagine how hard it was to cut a road here in the days before heavy equipment.

Marathon, midway down the archipelago, has been developed as a tourist center and has an airport and an 18-hole golf course, *Sombrero Country Club* (phone: 305-743-2551). Nevertheless, Marathon retains much of its original fishing-town character. There are more than 80 species in the gulf and ocean waters that can be taken with rod and reel or nets from charter boats or the Key's bridges. For information on the many fishing tournaments held throughout the year, contact the *Marathon Chamber of Commerce*

(12222 Overseas Hwy., Marathon, FL 33050; phone: 305-743-5417; 800-842-9580). The competition is tough and the fish are smart. *Hall's Diving Center* (1994 Overseas Hwy.; phone: 305-743-5929) is a good place to rent gear or arrange dive and snorkel trips.

At Bahia Honda Key, the 524-acre *Bahia Honda State Park* (near mile marker 33; phone: 305-872-2353) has 80 campsites, six cabins, picnicking, nature trails, and coral-free swimming. You can see a cross-section of Henry Flagler's old railroad bridge suspended high over the water. Other parts of the old road bed parallel the highway and are used as fishing piers.

Big Pine Key, the largest of the Lower Keys, contains 6,300 acres thick with mangroves, silver palmetto, and Caribbean pine. Tiny Key deer, once close to extinction, now number about 300 here; it also is possible to spot the endangered great white heron here. For more information on Big Pine Key, or any of the Keys between Marathon and Key West, call the *Big Pine Chamber of Commerce* (phone: 800-872-3722).

Last, but not least, is Key West. The southernmost community in the US and the point closest to Cuba, it combines Southern, Bahamian, Cuban, and Yankee influences in a unique culture that can be seen in its architecture, tasted in its often quirky food, and felt in its relaxed, individualistic atmosphere. Traditionally, fishermen, artists, and writers have been drawn to this tranquil slip of sand and sea. Ernest Hemingway, among the island's early devotees, lived here during his most productive years, when he wrote *To Have and Have Not, For Whom the Bell Tolls, Green Hills of Africa,* and one of his greatest short stories, "The Snows of Kilimanjaro." His Spanish colonial–style house of native stone, surrounded by a lush tropical garden, is now a museum with many original furnishings and Hemingway memorabilia, along with several six-toed cats alleged to be descendants of Hemingway's own pets. The *Ernest Hemingway Home and Museum* (907 Whitehead St.; phone: 305-294-1575) is open daily; admission charge. Among others who have been attracted to Key West are John James Audubon, Tennessee Williams, John Dos Passos, Robert Frost, and President Harry S Truman. Now a museum, Truman's *Little White House* (111 Front St.; phone: 305-294-9911) is filled with original furniture and artifacts. It's open daily; admission charge.

At the *Welcome Center* in Key West (3840 N. Roosevelt Blvd.; phone: 305-296-4444; 800-352-8538 or 800-284-4482) you can make hotel reservations, sign up for tours, arrange to go skydiving, or even make wedding arrangements.

To get your bearings, take the *Conch Tour Train* (phone: 305-294-5161), a 90-minute narrated tram ride that covers 14 miles, passing all the Key West highlights. The train leaves from Mallory Square and North Roosevelt Boulevard, next to the *Welcome Center* (see above), where there's free parking. Purchase tickets at the bright red-and-white kiosk on the corner of Duval and Front Streets. *Old Town Trolley Tours* (phone: 305-296-6688) also provides a great orientation. The narrated tours pick up passengers daily at 12 stops; the full-day ticket permits on-again, off-again privileges until the loop is completed.

Since Key West is best explored on foot, after your tour stroll past the houses whose wooden gingerbread architecture reflects the influence of Bahamian settlers and New England sea captains, and browse through the many galleries and crafts, shell, and souvenir shops. (Key West has the dubious distinction of having more T-shirt shops per square foot than any place outside of Orlando.) Information about a free, self-directed walking tour is available from the *Key West Chamber of Commerce* (402 Wall St., Key West, FL 33040; phone: 305-294-2587; 800-648-6269).

Visitors can choose from a number of boat excursions, including the *Fireball* and the *Pride of Key West,* which sail daily from the foot of Duval Street (phone: 305-296-6293 or 305-294-8704). The catamaran *Stars & Stripes* offers daily, six-hour excursions to a deserted island that include off-boat snorkeling, beachcombing, and bird watching; there's also a sunset sail. The boat departs from *Land's End Marina* (phone: 305-294-PURR; 800-634-MEOW—as in *cat*-amaran).

Unlike glass-bottom boats, *Discovery Tours'* craft have below-deck viewing rooms where passengers observe the coral reef and its inhabitants through eye-level windows lining the hull. The boats leave from *Land's End Marina* (phone: 305-293-0099) for thrice-daily trips. On the way back from the reef, the boat cruises by Mallory Dock, where an onboard sunset celebration takes place every night, beginning one hour before and lasting until one hour after the sun sinks below the horizon. Artisans, jugglers, flame swallowers, a high-wire act, an escape artist, and trained house cats are all part of the festivities.

At the *Lighthouse Museum* (938 Whitehead St.; phone: 305-294-0012), visitors can climb the 90-foot-tall 1847 lighthouse for panoramic island views and visit the furnished *Lighthouse Keeper's Quarters.* It's closed *Christmas Day;* admission charge. The *Audubon House & Gardens* (205 Whitehead St.; phone: 305-294-2116), where the artist John James Audubon worked on paintings of Florida Keys wildlife in 1831 and 1832, has original Audubon engravings, some of which appeared in his *Birds of America.* The lovely gardens showcase numerous tropical plants. Restored by the philanthropic Wolfson family, who hail from these parts, *Audubon House* also encompasses the home and belongings of a wealthy 19th-century sea captain and wrecker. It's open daily; admission charge.

Wrecking was an important industry among early Conchs. Wreckers were licensed salvagers who saved lives, ships, and cargo in the event of a shipwreck; the practice is explained through talks and pictures at the *Wrecker's Museum* (322 Duval St.; phone: 305-294-9502). The oldest house in Key West (dating from 1829 and also owned by a sea captain), it harbors furniture, documents, a charming furnished dollhouse, and ship models. The museum is open daily; admission charge.

The island's oldest house of worship, the *Cornish Memorial A. M. E. Zion Church* (702 Whitehead St., Bahama Village; phone: 305-294-2350), dates from 1864. The *East Martello Museum* (3501 S. Roosevelt Blvd; phone: 305-296-3913), housed in a Civil War fort, details colorful island history, including tales of weird inhabitants such as "the mad scientist of Key West," who "reconstructed" his dead girlfriend using wax and wire, hoping to bring her back to life. The museum is open daily; admission charge. Also of interest is the *Mel Fisher Maritime Heritage Society Museum,* set in a former navy warehouse (200 Greene St.; phone: 305-294-2633). It displays treasures and artifacts salvaged from the Spanish ships *Atocha* and *Santa Margarita,* sunk in a 1622 hurricane. On view are silver bars, gold chains, emerald and diamond jewelry, plus trade beads and shackles from the *Henrietta Marie,* an English merchant slaver, which sank in 1701. The museum is open daily; admission charge. The *Key West Aquarium* (1 Whitehead St. on Mallory Sq.; phone: 305-296-2051) has a collection of colorful local marine animals. It's open daily; admission charge.

As elsewhere in the Keys, fishing dominates the sporting life here. Both the *Gulfstream III* (phone: 305-296-8494) and *Back Country Fishing and Deep Sea* (phone: 305-296-8673) offer a variety of excursions in and around the Keys. But there are other options for active visitors. For snorkeling and scuba diving around the coral reefs, the *Key West Pro Dive Shop* (3128 N. Roosevelt Blvd.; phone: 305-296-3823; 800-426-0707) sponsors trips and rents gear. Golfers can tee off at the 18-hole *Key West Resort Golf Course* (6450 Junior College Rd.; phone: 305-294-5232). There's a resident pro. The area also boasts nine public tennis courts: The six at *Bayview Park* on Truman Avenue are lit at night; the three at Atlantic Boulevard and Reynolds Street do not have lights.

Blue Heaven (729 Thomas St.; phone: 305-296-8666) is one of Key West's most popular restaurants. Outstanding meals also are served at *Louie's Backyard* (700 Waddell Ave.; phone: 305-294-1061), either inside or on the spacious deck under a large shade tree, overlooking the ocean, and at the *Pier House* restaurant (see *Best en Route*), where the Key lime pie may be the best anywhere. Fans of Jimmy Buffett can stop at his *Margaritaville Café* (500 Duval St.; phone: 305-292-1435) for the famous thirst-quencher, a light meal, and the possibility of bumping into the singer, who appears here from time to time. And Hemingway fans never miss a pilgrimage to *Sloppy Joe's* (201 Duval St.; phone: 305-294-5717), the bar said to be once frequented by the writer himself; current regulars are not of the literary persuasion.

For information on Key West, contact the *Key West Chamber of Commerce* (402 Wall St., Key West, FL 33040; phone: 305-294-2587; 800-648-6269). For general information about the Keys, contact the *Florida Keys Visitors Bureau* (PO Box 866, Key West, FL 33041; phone: 800-FLA-KEYS).

BEST EN ROUTE

Below are some recommended spots for overnight stays in the Keys. Except where specified, all of the hotels listed are very expensive, charging $250 or more a night per couple in winter. Unless otherwise noted, hotel rooms have air conditioning, private baths, TV sets, and telephones. The island also has more than 40 guesthouses, most offering continental breakfast, tropical courtyards, and pools. Contact the *Key West Reservation Service* (628 Fleming St., Key West; phone: 954-340-4786; 800-853-9773).

Cheeca Lodge, Islamorada Low-key elegance makes this 27-acre seaside hideaway a romantic pleasure. There are 203 rooms and suites; facilities include a dining room and open-air grill, two pools, a manmade lagoon with a sand beach and waterfalls, six lighted tennis courts, and a nine-hole, par 3 golf course designed by Jack Nicklaus. "Camp Cheeca" has won awards for its environmentally conscious program for kids. Water activities—such as fishing, snorkeling, diving, and parasailing—also are available. Mile Marker 82, PO Box 527, Islamorada (phone: 305-664-4651; 800-327-2888; fax: 305-664-2893).

La Concha Holiday Inn, Key West In the heart of the Old Town, this restored 160-room, seven-story Art Deco hotel first opened in 1926. Chintz bedspreads, four-poster beds, lace curtains, and antique furnishings abound, although plumbing and electronic equipment are modern. There are two restaurants, four bars, a gift shop, and a pool. A daily sunset celebration (weather permitting) takes place at the rooftop bar. Rates in winter season run less than $250 a night—but not much less. 430 Duval St., Key West (phone: 305-296-2991; 800-745-2191 or 800-HOLIDAY; fax: 305-294-3283).

Hyatt Key West, Key West With its own private beach and marina, this four-story, 120-room hostelry in town offers a pool, a Jacuzzi, a small exercise facility, and two restaurants. 601 Front St., Key West (phone: 305-296-9900; 800-233-1234; fax: 305-292-1038).

Little Palm Island, access from Little Torch Key On a secluded island just off Little Torch Key, this charming, romantic hideaway, a member of the prestigious Relais & Châteaux group, is popular with honeymooners and couples. The 30 private, one-bedroom, thatch-roofed cottages have rustic but elegant furnishings. Other attractions include a pool, water sports, and a fine restaurant. No children under age 12 are allowed. Rte. 4, PO Box 1036, Little Torch Key (phone: 305-872-2524; 800-343-8567; fax: 305-872-4843).

Marriott's Casa Marina, Key West Built in 1921 by Henry Flagler, this is a charming full-service resort whose past guests have included Rita Hayworth, Ethel Merman, Al Jolson, and Gregory Peck. Along with its own beach, it offers 311 rooms, two restaurants, two pools, a whirlpool bath, three lighted tennis courts, a health club, and water sports. 1500 Reynolds St., Key West (phone: 305-296-3535; 800-228-9290; fax: 305-296-4633).

Ocean Reef Club, Key Largo Once a private fishing camp and now a posh tropical paradise, this 300-room exclusive—and expensive—resort boasts two 18-hole championship golf courses, terrific fishing, 11 tennis courts, and 145 hotel rooms plus accommodations in condominiums and villas spread out over 4,000 acres of land. There are seven restaurants, five lounges, and an Olympic-size pool; a daily supervised children's program is offered year-round. If you're into high-style living and have the pocketbook to back it up, this is the place for you. 31 Ocean Reef Dr., N. Key Largo (phone: 305-367-2611; 800-741-REEF; fax: 305-367-2224).

Pier House, Key West In the heart of the restored Old Town area, this comfort-ably upscale yet unpretentious deluxe property has 142 rooms, five bars, and three dining rooms (the *Pier House* restaurant is first-rate). Twenty-two of the rooms are in a separate health spa available to resort guests (also see *Sybaritic Spas* in DIVERSIONS). Other features include a manmade sand beach (with a section for topless bathers), a pool, a Jacuzzi, and a deck for sunset watchers. 1 Duval St., Key West (phone: 305-296-4600; 800-327-8340; fax: 305-296-7569).

Tour 9: Everglades National Park

Although known for its sea and sand, South Florida is also the site of America's only subtropical wetlands, the Everglades. This unique ecological system—the world's most delicate—is not far from Miami. The Shark Valley entrance of *Everglades National Park* is about a half-hour drive west of the city, and the park's main entrance, which offers access to the more interesting areas of Royal Palm and Flamingo, is an hour's drive south.

In most of America's national parks there's little more to do than arrive and open your eyes to be impressed. *Everglades National Park* is far more demanding. Here it helps to know something about ecology, and something about what you're looking at, in order to appreciate the full splendor of this magnificent marshy wilderness. Or, at least, it helps to have a child-like curiosity that aches to see that fabled reptile, the alligator.

Fed by the waters of huge Lake Okeechobee, the entire southern tip of the state was once more or less as the Everglades are today—a huge tract of mangrove swamps, seas of sawgrass, hammocks of hardwood trees, and millions of birds, fish, snakes, alligators, and insects (including 43 species of mosquitoes). As South Florida developed, the slow-draining waters of Okeechobee were channeled for irrigation and most of the swamps were drained. Bit by bit, South Florida dried out.

In 1947, alarmed by the destruction of these unique wetlands, the federal government set aside 1.5 million acres 30 miles southwest of Miami as *Everglades National Park.* Despite various (and continuing) environmental threats from urbanization, industry, and farming, the park survives. It's the third-largest of the continental US's national parks—2,510 square miles stretching to Florida's southern and western Gulf coasts. Although the Everglades are considered the nation's most threatened natural area by the *National Park Service* and various environmental agencies, there is reason to be at least cautiously optimistic about their future. Congress has extended the national park eastward by more than 107,000 acres to include and protect the northeast Shark River Slough (pronounced *slew*), whose flow of water had been chopped out of the water-starved park's original boundaries. In addition, South Florida's water management system of canals, levees, and dams is being modified to restore natural water flow and marsh conditions to this critical wildlife habitat to the extent possible. Park managers also are hoping that filtration marshes being created north of the park will cleanse pollutants out of the water that passes through them before entering the Everglades. There is still controversy, however, over whether preservation efforts thus far have been effective enough.

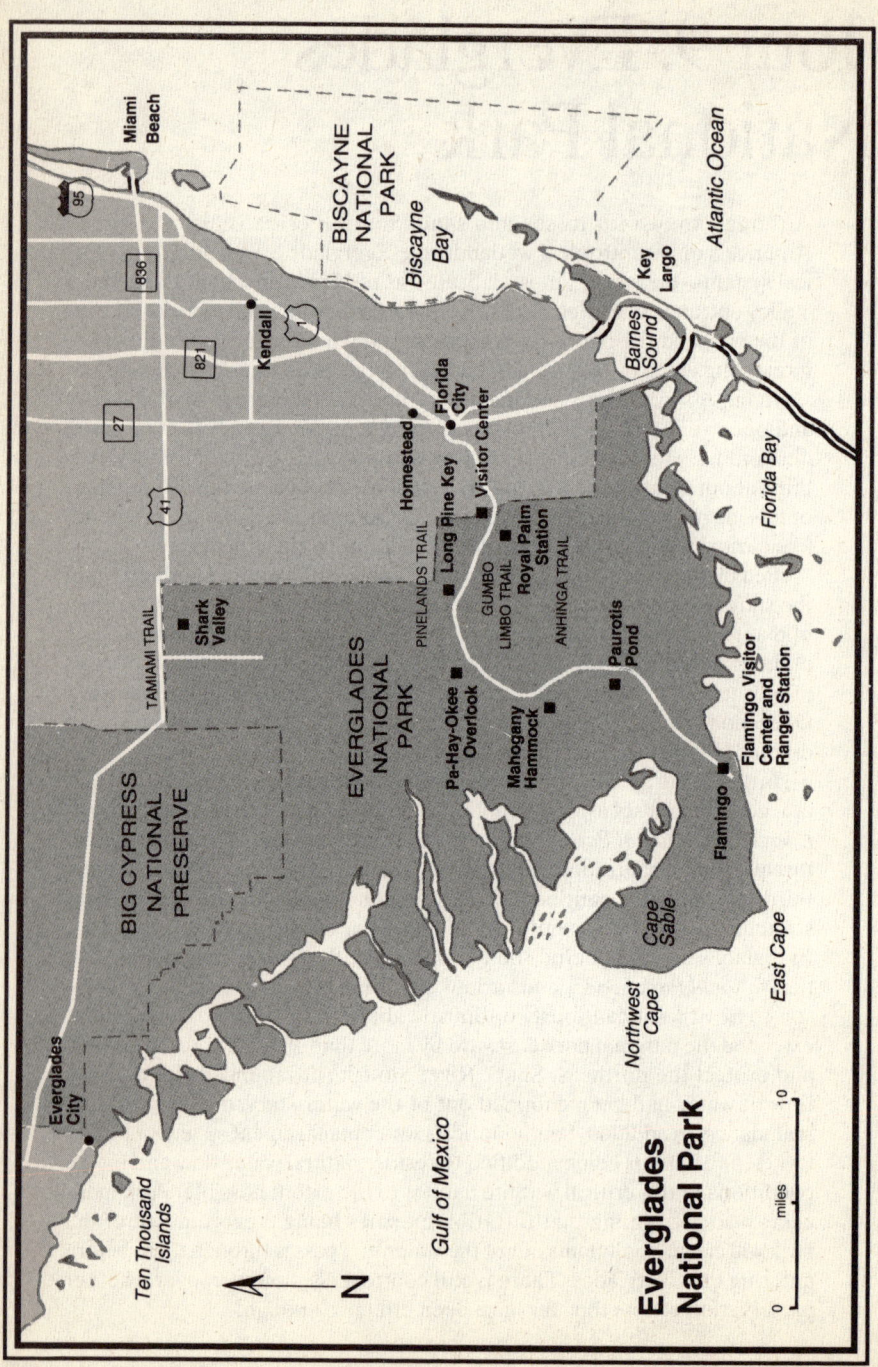

Everglades
National Park

You must understand the delicacy of the Everglades to enjoy the wetlands' understated pleasures. The area is actually a freshwater river (its Indian name is Pa-Hay-Okee, "River of Grass") 100 miles long, several dozen miles wide, and just inches deep during much of the year. This strange stream travels along an incline of only three inches a mile, moving so slowly that a single drop of water takes years to reach the Gulf from Lake Okeechobee. The slow river provides nourishment for a vast and complex system of life, and is a great laboratory in which to see the interdependence and sensitivity of an ecosystem. Where the earth rises a few inches, the plant life in the Everglades changes from sawgrass to hardwood forest. Where ripples appear in a pond, a small fish is eating mosquito larvae; a larger fish, a bream perhaps, will dine on the larva-eater; bass hunt the bream; gar will feed on the bass; and the gar is fodder for the alligator who originally made (or deepened) this pool by digging with his tail.

About 200 miles north of the Tropic of Cancer, the Everglades are the meeting point of subtropical and temperate life forms. In this, the region is unique in the US: Here you see mangrove, West Indian mahogany, and the poisonous manchineel tree, and in a nearby hammock rising from the sawgrass, pine and hardwood trees. Alligators, the rarely seen American crocodile, and white-tail deer share the same ecosystem, and schools of dolphins can sometimes be spotted from the coastal shorelines. Recreational fishing is permitted, but all plants and animals are protected by law from any molestation or harm by humans. (For general information, write or call *Everglades National Park,* 40001 State Rd. 9336, Homestead, FL 33034-6733; phone: 305-242-7700).

Plan to visit the Everglades during the winter to avoid being consumed by mosquitoes. In summer, some areas are so infested by these offensive insects that a pleasant visit is nigh impossible. Always carry insect repellent, regardless of the time of year (if you forget, you can buy it at the visitors' centers).

The Shark Valley area of *Everglades National Park* is most accessible from Miami and Ft. Lauderdale (about 20 miles west along the Tamiami Trail) and offers year-round tram tours (phone: 305-221-8455). Several ranger-led walks are offered from January through the beginning of April, and riding a rented bike along a path is a nice way to see the place. Lucky visitors will spot otters in early morning or around dusk, and alligator sightings are virtually a sure bet.

To reach the park's main entrance, drive about 30 miles south on Route 1 to Homestead, and then about 10 miles southwest on Route 9336. Stop at the *Robert Is Here Fruit Stand* (phone: 305-246-1592) along the way for the best strawberry shake on the East Coast; fruits and vegetables are also available. (This and snacks from vending machines are the only food to be found between Homestead and Flamingo, so pack a picnic lunch before leaving.) From the park's entrance follow the main park road for a 38-mile journey to Flamingo, on Florida Bay. Don't skip this drive; Florida Bay is a jewel worth the trek. There are several ways to see the 'glades: By car, driving to various stops along the road; on foot, following trails (some as short as half a mile) into the heart of things (with or without ranger guides); and by small outboard or canoe, following the water routes. Most of the park is under water, so it's a canoeist's paradise.

No matter how you plan to go, the first stop is the temporary *Visitors' Center* at the park entrance to see exhibitions on park wildlife and ecology and pick up information on guided tours, winter "swamp tromps" (more about these later), and park activities and rules. The *Main Visitors' Center* suffered severe damage from Hurricane Andrew in 1992. A new one is being built; it's scheduled to open at press time.

The next stop is the *Royal Palm Visitor Center* (about 2 miles beyond the temporary *Visitors' Center;* phone: 305-242-7700), with an exhibit on indigenous flora and fauna. The pond here on the *Anhinga Trail* is rich in animal life. Anhingas and ibis regularly hang out in the trees, alligators waddle out of the water and loll a few feet from visitors, snakes sun themselves on the grass, gars float in the clear water, and raccoons stroll by. Another well-known trail, the nearby *Gumbo Limbo Trail,* is missing its tree canopy—it was destroyed by Hurricane Andrew—but it's starting to grow back. A bit farther, Mahogany Hammock (see below) resembles the way the *Gumbo Limbo Trail* used to look; comparing these two places over time will reveal the often miraculous ways in which nature can replenish itself.

Beyond the *Royal Palm Visitor Center,* the road runs through pine forests. Continue to the *Pinelands Trail* (beginning about 2 miles from Long Pine Key), where you might be lucky enough to spot the delicate Virginia white-tailed deer. The prey of the Florida panther, they have been dwindling in number here in recent years. Note the pines along the *Pinelands Trail.* They manage to survive only because they are sturdily fire resistant. You may see a number of them with fire-blackened trunks. In both summer and winter, fires often sweep through parts of the 'glades. Many trees are killed, primarily the hardwood trees. It's nature's way of keeping a balance here; without the fires, the hardwood trees would soon gain ground over the pines and push them out. The pines survive as they burn only on the outside; their corky bark protects them. In summer, the saltwort marshes that flank many of the forests dry out and are torched by lightning, but since it is the rainy season, when water levels are relatively high, these fires do little damage. Fires caused by humans during the winter dry season do the most harm here.

The *Pa-Hay-Okee Overlook,* the next stop along the route, provides some of the best views and bird watching in the park. From here, you can see the expanse of sawgrass that makes up Shark River Slough, where alligators and fowl gather. ("Sawgrass" is actually a misnomer; it is not a grass but a fine-toothed sedge. Despite its delicate appearance, it has mean, serrated edges on three sides that easily slice clothes or flesh, so be careful.) The alligators are an important link in the chain of life in the Everglades. During the dry season—autumn through spring—they settle into sloughs and dig deep holes with their tails. In late winter, as the marshes dry out, fish get caught in these 'gator holes. This is crucial for the wading birds, which nest near these natural fishbowls and are thus assured a food supply. The dead-looking trees here are dwarf bald cypresses, some of them 100 years old, which sprout leaves at the onset of the rainy season.

Seven miles beyond *Pa-Hay-Okee Overlook* is Mahogany Hammock, the largest stand of mahoganies in the US and site of the country's largest mahogany tree. Boardwalks allow visitors to wander into it. You'll still see some Vriesia (bromeliads with red bracts) and Spanish moss growing on trees. The air plants, including orchids, are making a comeback after the 1992 hurricane. Beyond this point, the park was virtually untouched by the storm.

About 4 miles farther is Paurotis Pond. Here salt and fresh water begin to mix, and mangrove trees first appear. The mangrove is the only tree that thrives in salt water. It is a great colonizer and lives in a constant drama of creation and destruction all along the Gulf shore. It settles into the swampy salt water of the coast, and as it drops seeds and throws out breathing roots it captures material and actually begins "building" earth bulwarks against the sea. As seagulls and other sea birds collect around it, dropping guano, this earth becomes rich and fertile. Eventually, however, hurricanes sweep the coast, and everything is ripped out of the swampy ground and thrown inland.

Other ponds and trails beckon all along the main road. At Mrazek Pond, the water level ebbs as the dry season approaches, and hundreds of birds gather to eat the plentiful fish. Beautiful roseate spoonbills, with bright pink wings, share tree limbs with egrets, white ibis, and tricolored herons, among other species.

The main park road ends at Flamingo, where you'll find the *Flamingo Visitor Center and Ranger Station* (phone: 941-695-3092), a hotel, camp-grounds, a restaurant, a store, a gas station, a lounge, and bicycle rentals. Boats (including canoes, skiffs, and houseboats) are also for hire here for excursions into portions of the 'glades accessible only by waterway.

Slightly beyond this area is Eco Pond, an eight-acre manmade body of water drawn from the Flamingo Sewage Treatment Plant. The pond is the final stage of sewage treatment; the water is then evaporated and later returns to the Everglades as rain. Meanwhile, it provides a stop-off point for alligators and a variety of fowl, including gallinules and egrets.

Serious visitors to the Everglades should plan to spend most of their time out of their cars. For the less hardy, marked foot trails (usually board-walks) are a comfortable way to have an intimate experience in the 'glades; there are also tram rides available at Shark Valley off Route 41 (which skims the northern border of the park).

More intrepid visitors may want to join a "swamp tromp" or "slough slog" into the very heart of the marshes. These walking expeditions led by park naturalists are offered frequently from December through March. They really get you into things—quite literally. You'll need old clothes and shoes that you don't mind getting muddy and wet; waterproof, high boots are a good idea, for you'll be going into the water up to your knees. Bring plenty of mosquito repellent. There are several possible destinations, among them a 'gator hole, a tree island, and a major mangrove stand. Ask for schedules at the *Flamingo Visitor Center*.

The *Wilderness Waterway* is just about the most challenging test the Everglades offers an outdoors person. It is a 99-mile water trail that corkscrews through the Ten Thousand Islands area. Although the water lanes are well marked, there is sufficient room for error that travelers are asked to take all precautions when undertaking this journey. By powerboat it is quite possible to complete the course in about six hours. However, any serious nature observer will opt for the canoe and the serenity it offers en route. There are minimally outfitted campsites, each wryly nicknamed, along the water lanes: "Hell's Bay" ("hell to get into and hell to get out of"); "Onion Key," the bare-bones remains of a 1920s land developer's dream; and a crude pit outhouse and fireplace campsite known as "The Coming Miami of the Gulf." There are also shorter canoe trails, complete with camping sites. Overnight stays require a backcountry use permit issued at no charge by the *Gulf Coast Ranger Station* (Gulf Coast Ranger District, PO Box 120, Everglades City, FL 33929; phone: 941-695-3311) or the *Flamingo Ranger Station* (No. 1, Flamingo Lodge Hwy., Flamingo, FL 33034; phone: 941-695-3094). The waterways begin at Everglades City and extend to Flamingo.

The somewhat less athletic and daring boater might prefer to take a guided boat cruise. Excursions aboard the open-sided catamaran *Bald Eagle* or the schooner *Windfall* depart daily from Flamingo and sail among Florida Bay's islets or keys. They provide a fine opportunity to view Florida's blazing sunsets and watch the indigenous birds returning to roost for the evening; contact the *Flamingo Lodge* for reservations and information (phone: 305-253-2241; 800-600-3813). But the craft most visitors associate with the Everglades is the airboat. Though banned from *Everglades National Park* (the noise and gas fumes disturb the fragile environment), airboats may be operated outside the park. Near the Shark Valley park entrance, daily airboat rides are offered year-round at *Everglades Safari Park* (Rte. 41, about 9 miles west of Krome Ave.; phone: 305-226-6923).

For an overnight stay that doesn't involve camping out, try the *Flamingo Lodge* on Florida Bay in Flamingo, 38 miles from the entrance of *Everglades National Park* (1 Flamingo Lodge Hwy.; phone: 305-253-2241, 800-600-3813; fax: 941-695-3921). The only place to stay right in the park, it offers modern, clean, air conditioned, and inexpensive accommodations. Choose from 24 cottages with kitchenettes (but no TV sets) or 102 motel rooms (all with TV sets). There's also a suite with wonderful views; it sleeps six and has two baths and a kitchenette. There's a full-fledged marina where you can arrange guided fishing charters; and a screened-in pool, restaurant, and gift shop round out the amenities.

Whether overnight or just for an afternoon, a visit to the Everglades adds an intriguing element to the usual sun-and-fun Florida vacation.

Index

Index

NOTES

NOTES